Inhabiting the Other
Essays on Literature and Exile

Inhabiting the Other

Essays on Literature and Exile

Edited By
Sharmistha Lahiri

ARYAN BOOKS INTERNATIONAL
NEW DELHI

INHABITING THE OTHER
Essays on Literature and Exile

ISBN-81-7305-205-0

Published in **2001** by
ARYAN BOOKS INTERNATIONAL
Pooja Apts, 4B, Ansari Road, New Delhi-110 002 (India)
Tel. : 3287589, 3255799; Fax : 91-11-3270385

in association with
DEPARTMENT OF GERMANIC AND ROMANCE STUDIES
University of Delhi, Delhi

Computer Typesetting at Welcome Computers, New Delhi
Printed in India at B.B.N. Printers, New Delhi

Preface

Inhabiting the Other (Essays on Literature and Exile) is a collection of articles from different parts of the world presented in the International Seminar organised by the Department of Germanic and Romance Studies. The seminar centred around a common point of reference to the theme of exile and provided a forum for debate seeking to explore the issue with its manifold shades and nuances. In editing a volume such as this I incurred numerous debts. First, I would like to thank our Department at the university of Delhi for having provided the kind of help necessary when compiling a collection of essays whose contributors reside in various parts of the globe. My thanks go to Vibha Maurya as well as other colleagues for support and to Shaswati Mazumdar and Evelyn George for helping me with editing a few of the articles. A special thanks go to Manmohan Singh for helping me out with typing my manuscript. Last but not least, my thanks go to Vikas Arya who has extended steady support for the publication of the book.

Contents

SHARMISTHA LAHIRI

Introduction

As the title of the present volume suggests, literary texts predicated upon exile experiences have been brought together in this collection of essays with memorable instances from world literature. The feeling of uprootedness and alienation has been dogging the footsteps of man perhaps since the beginning of history, even without any physical uprooting from native lands, but it has acquired unprecedented intensity and dimension in the twentieth century. Two world wars, ethnic cleansing, economic deprivation as also a search for more conducive creative environments led people to flee their native lands, be it by imposition, or by voluntary choice. The rhetoric of migrancy has fired poetic imagination and has lent voice to the plight of the emigrant, the fugitive, the banished, the dispossessed and the recluse, while the dream of homecoming continued to burn. It is a discourse built around the sign of displacement, of shift in paradigms, of loss of history. It is sustained by a quest for rehabilitation which stretches across generations. In situations of multiculturalism it evinces a pattern of responses that trigger the construction of a variant idiom vis-a-vis the narrative of the dominant culture.

In going through the wide gamut of views articulated through the essays in question, exile emerges as a hydra-headed phenomenon and one is amazed at the array of issues it throws up for discussion, the changes it has brought to bear on the lives of nations and individuals and the process of formation of new communities even while some were pushed into the margins of society.

If one were to identify, from the maze of narrative material, one salient feature common to all experience of exile, it certainly could be the issue of identity, the quest of the self for its moorings, in history as well as in the immediate existential order of things. The image of the land of origin and the process of its transformation in the eyes of the displaced provided one of the principal sources of creative insight, vehicled into the sphere of general imagination through innovative textual strategies and a strongly nuanced narration. The disruption in communication allowed the exile the distance required to develop a fresh insight and a creative perspective on the familiar images. If dislocation entailed loss of identity and a cultural disorientation, coupled with yearning for one's homeland, the process of writing, by itself, signified a move towards redefining the Self while straining one's resources to forge a new identity. The émigré had to face myriad challenges like economic survival, fear of persecution and social discrimination. The loss of the linguistic community was another factor which removed the supportive base which had sustained creative development, but led to the acquisition of a new language, followed by a phase of acculturation with the new realities. Clearly, the exile's journey towards rehabilitation encompassed a dual objective: recognition and acceptance, aimed on the one hand at legitimation of cultural diversity and on the other at creating conditions for assimilation with the mainstream culture. Literature, in this context, is an embedded discourse and a narrative tool to negotiate one's position between two cultural realities. Through literary articulation the exile underlines his role as the spokesperson of the diverse and therein problematises the concept of cultural identities. With his expressivity he moves towards ending isolation and relocating the Self at the new site. In his seminal work on multiculturalism Charles Taylor calls it the *Politics of Recognition,* which could be logically extended into including definitions of political and juridical subjecthood with respect to multiculturally traditioned communities.[1]

An ethnopoetic element is implicit within the narratives of multiculturalism and exile. This follows from the basic assumption that an experiential expressivity is characteristic of the texts in question and each experience in exile is individual, depending on the historical specificites of time, space and circumstances that eventually led to the state of exile in each case. It is different in instances of inner exile. For some who did not choose the path of physical exile, withdrawal into the inner self akin to an inner emigration manifested itself in literary constructions apparently not related to the realities of the proximate outside world. This is not to obliterate the fact that the act of withdrawal, perceived as a mode of rejection of the prevailing norms, was by nature, an act of subversion. During the Fascist epoch in Italy, for instance, there was signification of ruptured communication in the hermetic poetry of the Italian writer Eugenio Montale in his works like *Ossi di Seppia (Bones of Squid), Occasioni (Occasions)*—minimalist, terse verses rendered inaccessible by his use of obscure words and constant allusions to the suggestions of a private mythology. Taking a stand against the directive principles of the official Fascist culture and shorn of material sustenance, the poet withdrew into a shell of supreme indifference and survived those turbulent years with dignity. Thus, writing, for an exile or an expatriate did not simply constitute an act of literariness, it was an act of social and political will. In her critique of Italian American culturalism, Renate Holub adopts a 'culture-specific methodology' and reads multicultural narratives along Gramscian lines.[2] In his "notes on linguistics", *Prison Notebooks, no. 29*, Gramsci refers to the multiple components of one's identity structured by linguistic experiences encountered by the body with respect to dominant or not-so-dominant languages and touches upon the universal desire to "speak the places where one's body has been". He also addresses the concern of cultural legitimation in his notes on philosophy and folklore,[3] conceptual tools which Holub refers to as "structures of feeling" and "universal expressivity".[4] Accordingly, we might observe that the multiple components structuring the narrative of the exile or the expatriate should be recognised in terms of -as Manuela Bertone says- "a richly compact set of responses to a common intellectual concern: the emergence of a sense of 'otherness', the awareness of a shared cultural past, the need to express both of them in artistic terms."[5] Thus the motivational imperatives underlying the Gramscian concepts of "structures of feeling" and "universal expressivity" may help explain the unique blend of the particular and the universal in the intricate weave of multicultural narratives and addresses some of the concerns voiced in the discourse of exile.

At this point it might be useful to reflect on certain paradigms that indicate the interconnectedness of multicultural narratives and the representational aspect of the texts on exile. In this context it is possible to locate the point of intersection in the categories of time and space which need to be factored into any appraisal of a discourse on exile. For, as evidenced by the pattern of responses, it is generationally distinguished. Daniel Aaron, in his text on culture studies, sets up a model which identifies three stages through which the ex-patriate, or in his term the 'hyphenate' (the dominant culture holds him at a hyphen's length), writer has to pass to reach 'de-hyphenation'.[6] The first phase writer wants to familiarise the reader with his cultural identity and employs very recognizable ethnic features in his narration to 'humanize' and demystify the negative stereotypes associated with the group. The second stage writer is less prone to conciliate the dominant group and is a militant critic of the hegemonistic politics of the mainstream culture. He 'reinvents' his ethnicity and adopts a policy of strategic essentialism to counter the essentialism of the dominant group. The third stage writer, having appropriated the language and the tools of the culture, feels himself part of the dominant group. A. J. Tamburri, an Italian-American critic, cites Aaron to point out that the third stage writer is aware of his cultural heritage but transcends "a mere parochial allegiance 'to bring' into the province of [general imagination] personal experiences which for the first-stage ("local colorist") and second stage ("militant protester") writers comprised the very stuff of their literary material"[7]. As a case in point we might cite the experience of Jhumpa Lahiri, the recent Pulitzer Prize winning author of *The Interpreter of Maladies,* who agrees that the question of identity especially for those who are culturally displaced is a difficult one. She mixed an attractive combination of local colour, characters and settings within the framework of western narrative tradition and, as critics remark, entranced her reviewers with the 'heady Calcutta flavour' of many of her stories in *The Interpreter of Maladies.* As a child of the Indian Diaspora in the United States, Jhumpa Lahiri illustrates the generationally graduated response to the issue of identity when she says that in superficial ways she is much more American than her parents; yet, it is difficult for those with her background to feel completely American either. One has to recognise that for the older generation the challenges of exile, loneliness, sense of alienation are more acute than they are for their children, a feeling which another expatriate writer Salman Rushdie tried to define when he said "it is an emotional baggage one carries wherever one goes", while explaining his nostalgic association with India. A reading of the multi-layered texts in *Shame* and *The Moor's Last Sigh* would render its purport amply clear.

Truly, writing under conditions of exile has been viewed as a defining category in literature. With the backdrop of a growing trend to engage with the texts of the other groups in the society as a separate category, to be viewed in relation to the paradigms of the mainstream culture, we take into consideration certain formulations in this context, brought into the discussion by the writers of Italian American descent who, together with the Black Americans and the Hispanic Americans, among others, constitute a sizable presence of 'otherness' in the cultural profile of the United States. Fred. L. Gardaphé, a renowned scholar of Italian American literature, introduces a variant to the model of Aaron by adopting Vico's theory of the three-fold division in the history of Italian American literature.[7] Gardaphé's classification points to the poetic mode of expressivity in the primitive stage and the mythic mode of militant ethnicity in the second stage, which engages in "a materialization and an articulation of the past". The third stage brings the philosophic mode of self-reflection and expression and the writer is confident and at ease with his ethnic background; he looks at the dominant culture "less critically but more knowingly" and even employs a parodic representation of his ethnicity. These three stages, in Gardaphé's formulation, have their parallels in modern and "contemporary socio-cultural constructions of realism, modernism and post-modernism."[8] Against reflections on the categories of Aaron and Gardaphé, Tamburri emphasizes on a cognitive Peircean perspective and traces the progress "from a state of non-rationality ("feeling") to practicality ("experience") and on to pure rationality ("thought") and concludes in terms of a two-fold evolutionary process—both temporal and cognitive, that may or may not be mutually inclusive."[9] Tamburri buttresses his argument with examples drawn from three texts by Italian American writers—*The Evening News* by Tony Ardizzone, *Benedetta in Guysterland* by Giose Rimanelli and *Umbertina* by Helen Barolini—and establishes the point that the temporal and the cognitive may not coincide at any given stage. Another reading in the evolutionary process is offered by Rose Basile Green who identifies, in the generational divide on approaches to literature, moments of "revulsion and counter revulsion."[10] She points out that the first generation settlers in their anxiety to obtain identity in the new land moved away from their cultural traditions whereas in a later phase the immigrants experienced a counter-revulsion and returned to the ethnic roots to affirm their cultural identity. The literary career of Italian American writer John Fante illustrates best how a writer oscillated between two worlds and tried to grapple with this cultural displacement. Between his two books, *The Road to Los Angeles* and *Wait until Spring, Bandini,* Fante changed his approach to the text and abandoned the former novel to retrace his cultural memory and recuperate the ethnic past. His character Arturo Bandini "must first rescue and deal with his Italian heritage" writes Ernesto Livorini, "before being able to move on in the underground literary world in the new land in which he was born."[11]

An interesting variation in these categories is found in the texts of Italian American women writers who fight a battle in terms of both gender and ethnicity. With a discernible subversive intent to debunk the popular stereotypes of Italian American women, many of these writers have used food as a necessary ingredient in their narrative and evolved an aesthetics of domesticity through an interplay of gender, genre and ethnicity. Helen Barolini, a prolific writer, turned to cook book, sourcing it from native family traditions, "to create", as critic Edvige Giunta points out, "a much more complex story, one that the reader must learn 'to read'."[12] The innovative style of her book *Festa* induces dialogization with the mores and lifestyle of the Italian people and serves as a text through which she "furthers her authorial assertion as a woman who cooks *and* writes." With her work Barolini reiterates her stand on the struggle that the women writers have to wage in order to have their voices heard, within the narrowing walls of the domestic space dominated by men at home; and outside, alleges Barolini, against the policy of "literary apartheid" practised by the dominant culture to keep the other groups in the margins.[13] In her novel *Umbertina* Barolini's female protagonist Tina is a third generation immigrant in the United States who goes into a bind over her loyalties while trying to negotiate her position between American and Italian cultures. As a telling testimony to her predicament of identity, during a voyage to Italy, she discovers that she is unable to decide her role between a tourist and a traveller.

In the final analysis any discussion on the narrative of exile and multiculturalism should necessarily pause to consider the relevance and significance of ethnicity as a primary impulse. With our little excursus into instances from Italian American literature, it is evident that the different forms of writing constitute a narrative strategy to affirm the right of the displaced to subjecthood. In an interaction between art and society, a reformulation of social and cultural issues perhaps is needed as a corrective strategy to intervene in the social text. Ethnicity represents one of the components of his/her identity and the positions of subjecthood and objecthood are liable to change with shifts in specific situations, time and space. The same Italian American male who enjoys a subject status at home is in turn relegated to objecthood when he confronts the dominant group, a situation which illustrates Gramsci's concept of non-monolinearity in relationships of power[14]. Ursula Apitzsch, well known in the field of European migration studies points out, in Gramscian line, the "ambivalence of the multicultural model" and shifts the focus on elements of hegemonic structures, for example, political economy, ideologies, instituions.[15] In a related outcome, in their study on the immigrant population in the United States, Nathan Glazer and Daniel Moynihan re-examined the cultural component of ethnicity and defined the ethnic group as "groupings of interests"[16] This concept of an "instrumental ethnicity' would militate against the anthropologists' theory of a 'primordial ethnicity' comprised of the essence of the individual groups, a sense of belonging, which would continue for generations in the family of the immigrants. [17] We recall here what Michacl M.J. Fischer observed on the issue of ethnicity and memory referring to ethnicity as "something reinvented and reinterpreted in each generation by each individual" in line with the "several components of one's identity."[18] In an analogous vein Werner Sollors elaborates that ethnicity is "an acquired modern sense of belonging", which is recreated or redimensioned in ethnic "kinship symbolism" in accordance with the historical specificities of time and place and evolves continually to face the challenges of reality in power relations.[19] It is said that in creating a Bachtinian universe of hybrid-glossia and plurivoiced discourse, the later generation writers of the Other groups often use their ethnicity as an ideological tool and adopt a strategy of essentialism in a voice similar to that of the dominant discourse. Reflecting on the situation, within the framework of the dialectics of power and subordination and considering the fluidity of hegemonic structures, perhaps it is necessary to look beyond the canons of multicultural narratives and rationally consider the bipolarised perceptions of the oft-repeated terms such as the centre and the margin, the dominant culture and the subaltern Other, or even take for granted the moral superiority of the latter over the former in a generalised context.

We have attempted a thematic grouping of the essays published in this volume trying to find the characteristic features common to experiences of similar kind. In the first part, we begin with the essays on early twentieth century writers who laid down the premises of the modernist preoccupation with the theme of alienation and exile. In this segment we have included essays on Joyce, Camus and Beckett; and followed it up by continuing our excursus right through the postmodern with articles on Kundera and Rushdie. In the second part, in an areawise study of the phenomenon we examine the many faces of exile in texts of Portuguese, Hungarian, German, Italian, Romanian, Yiddish and Hispanic literatures. These are mostly works of post-second world war authors in whom many of the earlier concerns continue to be paradigmatic.

PART 1

Beginning our observation with the early twentieth century writers, Joyce's formulations made a significant breakthrough in the art of writing; and created the framework for an aesthetics of alienation and deconstituted subjectivities that set the trend in the literature of his times. Lalita Subbu, in her essay titled 'Art, Exile and the Case of James Joyce—A Note' emphasizes on the centrality of the theme of exile in Joyce's aesthetics as it evolved through his urban short stories like *The Dubliners, A Portrait of an Artist,* his 'exploration of exiles' in *Exiles, Ulysses* and 'the final dismantling of language' in *Finnegan's Wake.* Lalita Subbu examines the circumstances that led Joyce to his so-called "exile" and merge his art into it through "complicated twists of history and aesthetics". She points out the existentialist dilemma inherent in the discourse and argues that the theme of continual "departure" from an earlier format is definitive—"be it country, language, community, religion, politics or gender." She concludes that "exile as confrontation with the Self is perhaps the most daunting artistic formulation of Joyce, for it implies that we are forever in exile from ourselves."

The notion of alienation from the framework of established conventions continued to shape twentieth century discourse and is a pervasive theme in the works of Albert Camus. Dominique S.Varma in her essay 'Albert Camus : Kingdom of Exile' presents the experience of Camus as a case of an encounter with exile in which one's own land becomes the Other. She links it with his emotional attachment to Algeria, the place where he was born, as against his country France which for him was the Other land. She refers to a collection of short stories *Exile and the Kingdom* and analyses the story 'Adulteress', with a linguistic key, to reveal the metaphysical dimension in Camus' discourse of the Other. In it, Janine, the female protagonist, a French national like the author, had to severe all links with her land and social milieu in order to be a "free and destitute sovereign of herself." The term 'adultery' here is interpreted etymologically as essentially an encounter with the forbidden Other and instead of an erotic adventure, Camus builds a metaphysical experience in his story of the French woman exile and the absolute Other, the Arab. Dominique Varma argues with textual references to establish the interconnection between Camus' title of the book *Exile and the Kingdom* and the signs of philological inferences drawn from the Old and the New Testaments embedded in it.

The modernist engagement with the theme of displacement and alienation that haunted the industrialized urban milieu of Joyce and Camus culminated into the theatre of the Absurd with Samuel Beckett as one of its principal exponents. Hema V. Raghavan in her essay 'The Exile in the Plays of Samuel Beckett' delves into Beckett's definition of the absurdity of existence and discerns a metaphysical aspect in his state of inner exile experienced when he was hiding in France, fleeing from the Gestapo. In her essay, Hema. V. Raghavan compares the positions of Camus and Beckett in relation to the notion of exile as a paradigmatic human condition and indicates that the Beckettian perception of exile is more frightening, as it "harbours no illusion of happiness or triumph for man who is confined within the limits of the *Absurd*". She quotes Camus to say that when rebellion fails, it ends in exile whereas "in Beckett the foreknowledge of failure which does not hinder rebellion turns his character into exile."

We conclude the first part of our volume with two essays, on Milan Kundera and Salman Rushdie, which take us right into the postmodern constructions around the notions of Diaspora and exile. In Kundera's words, the writer in exile is the one who through his act of remembering wages one of the defining struggles of our epoch: "the struggle of memory against forgetting", a task which, as V. Rajakrishan writes, James Joyce had set for himself, at the beginning of the century "to redeem the ruptured conscience of his race." In his essay 'The Land of the Dead in Salman Rushdie's *The Moor's Last Sigh*,' a novel that hints at a dark spirit of foreboding similar to Dante's portrayal of Hell, Rajakrishan locates the site of exile in the land of the Dead in the remote Spanish village of Benengeli. He argues that the Street of Parasites described in the book is emblematic of the limbo of exile which Rushdie experienced during his period of hiding, with the spectre of annihilation lurking around him. He puts in perspective the paradox between the time of history and the timelessness of exile in Rushdie's work and sees the writer learning to conquer "the shame of hiding his identity through his art."

Rosy Singh's readings of Milan Kundera's works in her essay 'Milan Kundera and Forgetting as a Metaphor,' reinforces our notion of exile as an ongoing experience, mediated by time. While during his early years as an émigré writer Kundera revealed his strong roots in the cultural milieu of his homeland relying largely on Czech characters and situations for his narrative material, his later works, for example, *Immortality* (on Goethe) and *Slowness*, display a tendency towards opting for a commonly shared European heritage. Rosy Singh analyses Kundera's *Lost Letters* and indicates the two levels, the historical "where the text serves as a frozen image within a temporal framework", and the immanent "where the discourse enters the realm of universal significance (...)" if considered as a metaphor for 'alienation' and 'forgetting'. Like Joyce, Kundera considers the past as a country which we have left and in *Testament Betrayed* he clearly emphasizes the role of the writer who can in turn fashion out of it an instrument of creative growth. In Kundera's experience, as Rosy Singh observes, "the feeling of estrangement related to the motif of forgetting goes hand in hand with nostalgia and perhaps even overtakes it", leaving the exile with a feeling of not belonging to any particular land to call his own. It is the world of the Postmodern where, as we shall see soon in the essay of Sonya Gupta, the centre has disintegrated and the migrant emerges through it as the truly universal man.

PART II

In this segment, exile experiences have been positioned into separate geo-political categories with a focus on the specificities of each in relation to literature.

The Portuguese experience is expressed in four essays by Maria Alzira Seixo, Alberto Duarte Carvalho, Fernando Cristóvão and Ana Paula Laborinhas. Maria Alzira Seixo in her essay on the 'Faces of Exile in Portuguese Literature' initiates a discourse on the concepts of parallel time in relation to exile, the time of Enunciation and the time of History citing instances from the recently published *Manual dos Inquisidores (Handbook for Inquisitors)* by Antonis Labo Antunes. Seixo points to the frequent situations of exile in twentieth century Portugal during the regime of Salazar and the compulsive voyages to the Portuguese colonies of Africa, and sees in the phenomenon of emigration "a complex situation involving several instances of memory", comparing it with Umberto Eco's definition of natural narrative and artificial narrative. With an exhaustive account of the presence of the theme of exile in different works in Portuguese literature across the ages, beginning right from the biblical narrative of Camoes in the sixteenth century, Seixo notes the tendency of the ex-patriate writer to reconstruct identity in the new land to end the situation of Otherness. She also refers to Portuguese writings in which expatriation is felt while staying in one's own country, as evident in the works of Egito Goncalves, Daniel Filipe etc., portraying homeland as a place of exile. Instances from the works of Jorges de Sena and Jose Rodrigues Migueis are cited to show how staying in distance from homeland makes the writer more perceptive of his cultural roots. Maria Alzira Seixo explores the notion of the split of the self as a typical element of Western modernity and relates it to the contemporary feeling of exile reflected in Portuguese literature, so that "recovering life is recovering home and homeland and travel becomes a positive displacement in search of knowledge".

Alberto Carvalho in his essay 'Travel and Metaphors of Exile in African Literature in Portuguese' focuses on the 'centripetal force of the African land' and indicates how elements of space, travel and metaphors of exile converge to endow the writing of the authors in this continent with certain common denominators. Carvalho puts his focus on the specific facets of the literature of Cape Verde, Angola and Mozambique and explains that "in aspects as diverse as thematic, the specification of genre and the distribution, [it] brings together all that is most representative that distinguishes this sector within the Portuguese-speaking space" while throwing light on the clear distinction between "the creative dynamics of the colonising enterprises within the African space." He points out that in case of the literature of Cape Verde, the Creole evolution of its cultural base and its Atlantic insularity led to particular leanings towards themes of oceanic solitude, economic migration and "yearning for the absent fatherland". Literature of the continental countries like Angola and Mozambique, on the other hand, grew out of mutually acculturative contacts between the African Black and the Portuguese and flowed with the images of a richly syncretic Mestico culture.

In his essay 'Two Exiles in the Contemporaneous Brazil', Fernando Cristóvão has engaged in the textual analysis of two novels of contemporary Brazilian literature: *O Amor de Pedro Por João* (1982) by Tabajara Ruas and *O Mar Nunca Trasborda (The Sea Never Overflows)* by Ana Maria Machado (1995). In *O Amor* the author recapitulates the struggle on the part of the writers in Brazil and Chile in the sixties and the seventies for the great revolutionary dream, a process that culminates in political exile and disillusionment bringing up the narration to the moment where exile coincides with ideological oblivion. He highlights a different aspect of exile in *O Mar* in which the socio-political angle shifts to 1995, in the story of two Brazilians living in London, working for a Brazilian mass media and yearning for the roots in a state of cultural exile. Cristóvão analyses the significance of the Portuguese term 'Saudade' — "a feeling of longing heightened by stay in a situation of cultural exile", which often lends clarity and vision to the image of one's homeland. We ought to point out here that this is an aspect which finds corroboration in the observations of almost all the authors in this volume as an attribute that the experience of exile brings to literary expression.

Ana Paula Laborinhas in her essay 'Camilo Pessanha and the Poetry of Exile' shifts the focus to the Orientalism of the noted Portuguese writer Camilo Pessanha and reads in it the signs of an intense aesthetic experience grown out of his exposure to the Chinese culture in Macau. The knowledge of Chinese poetry enabled Pessanha to discover its essential similarity with western symbolism in its use of sign, symbol and the aesthetics of a representational language that endowed poetry with a plural significance. Ana Paula Laborinhas too joins in the general consensus on exile and points out that the voluntary exile of Pessanha in Macau was an enriching experience and a necessary condition for his poetry as it "provided him with the space and distance necessary for his discourse on the identity of literature."

Speaking about Hungary, Margit Köves, in her essay 'Sunday Circle on Mondays : Exile in Vienna' examines the exile experiences of Hungarian intellectuals Georg Lukács and Béla Balazs, who like some other members of the Sunday Circle, an intellectual group in Hungary, left after the revolution of 1919 to meet again in Vienna on Mondays. With her keen analysis Köves draws our attention to the centrality of the categories of time in the works of Lukács and Balazs and points to the change from Sundays to Mondays as emblematic of the dislocation of time and space for the émigré. For Lukács, the concept of time evolved into a mystical experience of a subjective time, of memory and irradiation of hope. Margit Köves observes that exile was a positive experience for Lukács and Balazs who "set out from an idealist position to examine the concepts of Soul and Time and became radicalized in the process", and the varied cultural interactions opened a new dimension to the framework of their thought.

Coming to German experiences, Manfred Stassen narrates an instance of double exile, in his essay 'Neither Here nor there : Reflections on German - German Exile', encountered by the German poet Wolf Biermann who had emigrated to East Berlin on ideological grounds. Biermann, like many other Jewish socialist intellectuals, grew steadily alienated in GDR and subsequently migrated back to West Germany where he failed as a poet and lost a cause to fight, making it, in the words of Stassen, "a rich and famous failure, a crashed German Icarus." Manfred Stassen makes use of the mythcial imagery of Icarus taken from a ballad composed by Biermann in which the poet had a premonition that the Prussian Eagle would pick him up with its claws and drop him somewhere, which for him was *ou-topos* or nowhere, like in exile, and would turn him into a modern Icarus. This case study, in the German context, provides us with a phenomenal example where, contrary to the general trend, exile destroys.

In another essay on German literature, Shaswati Mazumdar delves into Brecht's years of exile and shows how the experience of exile and the anti-fascist struggle provided the material and intellectual resources for varied experiments with prose writing. She points to the genre of novel as the most easily translatable form and widely accepted by the writers deprived of readers and theatre-goers in an alien milieu. Shaswati Mazumdar analyses Brecht's *Fluchtlingsgesprache (Fugitives in Conversation)* which comprises a series of conversations between an intellectual and physicist Ziffel and the working class protagonist Kalle, both of whom enjoyed chatting in their common exile in a place where no one else spoke German. Thus, exile was shown to be an eraser of class distinctions in a common situation of dislocation. She locates Brecht's choice of form and content in the conditions and demands of exile and perceives a combination of criticism of Fascism and self criticism of the anti-fascist forces in exile as elements embedded in the textual strategy. With a focus on Brecht's use of satire as one of the chosen modes to represent history and an employment of hilarity "that liberates the oppressive and threatened condition of the two fugitives" Shaswati Mazumdar essays out in her analysis the subversive content inherent in the text.

Continuing with the theme of exile viewed against the background of Fascism, we present Stefano Fossati's 'Notes on *Fontamara*', a novel written by the Italian author Ignazio Silone during his period of exile. The theme of isolation is perceived as a perennial element and an issue central to the world and works of Silone. In both Shaswati Mazumdar and Stefano Fossati's expositions, the moral and the ethical dimensions of the experience is underlined in clear terms: the ethical in the self-criticism of the anti-fascist forces by Brecht; and the moral in Silone's projection of the isolation of the individual faced with his own conscience. However, the Italian Diaspora during the Fascist regime was never as overwhelming a phenomenon as in Germany and one important aspect of the fight against Fascism in Italy was opposition to cultural conformism and provincialism. Stefano Fossati explains that, for Silone in particular, exile helped to "stimulate in him the search for new cultural horizons". The description of Fontamara, a remote place in Southern Italy, reveals a desolate landscape indicative of the destiny of the author and Fossati presents Silone as an unusual figure in Italian literature who combined in his narrative an avowal for a "Christian message as well as a socialist commitment"; it was an ideology for religion without the Church and socialism without the political apparatus. By emphasizing on the characterization of the space in which the action takes place and the roles that languages of different social groups play within the society, Stefano Fossati highlights the two aspects of the novel which are particularly relevant to the theme of isolation.

We have a detailed description of the Romanian experiences in exile in an informative article titled 'God was born in Exile : Mircea Eliade and the Recuperation of the Sacred' by Mircea Itu. He throws light on the various facets of the life and works of the celebrated Romanian Scholar and philosopher Mircea Eliade, which blossomed and acquired a new spiritual dimension during the various phases of his life spent away from his country, in India and elsewhere in the west.

In an essay rich in linguistic references tracing the evolution of the Jewish language Yiddish under the impact of exile, Pratibha Bhattacharya refers to the Jewish history of perennial banishment and exile which continued right up to the twentieth century exodus from Europe. Pratibha Bhattacharya traces the history of modern Yiddish as a part of the process of Jewish modernization and refers to the significance of the different volumes of *Ashkenaz* in Yiddish, having a bearing on the themes of political and spiritual exile. It shows how through sheer determination and perseverance, "the Jewish people nurtured their state of exile into an intellectual and linguistic paradise and made Yiddish an insignia of their cultural autonomy".

The same centrality of the notion of time in the context of history that we have noted earlier, is in focus in the essay 'Exile as Recuperation of the past in Augusto Roa Bastos' *El Fiscal*' by Vijaya Venkataraman who analyses the Spanish novel *El Fiscal* by the Latin American writer Augusto Roa Bastos and defines exile as utopia, or "a space suspended in time, between two times, past and future." Venkataraman posits exile as "a vantage point from which the writer could make his writing an act of opposition to oppressive regimes." As against the loss of ability to communicate in a state of inner exile she projects the act of writing as an enabling experience and epistolary as the ideal genre which would help maintain link with one's lost country and send a message into the future. *El Fiscal* brings us a mediated past and allows a brief incursion into a particular moment in the history of Paraguay as a means of understanding the present. Vijaya Venkatarman connects the notion of time with the relativity of history and affirms the role of counter memory and its implicit subversive content in the rewriting of the past undertaken by the New Historical Novel in Latin American literature.

Sonya S. Gupta, on the other hand, in her essay on 'Exile as Ex-centricity: Juan Goytisolo's Rehabilitation of Moorish Spain' terms exile as a land without a centre and questions the validity of the traditional discourse of the centre and the margins, arguing that with distance in terms of time and space, rewriting history is essentially a rehabilitation of the Other as part of the discourse. In Goytisolo's work Sonya Gupta reads an attempt to demolish the negative stereotypes of Spanish Orientalism through a parodical representation of the same. Instead of being a book on Orient seen through the Western eye, she views it as a work where Goytisolo has Moorish Spain rehabilitated in the historical narrative of Spain. He parodied the Western discourse on the Arab Other and showed, in fact, "the universalist attribute of an exile in that he moved not towards utopia but *atopia*, in other words, to 'ex-centricity'."

In the last essay in the Hispanic segment, titled 'I Shall Inhabit My Name or Memory of Oblivion', Antonia Cabanilles analyses a trilogy: *Story of a Teacher, Women in Black* and *Power of Destiny* by Josefina R. Aldecoa and delineates the process of the gradual unfolding of an exile experience in which the story of the individual merges in the history of the collective into one composite whole. With her analysis of the style, structure and narrative technique of the text, Antonia Cabanilles identifies the two responses which represent two different situations in time and space, 'two historical moments', which span the narration between the points of view of the mother and the daughter, between the collective and the individual. While Gabriela, the mother, in a diegetic text, relives the collective past in order to justify her present and circumscribes the forces of oblivion, for Juana, the daughter, the narration is necessary to fill in the gaps in her individual identity, it is the 'mythification of a lost land: the land of birth'. This would correspond to our earlier description of the mythic mode or the Age of Heroes, mentioned by Gardaphé. Here, echoing the Lukacsian concept of subjective memory, the author says, "Memory was this mysterious spiritual faculty, which kept our individual as well as collective coherence together, and it had been provisionally liberating us from disintegration."

To conclude, the present volume aims to engage with the discourses constructed by and around the texts with a view to focusing not only on the trauma of exile, on the loss of language, traditions, one's cultural milieu or on the manifold forms of violence to which exile writing was subject but also on the challenges thrown open before exiled writers who transformed their experience from an impingement on their selfhood into a positive act of cultural significance.

NOTES

1. Charles Taylor, *Multiculturalism and the 'Politics of Recognition'*, Princeton, 1992.
2. Renate Holub, 'Italian American Culturalism : A Critique' in *Beyond the Margin*, Madison, N.J., 1998.
3. Antonio Gramsci, Notebook No. 29, *Quaderni del Carcere* (Prison Note book), Turin, 1977, pp. 2341-51
4. Renate Holub, op. cit. p. 53.
5. Manuela Bertone, *From the Margin*, Purdue University Press, 1991.
6. Daniel Aaron, 'The Hyphenate writer and American Letters', *Smith Alumnae Quarterly*, July 1964, pp. 213-217.
7. Anthony Julian Tamburri, *To Hyphenate or Not to Hyphenate, the Italian/ American writer : An other American*, Montreal, 1992 and his 'In (Re) cognition of the Italian/American writer : Definitions and Categories' in Differentia 6, 1994, pp. 9-32.
8. Fred. L. Gardaphé, *Italian Signs, American Streets. The Evolution of Italian American Narrative*, Durham, 1996.
9. A.J. Tamburri, 'Rethinking Italian American Studies', *Beyond the Margin*, op. cit., p. 248.
10. Rose Basile Green, *The Italian American Novel : A Document of Interaction of Two Cultures*, Madison N.J., 1974.
11. Ernesto Livorini, 'John Fante, The Saga of Arturo Bandini', *Beyond the Margin*, op. cit., pp. 95-96.
12. Edvige Giunta, 'Blending Literary Discourses', Ibid. p. 118.
13. Helen Barolini, 'Becoming a Literary Person Out of Context', Massachusetts Review 27, no. 2 1986 pp. 262-74.
14. Antonio Gramsci, 'The Southern Question' in *The Modern Prince & Other Writings,* 1926; 10th reprint, New York 1957, pp. 34-35.
15. Ursula Apitzsch, 'Antonio Gramsci und die Diskussion um Multikulturalismus'. Das Argument 191, 192, pp. 53-62.
16. Nathan Glazer and Daniel Patrick Moynihan, *Beyond the Melting Pot, ...*, Cambridge, MIT, 1970.
17. Clifford Geertz, *The Interpretation of Cultures,* New York, 1973; Harold R. Isasks, *Idols of the Tribe: Group Identity and Political Change,* New York, 1975.
18. Michacl M.J. Fischer, 'Ethnicity and the Post-Modern Arts of Memory', in *Writing Culture: The Poetics and Politics of Ethnography,* Berkeley, 1986, p. 195.
19. Werner Sollors (edited by), *The Invention of Ethnicity,* New York, 1989, pp. XII-XVI.

LALITA SUBBU

Art, Exile and the Case of James Joyce: A Note

The relationship between art and exile has always been a controversial one, more so in the case of James Joyce than other literary artists. In this brief paper, I wish, firstly, to examine the reasons that drove Joyce into so-called 'exile' and, secondly, to speculate on how he fictionalised this theme.

With Joyce the process is not simple. In defining a term like exile, one invariably asks a lot of difficult questions. Just to name a few: Is not exile actually another form of engagement and re-location? Does a writer have to be in a state of geographical 'exile' to exemplify this process? Is exile a representation of the writer's guilt? Does the choice of exile contain a politics which is insidious, even offensively elitist?

Some of these questions gain urgency while considering Joyce. As one cannot homogenize all exiled artists under one definition a glance at Joyce's life is more revealing, for our purposes.

Joyce's immediate move to Paris in 1902 was undertaken for the purpose of becoming a medical student—something which he did not become. Instead, he read, studied, wrote reviews, lived on little food. He had become disenchanted with the improvidence of his father. Joyce had to go into exile to escape economic distress. He was removed from the boarding school and his family shifted from a fashionable area, Bray, to the poverty and squalor of Dublin. His father had once had a substantial private income from a lucrative, undemanding post in the local government for nationalist services rendered to the Liberal Party. He fell from favour along with the decline of Parnell, the leading Irish nationalist who was trying to force Parliament to consider Home Rule for Ireland.

Joyce saw his father stubbornly retaining the social superiority he was accustomed to even after becoming poor. The habit of associating all misfortunes with the martyrdom of the mythologized Parnell forms one of the paradigms of *A Portrait*, but Joyce's critique of his father is seen in the demythologizing account of poverty that always accompanied it. The relationship of Parnell with Mrs. Kitty O'Shea and the discrediting of Parnell by his own Irish nationalist groups created in Joyce a fear of betrayal. It also intensified the awareness in him that even a hero like Parnell had feet of clay. This realism informs the characterization of all the exiled heroes of his novels, who are anti-heroic.

Joyce had to return from Paris to attend to his dying mother in 1903. The anguish of the exiled writer at losing one symbol of the family (the mother) creates the bitterness and pride upon which Stephen's exile is predicated in *A Portrait* and *Ulysses*. His mother's patient suffering led him to distrust the religion demanding such self sacrifice.

Then what is it? Buck Mulligan asked impatiently. Cough it up. I'm quite frank with you. What have you against me now?

- - -

Stephen, depressed by his own voice, said: 'Do you remember the first day I went to your house after my mother's death?' - - -

You were making tea, Stephen said, and I went across the landing to get more hot water. Your mother and some visitor came out of the drawingroom. She asked you who was in your room.

Yes? Buck Mulligan said. What did I say? I forget.

You said, Stephen answered, O, It's only Dedalus whose mother is beastly dead.

A flush which made him seem younger and more engaging rose to Buck Mulligan's cheek.

Did I say that? he asked. Well? What harm is that?

He shook his constraint from him nervously. And what is death, he asked your mother's or yours or my own? You saw only your mother die. I see them pop off every day in the Mater and Richmond and cut up into tripes in the dissecting room. It's a beastly thing and nothing else. It simply doesn't matter. You wouldn't kneel down to pray for your mother on her deathbed when she asked you. Why? Because you have the cursed Jesuit strain in you, only it's injected the wrong way. To me it's all a mockery and beastly. Her cerebral lobes are not functioning. She calls the doctor Sir Peter Teazle and picks buttercups off the quilt. Humour her till It's over. You crossed her last wish in death and yet you sulk with me because I don't whinge like some hired mute from Lalouette's.

Absurd! I suppose I did say I. I didn't mean to offend the memory of your mother.

He had spoken himself into boldness. Stephen, shielding the gaping wounds which the words had left in his heart, said very coldly:

I am not thinking of the offence to my mother.

Of what, then? Buck Mulligan asked. Of the offence to me, Stephen answered.

Buck Mulligan swung round on his heel.

–O, an impossible person! he exclaimed. (Ulysses, 14-16)[1]

The same motif is repeated in Joyce's play *Exiles* (1918), where the hero, Richard Rowan, speaks about his dead mother:

Richard : How can my words hurt her poor body that rots in the grave? D you think I do not pity her cold blighted love for me? I fought against her spirit while she lived to the bitter end. [He presses his hand to his forehead.] It fights against me still - in here.

Beatrice : [As before] O, do not speak like that.

Richard: She drove me away. On account of her I lived years in exile and poverty too, or near it. I never accepted the doles she sent me through the bank. I waited, too, not for her death but for some understanding of me, her own son, her own flesh and blood; that never came. (*Exiles*, 24)[2]

In *A Portrait of the Artist as a young Man* Joyce explores Stephen's resistance to serve any authority as well as the difficulty of 'defining' his exile.

— Cranly, I had an unpleasant quarrel this evening.
— With your people? Cranly asked.
— With my mother.
— About religion?
— Yes, Stephen answered.

After a pause Cranly asked:

— What age is your mother?
— Not old, Stephen said. She wishes me to make my easter duty.
— And will you?
— I will not, Stephen said.
— Why not? Cranly said.
— I will not serve, answered Stephen.

. . .

— Do you believe in the eucharist? Cranly asked.
— I do not. Stephen said.
— Do you disbelieve then?
— I neither believe in it nor disbelieve in it, Stephen answered.
— Many persons have doubts, even religious persons, yet they overcome them or put them aside, Cranly said. Are your doubts on that point too strong?
— I do not wish to overcome them, Stephen answered.

. . .

— Your mother must have gone through a good deal of suffering, he said then. Would you not try to save her from suffering more even it. . . or would you?

—If I could, Stephen said, that would cost me very little.

— Then do so, Cranly said. Do as she wishes you to do. What is it for you? You disbelieve in it. It is a form: nothing else. And you will set her mind at rest.

He ceased and, as Stephen did not reply, remained silent. Then, as if giving utterance to the process of his thought, he said:

— Whatever else is unsure in this stinking dunghill of a world a mother's love is not. Your mother brings you into the world, carries you first in her body. What do we know about what she feels? But whatever she feels, it, at least, must be real. It must be.

. . .

— Do you fear then, Cranly asked, that the God of the Roman catholics would strike you dead and damn you if you made a sacrilegious communion?

— The God of the Roman catholics could do that now, Stephen said. I fear more than that the chemical action which would be set up in my soul by a false homage to a symbol behind which are massed twenty centuries of authority and veneration.

(*A Portrait*, 238, 239, 241, 243)[3]

It becomes clear that the pride of the artist in exile is in fact an attempt to hide his guilt about his feelings for the family, especially the mother and the father. These feelings extend also to his two other guardians: the Roman Catholic Church and the Irish nation. Stephen's animosity towards these amounts to a rejection of them:

. . . he had heard about him the constant voices of his father and of his masters, urging him to be a gentleman above all things and urging him to be a good catholic above all things. These voices had now come to be hollow-sounding in his ears. When the gymnasium had been opened he had heard another voice urging him to be strong and manly and healthy and when the movement towards national revival had begun to be felt in the college yet another voice had bidden him be true to his country and help to raise up her languages and tradition. In the profane world, as he foresaw, a worldly voice would bid him raise up his father's fallen state by his labours and, meanwhile, the voice of his school comrades urged him to be a decent fellow, to shield others from blame or to beg them off and to do his best to get free days for the school. And it was the din of all these hollow-sounding voices that made him halt irresolutely in the pursuit of phantoms. He gave them ear only for a time but he was happy only when he was far from them, beyond their call, alone or in the company of phantasmal comrades.

(*A Portrait*, 84)

The image of Ireland as a female goes back to Yeats's play, *Cathleen ni Houlihan* where the nationalist audience of the play were frenzied on seeing the old woman playing Ireland suddenly being transformed into a young girl with the walk of a queen. Joyce's Ireland is more cynically represented. The old woman who makes tea in *Ulysses* is a "wandering crone with shrunken paps who is a lowly form of an immortal serving her conqueror" (*Ulysses*, 20).

Joyce would not forgive the manner in which his contemporaries sacrificed their intellectual freedom to the repressive demands of the Irish Roman Catholic Church. All nationalistic fervour is seen as essentially flawed by Stephen in *A Portrait*. Those Irish freedom fighters who achieved the Irish free state between 1916 and 1922 sought to build it on virtues of Irish nationality, Gaelic language and Roman Catholic religion, all of which Stephen seeks to avoid.

It is quite possible that Joyce sought exile in order to achieve a greater clarity of perspective vis-a-vis Ireland, with whom he was as engaged as Yeats.

Exile becomes the mode of self-justification as well as a self-image:

> Not the least vital of the problems which confront our country is the problem of her attitude towards those of her children who, having left her in her hour of need, have been called back to her now on the eve of her longawaited victory, to her whom in loneliness and exile they have at last learned to love. In exile, we have said, but here we must distinguish. There is an economic and there is a spiritual exile. There are those who left her to seek the bread by which men live and there are others, nay, her most favoured children, who left her to seek in other lands that food of the spirit by which a nation of human beings is sustained in life. (*Exiles*, 128-29)

If we wish to territorialize the phenomenon of exile in Joyce, the exercise is a tricky one. Exile is portrayed even within Dublin, as in the case of the early work *Dubliners* (1914) which Joyce wrote in Switzerland. One of the Dubliners, Eveline, in the story of the same name, tries to escape from her humdrum and sordid life of supporting her family. She thinks of going away with her lover Frank but she is condemned to life imprisonment by her own rootedness in Ireland.

Similarly, the story "The Dead" dramatizes the rich past in contrast to the tawdry present. Gabriel Conroy has to come to terms with the fact that his wife had a secret self that was passionate and romantic and which constituted her past. A man had died for love of her and her memory of the dead lover is much more potent than her awareness of Gabriel is.

A part of Joyce's preoccupation with exile derives its urgency from the cultural movement of modernism 1890-1940. In this movement art problematizes the status of the author, creates self-reflexive texts, introduces the themes of the metropolis, transnational capitals and border-crossings.

The new figures who embody homelessness, unsettlement, solitude and impoverishment, constitute the singular narrative of exile. Through the ideology of mobile émigrés and migrant quarters, the writing of Joyce becomes self-referential, mutually isolating and radically estranged. The metropolis, as Raymond Williams defines it, is a citadel for conservative art. It is also a global market with new, cultural technologies. In this terrain, those who represent the transplanted, the alienated, the deprived, leave behind "homelands" and contemplate them from afar. They belong now not to any new community but to a new community born of the new language they choose to employ.

In a confrontation with techniques of realism and naturalism, they choose other modes of representation like the stream of consciousness and free themselves to achieve the aesthetic autonomy of a work. The amorality of such art is an important aspect of Joyce's fictionalizing of exile, because it carries with it new challenges and new politics—particularly in the use of language:

> Now, at the name of the fabulous artificer, he seemed to hear the noise of dim waves and to see a winged form flying above the waves and slowly climbing the air. What did it mean? Was it a quaint device opening a page of some medieval book of prophecies and symbols, a hawk-like man flying sunward above the sea, a prophecy of the end he had been born to serve and had been following through the mists of childhood and boyhood, a symbol of the artist forging anew in his workshop out of the sluggish matter of the earth a new soaring impalpable imperishable being?
>
> (*A Portrait,* 169)

Joyce demonstrates his allegiance to at least three myths of exile. Firstly, Stephen incorporates the myth of the fleeing Dedalus and Icarus, craftsmen and artists, whom he resembles in the act of escaping the nets Ireland has thrown round him through silence, exile and cunning. Secondly, in a strategic glance back at Homer, the theme of exile closely underpins the wanderings of Bloom (like the wanderings of Odysseus in Homer) who is absent from Ithaca. Lastly, we can discern yet another myth—the old Testament myth of the Israelites who are in exodus. They are always searching for, and are always away, from their homeland. The Bible also offers us one more myth of the returned exile—the crucial tale of the prodigal son who is banished for his wasteful ways and who returns after a period of adversity.

In the first of these myths, (the Daedalus-Icarus myth), the reality of the present is not conducive for the artist's survival, and therefore necessitates exile. In the second myth, the development and personality of the writer as artist and hero can only develop away from his homeland, as that of Odysseus in his wanderings. In the third and fourth myths—

those of the exiled Israelites searching for Canaan and the prodigal who returns home, the familial obligations of the exiled figure are hinted at, as he has chosen to disregard them for a while and his return to the home becomes a paradigm of nostalgia and fulfilment at once.

Exile, which is enforced by the establishment and exile which is voluntary and willed, can have different representations. In Joyce's case, the self-image was all important. In his play *Exiles,* both Richard Rowan, the artist in exile who has returned and Robert, the lover of Richard's wife, swear a new amoral commitment to their friendship:

> A battle of both our souls, different as they are against all that is false in them and in the world... against the spectre of fidelity. . . the spectre of friendship . . . The blinding instant of passion alone . . . is the only gate by which we can escape from the misery of what slaves call life. (*Exiles,* 89).

Joyce's passion for his wife Nora (with whom he ran away from Dublin to Zurich in 1904, by whom he had two children and whom he married only in 1931), pushes him towards a representation of the marginalized husband and wife in *Ulysses.* In the new language of the art practised by writers in exile, different forms of radicalization and subversion are evident, even with a classic modernist like Joyce. These include the manner in which consciousness is pluralized in *Ulysses* (Bloom-Molly-Stephen), identity is repeatedly posited and destroyed in *A Portrait* (the diary of Stephen) and subject-matter itself is periodically discredited in *Ulysses.*

Clearly, the most interesting relationship between art and exile in Joyce is in the deconstruction of the idea of a modernist narrative where the self is constituted with finality. Since Joyce's novels enact the ultimate exile of language from its earlier state, there is presented to us an endless set of multi-voiced themes and dislocations and violations of language and gender. This kind of experiment is inherently political, for it destabilizes the Anglo-Saxon lexicon, as well as the concept of literary institutions. There are, instead, in *Ulysses,* instances of a free play of meaning, as in certain episodes where various English styles ranging from medieval to modern are used. The self is thereby announced, cancelled, announced again and beginnings and ends are simultaneously voiced. Whether it is a meeting between Stephen and Bloom, or breakfast between husband and wife, or Bloom admiring beautiful women in his wanderings, or attending a funeral, the subject of each episode is presented, withdrawn and presented again. The reader has to understand the nature of exile enacted by the language in *Ulysses*, for it has left behind any traditional or established codes of predictability. Words, signs, meanings and symbols are all reached for and simultaneously eroded in a writing that re-discovers and represents anew every moment.

This very act of writing creates a non-narrative method, for sequentiality, while it is maintained in the overall adherence to Homer, is deliberately destroyed. Molly Bloom's combined role as calypso and Penelope is most riddling, as is Stephen's closely worked theory about sons and fathers in the Scylla and Charybdis section of *Ulysses.* Here the ingeniously worked out theory redefines exile :

"The note of banishment, banishment from the heart, banishment from home . . . doubles itself in the middle of his life, reflects itself in another, repeats itself, protasis, epitasis, catastasis, catastrophe . . . [Shakespeare] is the ghost and the prince. He is all in all . . . Every life is many days, day after day. We walk through ourselves, meeting robbers, ghosts, giants, old men, young men, wives, widows, brothers-in-love. But always meeting ourselves (*Ulysses,* 213).

Exile as confrontation with the self is perhaps the most daunting artistic formulation of Joyce, for it implies that we are forever in exile from ourselves. The theme of exile can here offer an interesting rider to the "Penelope episode of *Ulysses* where the 'affirmation' (so-called) of Molly Bloom in her monologue has been hailed as the triumph of her family and her bond with Bloom. However, it is important to recognize that *what* she affirms as *"Yes I said yes I will Yes"* is not so much to Bloom, her sexual partner, as to herself, the *marginalized* and *marginalizing* woman of *Ulysses.* For it is no secret that if Molly is openly adulterous with Blazes Boylan and a score of other lovers, Bloom in his own way has replicated these acts mentally throughout various episodes, in continuity of Homer—such as *Nausikaa* or the *Sirens*. The important difference is that where the Homeric source emphasizes expediency, tactics of survival and the mystery of Odysseus' personality as epic hero, Joyce's work emphasizes, not just Bloom's sexuality, but his preoccupation with the verbalizing of his ardour. So *Penelope* seeks not only to reinstate the exiled Bloom and the exiled Molly as lovers, but to emphasize the transgressions they have both undertaken as agents of the family.

The logic behind enlarging the theme of exile and art to include all such subversion may seem at times too difficult to credit. But, increasingly with Joyce, the polarisation of terms like 'Irish,' 'European,' 'naturalistic' and 'psychological' continues to irritate the sensitive reader of his work. All exile is self-referential, whether induced or voluntarily undertaken. The language of the self is a language of exile, and in a space full of characters and words jostling for centrestage, the theme of continual 'departure' from an earlier format is definitive—be it country language, community, religion, politics or gender. The question of where it finally arrives is conjectural.

Right from his urban short stories like Dubliners, through his confessional *A Portrait,* the exploration of exile in *Exiles,* the grand framework of dismantled subjectivities in *Ulysses* and the final dismantling of language in *Finnegans Wake,* Joyce's case confronts 'art' with 'exile' in complicated twists of history and aesthetics. Our concerns today encompass the problematic nature of too-fervent nationalisms around the world. They also embrace the diasporic identities of writers freewheeling in new spaces of their own creation and how, because of circumstances they stay away from homelands while descrying them aesthetically. The issue of non-resident authors, the accustations of 'elitism' in such postures, the new consciousness and globalization of such writing has certainly transformed the act of writing about one's own country. In a global climate where being too blindly nationalistic has its own dangers and being too irresponsible and indifferent to the problems of one's own country in the comfort and publicity of a new, insulated identity as non-resident, diasporic inhabitant of another, global setting, Joyce's 'nationalism' and his 'exile' are unified by one clear graph—which is artistic. The developmental aesthetic of Joyce cannot be easily halted and his version of exile is the physical departure from the motherland, the insistent engagement with her in terms of memory, desire, history and language. Finally, the way in which Joyce enacts the meaning of exile is self-encompassing, for it involves an endless journey away from and towards Ireland, away from and towards himself—a journey that searches for the genesis of words, personality and nation simultaneously.

NOTES

1. Pagination refers to James Joyce's *Ulysses* 1922; rpt. Hammondsworth, 1968. All further references are to this text and page numbers are given within parentheses.
2. Pagination refers to James Joyce's play *Exiles* 1918; rpt. Hammondsworth, 1952. All further references are to this text and page numbers are given within parenthesis.
3. The edition I have used is James Joyce's *A Portrait of the Artist as a Young Man* 1916; rpt. London, 1992. All further references are to this text and page numbers are given within parenthesis.

DOMINIQUE SARFATY-VARMA

Albert Camus: Kingdom of Exile

A Biblical Paradigm in *Exile and the Kingdom*

Exile and the Kingdom, published in 1957, just a few months before his Nobel Prize, has a special place in Camus' itinerary. This collection of short stories seems to reflect in a minor mode Camus' preoccupation with the Otherness. The same themes that he has dealt with in a doctrinaire and vehement manner in *L'Etranger,* (The Outsider) his best known novel, are here enounced in subdued hues, with many more nuances, though with the same metaphysical violence.

First, one must note that three among these six short stories are set in Algeria, the French Algeria where Camus was born in 1913, of a rather poor family. Camus thus had the privilege of being one of the few French writers to belong to the authentic working class, a kind of privilege that Sartre, with all his politically correct discourse on the proletariat, may have secretly envied. Camus' father, whom he lost at the tender age of one, was a farm hand, a 'colon' working for other 'colons'. Camus always remained, physically, emotionally, sentimentally, extremely attached to Algeria, the land of his birth, a land where he was also a foreigner, an outsider. A land where, two years after the publication of *Exile and the Kingdom,* he, like any other Frenchman, would be considered an enemy. This land to which he belonged did not belong to him. Excluded from the high society of the true blue colonists, he was also excluded from the people of the land, for whom the French could not be but intruders. But Camus loved this land, even though he remained separated from its inhabitants. So whenever he speaks of the sensual beauty of the earth, Camus constantly refers to the Algerian landscape, be it the indigo Mediterranean or the white harshness of the Saharan desert. Exile for him is exile from Algeria, but Algeria is already a land of exile, since he is supposed to belong to another land, across the sea, unknown and not even desired. His fate was that he would meet his death in this 'other' land, France. Algeria would forever remain the land of life.

Though *Exile and the Kingdom* is the title of the anthology, it actually refers specifically to the first story, called 'The Adulteress'. A very interesting programme indeed, Camus being himself a fine specialist on the matter. Let's have a brief look at the story. The heroine, Janine, has been married for twenty-five years to a rather dull, ordinary looking salesman who has devoted his life to money and his money to his wife. They live a secluded life, not mixing with the other French colons, and even less with the Arabs. Marcel, the husband, is a frank racist who does not disguise his prejudices and contempt for the Arabs with whom to survive he is compelled to do business. He has not understood that the times have changed—the story is set in post World War II, shortly before the Independence Movement. He cannot afford such scornful behaviour, which indeed is returned in kind by the people he has to deal with.

As for Janine, the encounter with the Other (the absolute Other being the Arab) is placed under the sign of fear. For the first time, to accompany her husband on a business trip, she unwillingly leaves the secluded middle-class comfort of their small flat on the Algerian coast and discovers a new unknown foreign world down South in the desert. There she is forced to confront her preconceived images of yellow sand and palm tree with the reality of the cold winds, dust storms, arid whiteness of desolate plateaus, sleepy towns with majestic burnous-clad silouhettes, like a traveller from outer space discovers the rocky mountains of a faraway planet. The desert becomes the mirror of her life, a life she is now forced to assess.

With the title 'The Adulteress', Camus leads us into the expectation of some classic love triangle, setting up the decor and characters, a woman aware of her frustration and of her charm, a sleepy busy husband, and coming out of nowhere, in a bus sailing in a dust storm, a good-looking French soldier, a sort of Gary Cooper in *Marocco*, the Foreign legion type, endowed with the beauty of a desert animal, the 'jackal-soldier' in Camus' words. A perfect setting for adultery. Incidentally, though adultery seems to our ears close to adult; and though we may be tempted to associate adultery with adulthood and somehow legitimate adultery as the archetype of adulthood, in fact the two words have different roots. Linguists in this case have used their scholarship as a kind of censorship for the benefit of the moral values we are supposedly in need of. Adult is the past participle of the Latin *adolescere*, which means to grow, and adultery comes from the Latin *ad ulterare*, or *ad alterum*, strictly speaking, *ad*, towards, *alterum*, the other. Indeed adultery is intrinsically an encounter with the forbidden Other. So while the reader is hoping for a forbidden encounter with the Gary Copper type soldier or may be a much more daring, more scandalous encounter with a majestic enigmatic Arab, Camus plays the literary trick of leading us, not to some B grade erotic adventure, but to a metaphysical experience, which is as much of a surprise for us as for Janine. With Camus' solid reputation of agnosticism, or rather straight atheism, with his existential denial of all transcendental references, it comes like a bodyblow; and the reader may feel frustrated, or at least disappointed by the non-fulfilment of the promise enticingly presented in the title. No doubt, however, that in our times, metaphysics is at any rate more taboo than sex. God would be even more taboo, but the word God is absent from the story, though the concept, as we shall see, is not that far off. In fact, this 'adultery' is the experience of the ultimate Other.

We can legitimately wonder how adultery would be connected with 'the Exile and the Kingdom'. Let's go back to the story. Janine feeling frightened and strange in this foreign land, realizing the nothingness of her past life, scared by her fear of death, could very well drop everything of her meaningless, absurd existence and run away from her accepted and admitted insatisfaction towards true pleasure, true passion, true completion. In other words, exchange boredom for folly. And the reader, like in a classic novel, could, by proxy, live her madness and forget his own reasoned passivity. But in this instance the reader cannot find catharsis in the heroine's passion, cannot compensate with Janine's transgressions his own unfulfilled desires. On the contrary, Janine becomes the counter-example of someone who is exiled from herself, exiled from her true feelings.

This exile would have remained abstract if Camus the atheist had not linked his heroine's experience to the old paradigm of the Exile and Kingdom, but in a totally secular way. Through some inescapable workings of childhood memory, when one imbibes all concepts and even the religious ones, the dual Biblical paradigm reappears in a metaphor of where do we belong, do we belong anywhere, is there any place in the world that we can call ours, can we appropriate any land as the immutable territory of some more or less distant ancestors? Old but still up-to-date questions.

Janine realizes her own exile on earth when from an old fort overlooking the dunes, she discovers, at the frontier of the desert, the black tents of a nomads' camp etched in the cold light of a winter sunset. Dual worlds, the nomadic and the sedentary, the black tents and the white terraces stained with the blood-red of the drying chillies. Another Biblical conflict, Abel the wandering pastor and Cain the sedentary civiliser, Cain the murderer, Cain the first builder of cities, the initiator of civilisation. One may recall that what provoked Cain's jealousy towards showing an open preference for the wandering pastor over the agriculturist.

Faced with the paradigm of the parallel worlds of the tents and the solidly built houses and the mere beauty of the landscape, Janine experiences an emotion which not even the most handsome dream lover could give her.

There, further South, at the point where the sky and the earth joined in a pure straight line, there, it suddenly seemed to her, something was awaiting her, something she had ignored till this very day and of which she had never ceased to feel the need.

There lies the Kingdom. Exile and Kingdom form two parallel antithetic worlds. Exile, *exilium* in Latin, means banishment. One is always banished from somewhere. The kingdom is the consecrated demarcated piece of land under a supreme authority. For a hardcore convinced Republican like Camus, the Kingdom obviously cannot have a political connotation, but a mythical meaning. It is the kingdom of fairy tales, beyond time, where revolution of course is unthinkable. It is the kingdom of the promised land, the kingdom of the Gospels, a kingdom freed of kings, a kingdom of god without god. Camus lets the exiled Janine dream about the kingdom, a parable which he must have heard in his childhood and kept hidden in the closet of his mind. One may though expect from Camus at least a touch of blasphemy, like what he aims at in the second short story of the book called 'The Renegade' where a missionary at the frontier of death, tortured by the savages he wanted to convert, proclaims his own conversion to the Others' fetishes and cries out: No, "God does not speak in the wilderness." But in 'The Adulteress', there is no such obvious blasphemy.

In fact, the simple frustrated middle-class woman has in the desert a kind of metaphysical revelation. The vision of the nomads liberates the repressed emotions that she had kept concealed even from herself. They incarnate a freedom of body and mind that she feels incapable of achieving, but that she can experience for a moment through the inaccessible others.

For ages incommensurate, on the arid land, scraped to its bones, of this inordinately long territory, a handful of men had unceasingly been plodding along, who possessed nothing but served nobody, free and destitute sovereigns of a strange kingdom. Janine did not know why this idea was filling her with so sweet and vast a sadness that it was forcing her eyes shut.

The sadness which Janine enjoys, is a mixing of pleasure and pain, a kind of nostalgia, not for something which would have happened in the past, but of something suddenly appearing like a piece of an improbable future. Like the recognition of an impossible love. The secular Camus makes her succumb to a sensual illumination, an opening, for a brief moment, of her senses and her mind, like a treasure offered in a casket already about to close up.

She only knew that this kingdom, from time immemorial, had been promised to her and that it would never, though, be hers, never again, except at this fugitive instant perhaps when she opens her eyes again on the sky suddenly still and on its streams of clotted light, as the voices coming up from the Arab town abruptly fell silent. It seemed to her that the flow of the world had just stopped and that, nobody, from that very moment, would grow older nor die. In all places from now, life was suspended, except in her heart where somebody was at the same time crying of pain and wonder.

What Camus calls 'the knot in her heart' loosens. The wonder is accompanied with pain, the pain of an ephemeral and everlasting discovery. Janine's tears are tears of pleasure since the unimaginable is now at 'eye reach'. The kingdom is lying in front of her, the kingdom of pure freedom, beyond the laws, conventions, segregations she has been living with. We are in exile when we are foreigners in a land, be it our land, our nations, our native land, but one is also in exile when one is banished from one's own inner self.

Now it is high time to recall that in the Judeo-Christian world where Camus was born, where Janine belongs, exile has a very long history. Even the non-believers know that in the Bible, exile starts with the beginning of time, or rather that time begins under the sign of exile, when Adam and Eve are banished, exiled from Paradise. From the East of Eden, Adam's descendants begin their peregrination, their long march into history. *Exilium* in Latin means 'to walk,' 'to go' (the root *il* or *ul* in *ilium* means 'to go'), *ex*, of course, meaning 'out of', from a point but spatial and temporal. Literally, the exiles, i.e. the whole human race, have to accomplish a journey out of Paradise since the moment they are born. The *ex* of exile is a definition of life.

Exile is also a one word definition of the Old Testament. 'The Exile and the Kingdom' together cannot be but a Biblical reminiscence, as these two words summarise the Old and the New Testaments. Though *The Book of Exile* forms one part of the Old Testament, the Old Testament is itself a Book on Exile. The destiny of the Hebrews and by extension, of all their relatives — the human race as a whole, has for name, Exile. Exile is the main threat in the Prophets' mounts, Jeremiah, Ezekiel, Amos, Daniel... And the story and history of the Hebrews is this journey from one exile to another. Interestingly, the two principal kinds of exile are covered and abundantly described in the Bible, one is the voluntary exile, self chosen for economic and political reasons, the other one is the banishment or forced exile suffered under historical and political forces. The first exile in the Bible historically dated 745-725 BC is the self imposed or rather self decided one. Joseph and his brothers leave Judea for Egypt. They decide to temporarily settle in Egypt for economic reasons: famine, lack of food, non-availability of work. They remain in

Egypt of their own free will, but because of a political change, new pharaoh, new laws, they become slaves under the dictat of the new ruler. The departure from Egypt is called Exodus, *exodos* being the Greek word, *odos* signifying 'way', and *ex* 'out of', *exodos* means the way out. For the exiles, exodus is finding the way out. The exodus is the escape from, the liberation from exile, the positive face of exile. This liberation is Moses' job in the Bible. The exodus is how the Hebrews are rescued from Egypt under Moses' direction and how they are given a pattern of worship on the form of the Tabernacle, this special tent sheltering the Ark of the Covenant. The second Exile is the forced exile, the banishment. In 597 BC, Jerusalem is besieged and captured, the Hebrews, king and citizens, are deported to Babylon. This exile begins with violence and ends in violence, with little participation of the Hebrews. The exile ends because in the cycle of violence, Persia conquers Babylon and the exiled Jews return to rebuild Jerusalem. One has to underline that according to the Bible they are partly responsible for their unchosen exile. The Bible is rather clear on that point, the Prophets had warned the Hebrews: those who don't follow the laws (the divine and mosaic laws) will be punished by exile. So what is also underlined is that the inner order can restore the outer order, a lesson in responsibility that was very dear to the philosopher Emmanuel Levinas. Levinas, a phenomenologist and Talmudic philosopher likes to quote the 119 Psalm: "I am a stranger on earth, don't hide your commandments from me." And God says: "You are a stranger on earth, domiciled in my place." In other words, the earth and a *fortiori* the land does not belong to man. So exile which is the general condition of man on earth can be worsened by the historical exile, but in Levinas's interpretation of the Bible, not when ethics reign.

Now if Exile is a name for the Old Testament, Kingdom could as well be a generic term for the New Testament. The 'Kingdom of God' is the central message of the New Testament. "He went down about all Galilee preaching the gospel of the Kingdom." (Matthew, 4, 23). What is translated by Kingdom? As is usual in translations, the meaning can be distorted. One knows that the 'original' New Testament is in Greek, but it could not have been originally pronounced in Greek, since Jesus' language (and the language of the people then) was Aramaic. There is a lot of discussion in authorised circles and specially in the less orthodox ones about what Jesus has really said and about whether the original teachings would even exist somewhere. Anyway, what has been translated by 'Kingdom' is the Latin *Regnum*, itself translated from the Greek *Basileia* and certainly from the Hebrew and Aramaic words: *Malkuth*, *Malkutha* (cf Malik). *Malkuth*; and its Greek avatar *Basileia*, means kingship, rule, sovereignty. In this occurrence, Kingdom does not stand for a geographical area nor a political system or group. *Basileia* which was the main object of Jesus's predication, is not kingdom in fact, but reign. "Let Thy kingdom come." The coming of the kingdom is the *parousia*, presence or appearance of a great person (darsan). It means the Reign or establishment of Principles.

It may seem a long digression, but the two concepts of Exile and Kingdom are interconnected. In brief, the exiled has to re–establish the principles in himself. Christian predicators and preacher-philosophers have used this dichotomy as a symbol. Augustine in his commentary on the Gospel of John says:

> At the present time, then, before we come to the land of promise, namely the eternal Kingdom, we are in the wilderness of Tabernacles.

In other words, we are in exile as long as we have not reached the Kingdom.

I believe it is not stretching too far to say that Janine, Camus' heroine, has in the desert, her wilderness, her vision of the Tabernacles. This revelation, however fugitive it may be, is to transform her life. The last part of the story describes the adultery of Janine, her approaching the Other. Like for a rendezvous with a lover, she leaves at night her husband in the conjugal bed and rushes out in the night towards the old fort. Camus the atheist describes Janine's experience as a sensual, mythical encounter, which Camus calls 'deliverance' (moksha?).

> She wanted to be delivered, even if Marcel, if the others were not to be delivered." She responds to a "silent call that after all she could from her own will stop or perceive, but whose meaning she would never know, if she did not immediately respond to it.

In Camus' words, the end of exile, the apprehension of the kingdom is like, or rather is a sexual experience. To come out of exile, one has to listen to, follow, one's senses. Janine's experience is not only a compensation of a sexual desire, but a coming to wisdom through sensuous experience.

> In front of her, the stars were falling one after the other, their light getting extinguished among the stones of the desert, and each time, Janine would open out a little more to the night. She was breathing, forgetting the cold, the weight of all living creatures, the maddened clotted life, the long anxiety of living and dying. After so many years when, fleeing her fear, she had been frenetically running around without aim, she was at last stopping. At the same time, it seemed to her she was finding her roots again, the sap was flowing up in her whole body which had ceased shivering… . Then with an unbearable gentleness the water of the night began to fill Janine, overcame the cold, little by little came

up from the obscure centre of her being and overflowed in continuous streams to her moan filled mouth. The moment after, the entire sky was laying on her overturned upon the cold earth.

The whole sky has become the lover.

Thus Camus shows the way out of exile, out of the fear of death, Janine's exodus, his exodus, Camus, who is not exempt from machismo, whose heroes are men and males, needed a woman, for he could not have translated otherwise such a forbidden (in his own eyes) experience. His only heroine helps him transgress his own ideological correctness, define may be his sole mystique, the opening to the language of the senses. For this sensuous encounter is also clearly a mystical one, one he would not have allowed himself nor any male hero.

This is the point where there is no exile any more, no kingdom even, mere sovereignty on oneself in the form of a complete surrender of oneself. Janine does not belong to any husband, society, nation, code of behaviour. She has become, like the nomads, a free and destitute sovereign of herself. That is for Camus the exiled the true advent of the 'kingdom'. His proudly 'heretic' allegiance to the Kingdom, a hymn to the glory of the senses. The exodus is through the individual's inner power and disruptive sexual force which can drive people out of imposed kingdoms, out of forced or accepted rules, in an almost universal prayer.

REFERENCES

Albert Camus, L'Exil et le Royaume, 1957.

Albert Camus, L'Etranger, 1942, Le Mythe de Sisyphe, 1942.

Emmanuel Levinas, Humanisme de l'autre homme, Entre Nous

Augustine, *Gospel of John*, Vol. I.

Walter Brueggemann, Hopeful Imagination: Prophetic voices in Exile.

Peter F. Ellis, *The Men and the Message of the Old Testament*.

E.W. Nicholson, *Exodus and Sinai*.

Charles H. Dodd, *The Parables of the Kingdom*.

George E. Ladd, *The Gospel of the Kingdom*.

D.A. Carson, *The Sermon on the Mount* (Matthew).

HEMA V. RAGHAVAN

The Exile in the Plays of Samuel Beckett

Presenting the case of Beckett in relation to the theme of exile in the European literature of the twentieth century this paper does not deal with a writer who was forced to distance himself from his home, from his countrymen and from his milieu, but who voluntarily chose to move out of his native land. Hence his writings are not the literary articulations of the experience of an exile expressing nostalgia,deep pessimism and despair. The concept of exile which I shall explore in Beckett's plays does not relate to any intense painful experience of a writer who had fled from his country or who wrote in response to his condition of being an exile.

To begin with, we take note of the fact that Beckett moved out of Dublin when he was twenty-five and spent his next five years moving about Europe till finally settling in Paris in 1937. He took an active part in the French Resistance and was hiding from the Gestapo for the next two and a half years. During this period, he was, as he himself said, "on the trot" liable at any moment to be recognised and executed or sent to almost certain death in the concentration camps. Thus Beckett, more than anyone had during these years lived as an exile, close to death, experiencing suffering, hardship and fear along with a fierce determination to stay alive and go on which we find reflected in all his works. Beckett who described himself as "a man whose world has no outside" said that "it is impossible for me to talk about my writing because I am constantly working in the dark... I can only estimate my work from within".[1] Beckett in this sense was for a brief while an exile from his adopted home in Paris and it was during this period that he wrote his second novel *Watt* set in the country round Foxrock, Dublin where he had been brought up early in life. All his works written before and after this period of semi-hiding to escape the Gestapo are expressions not of a physical exile but those of a metaphysical exile, of one who had retreated into an inner world, an inner emigration with a determined quest to find a meaning in existence in pursuit of some significance for himself and the world he inhabited. At the end of his first phase of fictional writing, Beckett arrived at the three following fundamental truths about Man and his existence:

1. Man is a rational being who constantly endeavors to rationalise the irrational.
2. Man cannot refrain from seeking the impossible answers to the questions, "where now? who now? when now?"[2]
3. Man becomes the *Unnameable* who neither has an identity nor can give himself one. All his efforts at articulating the 'I' expose the limitation of his rationality. Man ends up with the discovery that there is nothing to reason, no power to reason, no desire to reason together with the inordinate compulsion to reason even as he is framed within an absurd and irrational system. *The Unnameable*, the last novel of the trilogy and the last one of his first phase of writing ends thus:

...you must go on, I can't go on, I'll go on, you must say words, as long as there are any, until they find me, until they say me strange pain, strange sin, you must go on, perhaps it's done already, perhaps they have said me already, perhaps they have carried me to the threshold of my story... *you must go on, I can't go on, I'll go on.*[3]

The Unnameable ends here with his unresolvable dilemma where *to be is to ask questions as to why time does not pass; where to ask questions is to use words that have no validity* except to give the questioner his consciousness of an existence that disappears within words and yields no further clue to the essential self. The cycle starts with questions once more: Where now? Who now? and When now? and in the silence that ensues, the 'going on' continues in a distinctive voice that denies the voice itself.

Thus exiled from his self, Man in Beckett's plays (the next phase of his writing) and in his later fiction abandons his quest, moves out of the world of society and fellowmen and seeks isolation. There is nothing more that remains for Beckett's fictional hero except words, silence and the eternity of living within an absurd universe. Beckett's concern shifts from the quest after self to a quest after endurance in a world that offers him no certitude except that of suffering. Beckett's writings in his second phase are not as despairing as his early fiction, but they make a fresh departure towards deriving a *modus operandi* to live with an awareness of the absurdity of existence and of the suffering it entails with no hope of deliverance.

This awareness leads to protest and rebellion, but the awareness of any possibility of success leads his characters to a state of mental exile to a kind of rebellious co-existence with the Absurd. The Beckettian exile does not negate the world nor moves out of it. He lives in it with a rebellious determination to countenance the suffering of living by a bold acceptance of it.

Beckett has been classified as a dramatist of the Absurd who focuses upon Man's relentless protest and rebellion against human condition—where to be born is a compulsion; to suffer is an obligation and to die is to re-start the whole cycle.

In this context it is useful to recall Camus' definition of the absurdity of existence as "the exile of man from a universe suddenly divested of illusions and light."[4] Camus' absurd heroes in his early plays like Caligula, Martha and Don Juan represent his image of the Absurd Man who fails to reconcile himself to the absurd order and therefore pursues a life of wilful negation. Most Absurd dramatists of the post-World War era express this aspect of man's relationship to the Absurd and reduce him to a farcical figure in his futile and negative attempt to deny meaning in a meaningless existence.

But some of the Beckettian characters—whom I term as Beckettian exiles—have dignity and strength to co-exist with the Absurd. These characters of Beckett come close to Sisyphus, Camus' later image of the Absurd Man in his endless and futile toil to roll the stone up the slope. Camus contends that Sisyphus is happy because he surmounts his fate through scorn and contempt. In his book *The Rebel* written years later, Camus pursues the idea of Sisyphus, of rebellion as a possible means to triumph over the Absurd. Camus' admiration for Sisyphus who is 'on the go' is in contradiction to his earlier view of Man's relationship with the Absurd as something that can never be triumphed over through defiance and scorn. But the later Camus suggests an affirmation of the worth and value of man who courageously rebels against his fate.

However, Beckett has a far more frightening perception than Camus that harbours no illusion of happiness or triumph for man who is confined within the limits of the Absurd. Beckett's exiles have the Sisyphic scorn and anger against their miserable condition of existence and their angry response is to remain indifferent to the absurd suffering. Their clarity of perception makes them aware of the fully doomed state of their existence and the futility of all their efforts to extricate themselves out, but such awareness does not alter their state of rebellion. The world can march on inexorably to a state of extinction but the strength exhibited by these characters to march on without flinching gives them a perennial dignity. They refuse to be intimidated and cowed down by the Absurd. Their rebellion is a spontaneous protestation with no planned issues before it. It is here that Beckett diverges from Camus' concept of the Absurd rebel. Camus draws a distinction between rebellion and revolt, the former leading to the latter where the revolt is an aspiration towards the establishment of new values. In an analysis of Camus' thought, Maurice Friedman comments:

...If he believes in nothing else, the Absurd Man must at least believe in his protest, his rebellion. In so doing he is demanding order in the midst of chaos, and unity in the very heart of the ephemeral.[5]

This is what Camus' Man does— demanding order in the midst of chaos through his protest and rebellion. Beckett's characters, conversely do not accommodate any hope or value in their rebellion. Their rebellion arises when all illusions fade including the illusion of any possible success for the rebel. When rebellion fails, says Camus, it ends in exile. In Beckett the foreknowledge of failure which does not hinder rebellion turns his character into exile. These are not exiles in Camus' sense of the term—of becoming an alien or a stranger—but in terms of indifference to and non-involvement in the Absurd happenings around them. Unlike Camus' rebels who combine a vision of nothingness with a positive value (of being happy/triumphant) Beckett's rebels meet the absurdity of existence by a courageous exile into suffering without anticipating any form of happiness or positive value from such an action. Beckett is sometimes bracketted with early Camus on the basis of the commonness of their vision of the Absurd. But Beckett goes even farther than the later Camus' positive affirmation of rebellion to postulate a state of exile in which there is neither negation nor affirmation.

Beckett's characters present a composite picture of the suffering Man who has no other means to express his indignation except through total indifference to his miserable state. They know that rebellion is an essential attribute of mankind, but viewed in the context of the absurdity of existence, it turns out to be futile and meaningless. But what option does man have? He has to rebel and simultaneously admit that to rebel is to fail, but to shrink from it is desertion. These characters have the dauntless resoluteness to compensate for their decaying physical powers and they establish their superiority over suffering by adopting a cavalier attitude towards it. Though they never triumph over the Absurd, their sneering contempt towards its arbitrary infliction of existential pain has an enabling power to help them make light of their suffering and gain greater strength to resist further aggravation. These are the true rebels who exile themselves to suffering. These rebels withdraw all other illusory options of submitting meekly to the Absurd or clinging to illusory hopes of a possible salvation through the arrival of a Godot. They exemplify the spirit of a true exile whose voluntary withdrawal from the world of illusions evidences the mood of rebellion in them. In a unique and paradoxical way these rebels-turned-exiles combine an active spirit of rebellion with a formidable and courageous acceptance of suffering.

It is here that Beckett's drama comes close to the original tragic drama of the Greeks where, as George Steiner points out, "the spheres of reason, order and justice are terribly limited and that no progress in science or technology can enlarge their relevance."[6] Outside of man is the force—call it by whatever name— God or Godot, Fate or the Absurd. It is a force against which man is a cipher, a small nothing and man cannot deny his nothingness. Some of the Beckettian characters accept their nothingness not by means of abject surrender, but through indifference and nonchalance. Beckett's perception of the isogenic equation between existence and suffering constitutes the fundamental tragedy of Man. His plays are in line with the Greek tragedies of Oedipus and Antigone and the Shakespearean tragedy of King Lear dealing with the constant struggle between Man and the Absolute and the ultimate defeat of Man. In all these cases the situation is imposed on Man and he is forced to respond. The only difference is in the choice put before him. In the earlier tragedies, the choice is between two orders—both moral in the case of Antigone and between good and bad in the case of Lear where the voluntary choice of the bad leads to Lear's destruction.

Beckett's drama, however, is one of choicelessness. His first play *Waiting For Godot* demonstrates the absurdity of both waiting and not waiting. To wait or not to wait when both are absurd is the dilemma of the two tramps. There is little freedom of action—what Rosette Lamont refers to as "the choice of choicelessness".[7] The two tramps, Vladimir and Estragon do not have any awareness of this choice of choicelessness as they wait for a Godot to come and relieve them of their misery. Strangely enough it is Pozzo who secures this awareness and remains impervious to his loss and suffering at the end. He never waits for any Godot to come to his aid. He revels in his abysmal suffering and displays a rare degree of fortitude to endure without recourse to illusory waiting for succour and relief. Pozzo moves towards a timeless reality that makes a mockery of all illusory hopes of salvation. His entry and exit in both the Acts with a war-like cry "ON" gives his rebellion an affirmation. He who is on a losing end from the beginning, deprived of his physical possessions such as his briar, his vaporiser, his whip and his watch, is the one to gain a sense of awakening consequent upon the physical change he suffers between the two Acts. The final loss of his sight helps him in a queer way to see into the future. He recognises the absurdity of the linear concept of time and to Vladimir's insistent questioning pertaining to time - as to when he went blind and when his menial Lucky went dumb -, he replies furiously:

Have you not done tormenting with your accursed time? When? When? One day we become blind, one day we go deaf, one day we go dumb, one day we are born, one day we die, the same day… .[8]

Pozzo has moved away from his earlier narcisstic arrogance and pomposity and shows himself to be a courageous rebel who could exile himself from the world of illusions and hope to a world where to "pine, shrink, and dwindle" is the only certitude. He is able to face the Absurd in all its awesomeness marked by depletion and decay. His cry 'ON' at the end of his visits is in contrast to Vladimir's pathetic cry "I can't go on. What have I said?" [9] The point of similarity is that both have to go on. Pozzo's 'ON' is without Vladimir's abject surrender to Godot and makes a mockery of the metaphysical arbitrariness that controls human existence. It is a rare display of endurance that transcends servile passivity and grovelling submission.

The other Beckettian rebels-turned-exiles are Hamm in *Endgame*, Dan Rooney in *All That Fall*, Winnie in *Happy Days* and the Old Man in *That Time*. Hamm's "Me to play" (Beckett himself said in one of his rehearsals of *Endgame* that " Hamm says 'no' to Nothingness"[10]), Dan's acceptance of the choiceless imperative to move on without a stop, with no prospective haven to reach and Winnie's refusal to negate life through her resolve to remain cheerful despite being buried in the sand exemplify the spirit of the Beckettian rebels who exile themselves to suffering. These men and women withdraw all other illusory options of submitting meekly to the Absurd or clinging to illusory hopes of salvation through the intervention of a Monsieur Godot. These higher rebels can be classified as exiles where the term 'exile' is not to be misconstrued as being away from one's fellow beings or one's region or nation but to be looked at in its conceptual sense of voluntary withdrawal from the world of illusions to register their defiance. The Beckettian exile refrains from action but his non-action arises out of knowledge of the futility of action in the context of the Absurd. His protests are not impulsive, but well deliberated course of action within the limits of human potentiality. He does not rebel with the desire to make his shattered world whole, nor to vent his anger on the Absurd but to gain for himself a direction that would enable him to live with suffering on his terms. Instead of a futile attempt to thwart suffering, the Beckettian exile attempts at nullifying the effect of suffering through an acceptance of the same in a mood of defiance. It is thus the exile expresses his feeling of contempt for the irrational metaphysical order. By voluntarily enduring suffering, by exiling himself to the world of suffering without hope, without illusions, he rises above the threshold of suffering to eke out some small measure of dignity for himself.

The tragic sense of life which is the legacy of the Greek genius has once again surfaced in Beckett's drama. Beckett, like the Greek poets, deals with the fundamental predicament of human existence and asserts that the forces that shape or destroy our lives are beyond the governance of reason or justice. Antigone and Oedipus marched towards their disasters in full awareness of their doom. There can be no material compensation in Greek tragedy. All we notice is that there is an ironic abyss between man's knowledge and action. Yet in this awareness, in his acceptance of suffering, lies man's claims to dignity. Powerless and broken, the Greek tragic hero moves on and gains stature and is ennobled by the vengeful ire of the gods. The Beckettian character accepts his wretched state as part of human condition. He has the Greek hero's courage to remain nonchalant and indifferent to the absurd happenings around him.

His fight implies a total acceptance of the harsh realities of life with faith and courage to endure what cannot be cured. The wounds are not healed and there are no remedies. But the mind, as I.A. Richards says, does not shy away from anything, nor does it protect itself with any illusion; it stands uncomforted, alone and self-reliant. It is this aloneness, this awareness of hopelessness, this resistance to illusory comforts, this refusal of crutches of any kind that make the Beckettian exile.

NOTES

1. Quoted in Reid, Alec: *All I Can Manage More Than I Could* (Dublin: The Dolmen Press,1968), p. 53.
2. Beckett, Samuel: *Molloy, Malone Dies, The Unnameable* (London: Calders (publishers) Ltd.,1959), p. 293.
3. op.cit., p. 418.
4. Camus, Albert: *The Myth of Sisyphus* (Hammondsworth:Penguin Books,1975), p.13.
5. Friedman, Maurice: *To Deny Our Nothingness: Contemporary Images of Man* (Chicago & London: The Univ. of Chicago Press,1978), p. 335-36.
6. Steiner, George: *The Death of Tragedy* (London: Faber & Faber Ltd.,1961), p. 8.
7. Lamont, Rossette: "Beckett's Metaphysics of Choiceless Awareness" in *Samuel Beckett Now* (Chicago & London: The Univ. of Chicago Press,1970), p. 199.
8. Beckett, Samuel: *Waiting For Godot* (London: Faber & Faber,1956), p. 89.
9. ibid.
10. Cohn, Ruby: *Back to Beckett* (New Jersey: Princeton Press,1973), p. 152.

RAJAKRISHNAN V.

The Land of the Dead in Salman Rushdie's *The Moor's Last Sigh* and Some Reflections Based on Indian Response to the Theme of Exile

As the saga of the Zogoiby family approaches its end in Salman Rushdie's *The Moor's Last Sigh,* the novelist, performing one of his cunning tricks, prepares the reader for a fresh surprise. There is a detective element that runs through the description of the decline and downfall of the Zogoiby family (reminiscent somewhat of the tragic prophecy concerning the Buendia family which is fulfilled at the end of Gabriel Garcia Marquez's *One Hundred Years of Solitude*) which is played up for exaggerated effects in the last part of the novel. In the first place there occurs a change of scenery in the novel's fourth section, from the teeming Indian city of Bombay to the curiously withdrawn Spanish village of Benengeli, with a corresponding shift in the narrative code, style and imagery. Having shown the ways in which the grand narratives of history disintegrate under pressure from forces having an ancient and primordial appeal, Rushdie quietly switches over here to the conventions of fairy-tale fantasy. An air of decadent lyricism erupts into his prose, in keeping with the spirit of the new place he conjures up from another continent and another time. While working towards the denouement of the crazy story of the Zogoiby family parodying the strategies of 'crime mystery' novels, the novelist attempts to resolve some of his grandly orchestrated themes, as the narrator is given the last opportunity for untying some of the paradoxes in his life which have pursued him for long.

A fugitive from law, the Moor arrives in Benengeli to escape the guilt of a murder which he thinks he has committed and in pursuit of the stolen paintings of his mother Aurora Zogoiby. As he ruefully recalls while languishing in the tower on the hilltop, he misjudged almost all the encounters he had on his trip to this outlandish Spanish village, from the time he boarded the plain in Bombay. The people he met were putting up a show (though one person did warn him), the signs were deceptive and the fact of the matter was that he was being led into the trap laid for him by Vasco Miranda, the one-time friend of the Zogoiby family now turned into an avenging fiend. Perhaps there was in the Moor a latent feeling of life-weariness which coincided with the mood of this village, the sense of the ending of a family legacy and as historical epoch, which found its outer expression in the twilit stupor that pervaded the life here.

The sense of unreality which started weighing upon the Moor as he moves through the new landscape is suddenly quickened on finding a thoroughfare known as the Street of Parasites. It is inhabited by expatriates from different nationalities and cultures. There is not a single Spaniard to be seen here. A voice tells the Moor that the eyes of the people who crowd this street are empty. Those who inhabit the Street of Parasites are lost souls in alligator shoes and sports-shirts with crocodiles over their nipples. They are already in Hell and they are not aware of this. Because their pensions and allowances are paying up, they refuse to lie down in their graves. So these parasites walk up and down the street, eat and drink and gossip about the hideous minutiae of life. Incidentally there are no mirrors to be seen here. If there were, none of these trapped shades would be reflected in them. What these sinful creatures require is compassion. The Moor's first reflections on coming across this gathering of fugitives are somewhat revealing.

> 'Perhaps these expatriates are the Moors,' I thought. 'And I am one of them, after all, arriving here in search of something that matters to nobody but myself and staying, perhaps to die.'[1]

One cannot fail to see that the Moor's instant identification with the 'international riff-raff' who occupy this infernal maze is called up by some strong psychic compulsions and political imperatives. He has obviously burnt his bridges in the home city of Bombay. The series of explosions which shook Bombay in the wake of rising communal violence following the demolition of the Babri Masjid have blown to bits whatever was left of his family and its fortunes, leaving the Moor with little options regarding his future. A way of life had almost come to an end, a fragile, cosmopolitan culture, with its mixture of the beautiful and the ugly, which the Zogoiby family had represented, now stood on the verge of extinction. Post-Masjid India carries unwholesome prospects for the Moor and his tribe. The incredible transformation of the myriadly wonderful city of Bomaby brought about by the saffron brigade led by Raman Fielding signalled a prospect which the Moor had always looked upon with some metaphysical dread: the defeat of multiplicity by singularity, of the Many by the One. A 'putsch' from the iron-clad, ultra-Right groups claiming monopoly over Hindu nationalism, which made a shameless use of religious symbolism to reinforce their revivalist appeal, had knocked at the bottom of India's composite culture. Earlier in the novel, while meditating upon the wreckage of his relationship with Uma Saraswati, the Moor tells the reader that his lovc-life has become a 'bitter parable' for him. Uma, with her multiple selves, her artistic imperative to compensate the poverty of the real with garish fantasy and finely shaped lies; and her love of extremes in matters of the heart which lent her an enigmatic appeal, represented the modernist idea. The Moor came to believe that her humiliation—and violent end—represented in some sense a defeat for the pluralist philosophy. Coming in the wake of her tragic death, the rise to power of Raman Fielding, the Plato of the Underworld, now transformed into the high-priest of a new-Fascist gospel, appeared to have completed the disfiguration of the public reality in the city of Bombay and heralded a sequence of events which led to the Moor's final disenchantment with the Indian scene. A vertical communal divide seems to run through the Indian subcontinent, which jolts smaller groups and rootless cosmopolitans into an awareness of their marginality and growing irrelevance.

Bereft of a home, pursued by memories of real and imagined crimes, unable to recover from the loss and disappearance of almost everything—emotional ties, cultural moorings, values and institutions—which had lent a degree of coherence to his otherwise discontinuous and embattled existence, the Moor finds a resting place and a place to die too, in Benengeli. In this limbo of exile, he had found his Mooristan.

The German expatriate Gottfried Helsing, who introduces the Moor to the bizarre secret of Benengeli, tells him the strange story of the ex-Mayor of Benengeli. During the Civil War he took up the republican cause. After the war, fearing persecution by Franco he decided to go into hiding. In his house there was a small alcove behind a wardrobe and there he spent his days. At night his wife would shut the shutters and he would emerge. This went on for thirty years, until the general amnesty. By the time he came out into the open, his beloved Benengeli had become the preserve of all the floatsam-jetsam scum of the earth. Those of his generation who were still alive cold-shouldered him on account of past political differences. There was little that was left of his family. In the end he was reduced to sitting in the Street of Parasites, among the expatriates, because there was no longer a place for him among his own people. He had become a rootless stranger, too.

This story is apparently narrated here as yet another element that goes into the shaping of the narcotic quality of life in the Andalusian village, but there is perhaps something more to it. We have reasons to think that, in his presentation of the man who went into hiding for thirty years and emerged, only to find that the reality around him had changed out of recognition, Salman Rushdie had communicated some of his own deep-seated fears and misgiving over the effects of his long-stretched-out exile. Long absence from home and separation from one's people, turn the exile into an eternal outsider and his plans of rebuilding his life after his return to the native land sometimes go awry because he soon discovers that he simply cannot start from where he left off.

The archetype of the man who returned home triumphantly at the end of exile is Odysseus, the hero of the Homeric epic. Odysseus had a loyal wife who waited for him and could draw on the trust and support of his subjects and former associates. But in modern times many who have chosen to go back to their native country at the end of a long exile have found that in the altered scheme of things there, their return is of small consequence. This, for instance, illustrates the plight experienced by Alexander Solzhenitsyn, the greatest political exile of our century, after he returned to Russia. Once the initial enthusiasm generated by his arrival wore out, Solzhenitsyn discovered that the realities in post-Communist Russia defied his prescriptions. His prophetic airs were not taken seriously by many, while there were few takers for his political plans. For the people of his generation who are still alive, his presence inspires some degree of confidence and hope. But a new generation has sprung up in Russia, which speaks a language somewhat alien to him, for whom, Solzhenitsyn is more like a hovering legend from another time.

In his description of the dreadful incarceration of the Moor in the fortress of Vasco Miranda, in the company of the Japanese artist Aoi Ue, the novelist seems to have drawn upon some well-known fairytale motifs. We have here a disfigured, yet adventure-spirited and imaginative prince and a frail and charming princess trapped by an evil spirit in his decayed mansion. The 'Lario Sisters' who lured the Moor into this unearthly place at the bidding of Vasco remain blindly loyal to their master till the end as in a ghost story. The prince and the princess, through patience, hard work and mutual affection, manage to survive their ordeals spread over an unending stretch of time. The outcome of this fairy tale is not entirely happy. The evil spirit, having forced his prisoners to complete the tasks he had assigned them, chooses to kill the princess. But in his hour of triumph, his charms suddenly vanish and he cracks up. The prince, exhausted in body and spirit, thus gains back his liberty.

For the Moor the high point of his captivity comes when Vasco Miranda announces his decision to postpone his execution for a time, so that both of them can re-live the old times together. The Moor is ordered by him to recount the 'sinful saga' of the Zogoiby family.

> Every day after that, he brought me pencil and paper. He had made a Scheherazade of me. As long as my tale held his interest he would let me live (421)

It is through performing the role of a modern-day Scheherazade that the Moor manages to live through the daily shame which his imprisonment brings him and lend some meaning to his existence. Lying in a circular cell in shackles, he goes on reconstructing the past, arranging in his imagination the events and characters who figure in the mind-boggling family saga. His fellow-prisoner, Aoi, who has been bidden by Vasco to work on a painting, applies herself to her task with even more self-discipline and dedication. In fact it is Aoi who teaches the Moor how to wrench some element of order and dignity from the abysmal living conditions around them. Together they discover that artistic activity is what keeps at bay the thoughts of the humiliation which is practised on their image of themselves by their captor and the horror of impending death. "We are greater than this prison," Aoi reminds him. She cautions him not to allow their captivity to define them.

It is a measure of the success of the Moor's narrative art that he is able to keep Vasco amused in the story in which the latter plays a prominent, though ambiguous role. In fact Vasco is trapped as a character inside the Moor's fiction. The Moor succeeds in bringing his family chronicle up to date before his final confrontation with him. Again, the Moor's story outlasts his tormentor. Vasco who is transformed as a character in the novel which the Moor is composing dies in an unexpected manner during the violent climax of a scene which is visualized in terms of the Bollywood remake of a cowboy movie. Interestingly enough the loop of the Moor's remembrances unfolds against the background of the screaming violence of the 'avant-garde' music played by Vasco in his tower.

Are there shades of the Iranian despot who pronounced the sentence of death on Salman Rushdie lurking in the portrayal of the hideously comic and puffed up figure of Vasco Miranda? Could the last section in *The Moor's Last Sigh* be read as the author's indirect comment on the conditions of his own exile and isolation, in which his morbid fears of persecution by an unforgiving enemy loom large? Using as a narrative device a deliberately contrived situation which lies in the realm of caricature and grotesque fantasy, does the novelist suggest here something like the ultimate triumph of art over the vengeful obsession of a demented fanatic?

While the questions would remain in the realm of conjecture, we are tempted to pursue some clues provided by the novelist himself. There is a funny description of Vasco Miranda in his 'Sultan outfit' appearing at noon in the cell of the Moor and Aoi, with a revolver in his hand, ready for a showdown. Again the village of Benengeli is said to have been the Southern retreat of Franco once. There is perhaps more than a causal hint in the association of the place, where the 'mad folly' of Vasco is located, with the memory of a hated dictator.

The Moor's Last Sigh, with its abrupt shift of narrative codes and whimsical mix of styles, calls for an extremely supple interpretive strategy. In terms of the political nuances it carries, this novel is a sigh cast upon a vanishing culture and a vanishing world. What lends some sort of desperate urgency to the voice of the narrator in the novel is the fear that the climate of religious fundamentalism which has caught on in India in the nineties is corroding some of the first legacies of collective living in the country and the conduct of its polity. The novel also contains enough suggestions regarding Rushdie's growing realization of the ways in which his life in exile is affecting his creative sensibility, how it has caused to distance him from the realities of the living present. There are certain reflexes which condition the working of the imagination of the expatriate writer which Rushdie has in every likelihood started experiencing with keener pangs in the harrowing confinement of his secret hiding. The situation here is of a kind that the South African poet and writer, Breyton Breytenbach, has summed up with poignant precision in this fashion:

> You live and you write in terms of absence, of absent time (or in terms of questioned present time). Not an imagined or remembered existence, more an absent presence. A state of instant reminiscences. With your tongue you keep searching for the after taste of remembered delicacies, and you well imbue the tasteless fibres with an unexpected refinement. But the tongue keeps clacking against areas of dead palate. Your relationship with the world around you is that of the foreign observer.[2]

In the four-part symphonic structure of the novel the last section is designed in a special manner so as to orchestrate the grand themes of vengefulness, art and exile. The reference to Chirico which occurs in the course of the description underscores the surreal nature of the landscape where the action is laid.

The phantom image of the land of the dead conjured up by the novelist is perhaps revealing of certain existential traits that go with the imagination of the exiled writer in modern times, which are shared by some of Rushdie's leading contemporaries. I wish to recall here the near hallucinatory vision of Prague under Soviet occupation as a 'city without memory' invoked by Milan Kundera in his novel on the horrors of Stalinism, *The Book of Laughter and Forgetting* (1981). Kundera, writing in exile in Paris, likens the conditions in Prague after the siege of Czechoslovakia by Soviet Union to those described in Kafka's novels. In Kafka's works Prague exists in an utter vacuum. People there don't remember anything, they have no past to recall. The same sort of oblivion seems to have descended upon people in present-day Prague. The effort to invent a new history and to manufacture a new culture was at the root of all the repressive measures undertaken in the satellite country of Czechoslovakia by the Russians who, in Kundera's words, "wanted to erase hundreds of thousands of lives from human memory and leave nothing but a single unblemished age of unblemished idyll."[3] In a haunting epithet the novelist describes Svobodo Husak, the puppet ruler installed by the Soviets, as the 'president of forgetting.' He dismissed some 145 historians from the universities. Monuments were demolished and street names changed with alarming rapidity. Retrospective writing and redrawing of history proceeded apace, as in other totalitarian Socialist countries, as part of the process of organized forgetting. As a consequence of this so many came to believe, in a manner that has happened nowhere, that a past which is denied or rather disowned no longer exists and has never existed.

The writer who was forced to leave the country and lives in exile is the one who remembers. Through his act of remembering he wages what Kundera considers as one of the defining struggles of our epoch: the struggle of memory against forgetting. As far as the émigré writer is concerned, his geographical sense of distances and isolation enables him to view in perspective the predicament of his people who having lost their significant connections with the past and being confronted with sudden gaps and silences in their immediate view of reality, are left to lead an empty life. His art thus becomes the defence against collective amnesia. Upon him has fallen the new variation of a task which, at the beginning of the century, James Joyce, around whose art developed the modernist poetics of exile, set before him: to redeem the ruptured conscience of his race.

Salman Rushdie's postmodern construction of the figure of exile in *The Moor's Last Sigh* might inspire one to search through some of our ancient epics and Puranas for precursors and prototypes of the castaway traveller. The worlds's first exile according to the Christian belief, Adam, has no counterpart in our tradition. There is nothing corresponding to the story of the Garden of Eden and man's first sin and fall and expulsion from paradise in Hindu mythology. In our Puranas and legends we vainly look for an outcast figure, condemned for a life of fugitive wandering, resembling, say, the Prodigal Son of Flying Dutchman. The image of a home that has been lost beyond recall, casting upon man the curse to drift for numberless years, which is central to the Western consciousness and is best summed up by the title of the famous American novel, *You Can't Go Home Again* is absent in our mythic tales and classical literature. Exile surely forms a principal element in the story structure both in *Mahabharata* and *Ramayana* where the protagonists are made to undergo banishment from their kingdoms for an allotted period. If we take a close look at the ways in which Rama experience his stay in the forests or the Pandavas go through their life of wandering and mendicancy, it could be seen that the joys of exile balance its hardships and perils. For Rama and the Pandavas, exile seems to provide an opportunity for an exposure to a mode of being which is refreshingly different from life in the palace, with its sordid intrigues and power struggles. During the years of their banishment from their kingdoms, the protagonists in *Ramayana* and *Mahabharata* discover the beauty of the landscape, meet with strange and interesting people, visit holy places and run into dangers which they overcome with their physical prowess and strategic skills. Apparently Vyasa and Valmiki have used the experience of exile as a means for the spiritual maturation of their central characters.

Perhaps the legendary character who comes closest to being the Hindu archetype of the figure of exile is Aswatthama in *Mahabharata*. As it is well-known, Aswatthama personifies revenge in its stark and obsessive form. He committed the worst of all sins, *brahmahatya* (Killing of a Brahmin), for which an extraordinary curse was laid upon him. A man of noble birth and an accomplished warrior, Aswatthama was suddenly transformed into a hideously ugly figure, afflicted by diseases and his body festering with wounds. He was condemned to wander alone in desolate places and deep forests for three thousand years with the mark of the sinner upon him, never finding a place in human community. It appears that the only occasion in *Mahabharata* where the epic poet has touched on the tragic terror attendant upon the condition of exile is to be found in his description of the punishment meted out to Aswatthama by Lord Krishna. It is worthwhile to recall here that a modern Malayalam novelist (Madambu Kunhikuttan) harked back to this archetype while portraying the accursed destiny of his protagonist, a person of learning and sensitivity, who inherited a rich tradition but whose basic traits led him relentlessly to path of *adharma* (wrong behaviour).

It has been borne out by the course of history in the present epoch that the experience of exile sometimes takes on forms which are less explicit and direct, but painful and cruel nonetheless. What has come to be known as 'internal exile' has lent a new dimension to our notions of migrancy and metaphysical un-belonging. In am reminded here of the way in which the Indian cartoonist-turned-novelist, O.V.Vijayan, responded to the horror of the Emergency. Vijayan's cartoons, etched with black humour, had often tended to caricature the leading individuals and political processes during the 'Indira epoch' in Indian public life. During the Emergency he stopped drawing as a gesture of protest. A totalitarian regime exiles humour among other things, and the art of the cartoonist has little luck in a State where all laughter has died down in obedience to the wishes of a self-obsessed ruler.

Historians of literature have paid attention to the phenomenon known as 'inner immigration' which characterized the literary milieu in Germany in the late thirties. At the height of the Nazi power a few prominent men of letter fled Germany, while many chose to remain in the country. Among those who stayed back, some were banned from publishing. Several others, sensing the extreme pressure of the events taking place around them, bade a temporary farewell to their vocation, realizing that it was impossible for them to be honest to their vision of truth in the prevailing state of national hysteria. They knew that their art could never cope with the incredible reality of the concentration camps. A retreat into a world of one's own seemed to be a compelling option to these writers, as the barrier between the external political reality and the way one chooses to live private life of the mind appeared insurmountable.

A noticeably similar response arose in Soviet Russia a few years prior to the practice of 'inner immigration' by German prose writers and poets in Hitler's Germany. Issac Babel, the writer of Kossack tales credited with a Hemingway-like prose, who disappeared in forced labour camps during the purges, spoke before the time of his arrest of the 'genre of silence.' This seemed to him a temptation that awaited the writers who were confronted with the organized fear induced by the Soviet Communist Party in all walks of life. The writer was no longer free to express himself fully and the instrument he wielded, language, had been encrusted with half-truths and lies. The election of metaphysical silence looked like the only honest remedy open before Babel, who was benumbed by the mystique of terror which was growing daily around him. The curious affinity exhibited by German and Soviet writers in their preference for inner exile is also a pointer to the parallel courses ran by Nazism and Stalinism, which has been attested by some Western historians in recent years.

Vaclav Havel passed through a similar phase in the seventies and eighties during the course of his confrontation with the puppet regime installed by Soviet Union in Czechoslovakia after the failure of the Prague Spring in 1968, the memories of which he has recorded in his book *Living in Truth* (1986). As a practitioner of the Theatre of the Absurd, Havel could very well perceive the comic, nightmarish levels which public reality had touched in his country under an ideology which feigned the monopoly of truth. The media constantly lied to the people and the ordinary masses had little access to factual information. Language became cluttered with jargons and bombast and culture was turned into a timid State-sponsored activity. As one of the leaders of the dissident movement who was made to undergo constant prison terms, Havel discovered that a retreat into silence was the one way in which he could keep at bay the redundant falsity of the public rhetoric which prevailed in the besieged Czech society and preserve the integrity of his life in the theatre.

It would seem in retrospect that it is the strange case of Salman Rushdie, who has been rightly described as one who is doubly exiled, that has rendered the rhetoric of migrancy somewhat central to our literary discourse. Rushdie is surely symptomatic in many ways, chiefly of a temper which has persisted in twentieth-century literature from the time of the modernist revolt (remember the generation of James Joyce, Thomas Mann and Herman Broch), through the postmorden constructions around the notions of diaspora and exile. He is a writer whose psychic traumas impel him to equate with Hell the non-man's territory where the 'expatriate vermin' is fated to live. It is the hell of Otherness where one experiences the loss of the little patch of earth where one was born and the familiar sky of one's childhood and adolescence. It was Victor Hugo who called exile 'a long dream of home.' What if this dream looks unrealizable at any point of time? And like a lengthy death sentence, exile persists? Somewhere in his novel *Shame,* while speaking about the condition of migrant people Rushdie states that they have 'floated upwards from history, from memory, from Time.' The social despair, loss of identity and solipsism of the migrant, or the exile sometimes take on such paranoid forms that he feels like moving about in a realm where the gravitational laws of earth do not count. The writer-in-exile thus finds himself sleepwalking through life, he drifts across an uncharted time-zone punctuated by fleeting spectral encounters with the Executioner. His intellect, to quote Rushdie again, has to 'root itself in itself' since it has been deprived of nourishment from the soil where it grew. It is most activated when it apprehends reality in some eerie, disembodied forms.

NOTES

1. Salman Rushdie, *The Moor's Last Sigh,* London: Jonathan Cape, 390. All further references to the novel are from this edition and are included in the text.
2. Breyton Breytenbach, "You are an Outsider," in John Simpson (ed.), *The Oxford Book of Exile,* Oxford/New York : Oxford University Press, 1995, 229.
3. Milan Kundera, *The Book of Laughter and Forgetting,* translated by, Michael Henry Hein, New York: Penguin, 1981, 24.

ROSY SINGH

Milan Kundera and 'Forgetting' as a Metaphor

Milan Kundera, a widely read contemporary novelist and essayist, was born in 1929 in Bruno, the second largest city of former Czechoslovakia or Bohemia as Kundera prefers to call it. The 1960s in Bohemia were marked by a relative degree of artistic freedom, unknown to this nation since the 1939 Nazi occupation due to which the Czech state had ceased to exist. In 1945, even before democracy could take roots, Bohemia fell victim to the Cold War and was thus incorporated into the Soviet communist empire. Kundera was lucky to have embarked on his writing career in the period of the Czech history, commonly referred to as Prague Spring (1959-68), under the leadership of the tolerant government of Alexander Dubcek, that was experimenting with 'communism with a human face'. It was hence, only in the 1960s that writers such as Franz Kafka, James Joyce and Proust, considered 'decadent' in the paradigm of Socialist Realism, were openly discussed and debated upon. Kundera thrived in this atmosphere of academic freedom and tolerance. Some of his works were published in this period of brief 'thaw', also called a period of 'soft dictatorship'. But as half-a-million Warsaw Pact troops marched into Czechoslovakia in August 1968 and occupied it, any expression of disagreement with the official ideology was out of question. Kundera also suffered the imposition of censorship rules under the strict enforcement of the doctrine of Socialist Realism, promoted in literature by the Russians. Socialist Realism was originally meant to differentiate pre-revolution art from post-revolution art in the then Soviet Union. However, it soon degenerated into a dogma. In the application of this doctrine, the various characters a writer was expected to portray were, broadly speaking, classified into the positive, the negative and at the most a third wavering one. The positive character was invariably a hardworking, committed worker; the negative, mostly a capitalist or his sympathiser; and the wavering character would be an old worker or a bourgeois intellectual, sceptical of the new system based on collectivisation. No good writer worth his salt would or could produce literature that was so simplistic in its various social categories! As a consequence, works of several creative artists were banned. Imagine a small country like Czechoslovakia banning as many as hundred and twenty artists! Various writers responded in different ways to this repression. Bohumil Hrabal, a popular Czech writer, being old and sick, was the most vulnerable. He succumbed to the pressure and gave an interview praising the Russian occupation and the communist system. The ban on his works was consequently lifted and he was then allowed to publish some of his works. Václav Havel, a writer and also a political dissident, was offered emigration to the U.S.A. He rejected the offer, preferring to go to prison instead. Kundera and his wife migrated to France in 1975, when things became too difficult for him in his native land. In 1981, he took French citizenship.

After the Velvet Revolution[1] of 1989, Czechoslovakia stands divided into two independent states, the Czech Republic (of which Havel is the President) and Slovakia. The Czech Republic is all set to assimilate into Western Europe. It has already joined the North Atlantic Treaty Organisation (NATO) and the European Union. However, this is not really a radical shift from the East to the West, for, historically and culturally, Czechoslovakia has always been more Western than Eastern. It had been part of the Holy Roman empire and also part of the Austro-Hungarian empire till the World War I. Germany had been a dominant language here for a long time till the Nazi invasion made it and its speakers extremely unpopular. Kundera belongs to the school of thought that advocates the concept of Central Europe as a cultural and historical entity different from both the concepts of Eastern and Western Europe. This entity comprises, according to him, Hungary, Poland and Austria, besides Czechoslovakia, i.e., all former members of the Austro-Hungarian empire that lasted for about half a century.

Frequent political changes in the Czech state (monarchy, democracy, fascism, communism and now again democracy) have left their mark on Czech writers of the twentieth century. They have given a distinct character to their work and conditioned their responses. It is thus easy to understand why Czech literature abounds in satires, political themes and motifs. In a set-up where direct criticism is not allowed, political jokes, black humour, erotic jokes, graffiti etc. become an outlet for suppressed emotions. Milan Kundera is also to be read in this context. Kundera's profound antipathy towards the Russians and the communist system, as practised in his country, appear frequently in his narratives. In an environment where Marxist ideology failed to deliver and live up to the expectations of the people, it is but natural that it ended up as a butt of jokes. Yet it would be naïve to assume that Kundera's popularity rests on this aspect alone. If today Kundera has a niche in world literature, it is because he sheds some light on the multidimensional facets of human existence. His appeal to readership the world over lies not so much in his anti-communist stance as in his deep insight into the enigma of existence. He thematises in his narratives the human condition, which has a universal appeal about it, whether read in Eastern or Western Europe or in a developing country like India. The 'system' often provides no more than an ideological ambience to his existential themes, as illustrated by this interesting dialogue from his book, *Testaments Betrayed*:

> Are you a Communist, Mr. Kundera?
> No, I'm a novelist.
> Are you a dissident?
> No, I'm a novelist.
> Are you on the left or the right?
> Neither. I'm a novelist.

Kundera has been living in Paris for more than twenty five years now and the French like to call him a French writer. After all who would not like to be associated with fame, particularly when France today lacks literary giants like Albert Camus or Jean Paul Sartre! Yet Kundera's writings have more in common with Central European writers, particularly the Czech and the Hungarian than with the French tradition. His works may be viewed in the continuity of the tradition set by Franz Kafka, Jaroslav Hašek of *The Good Soldier Schweik* fame and Bohumil Hrabal, where the political and the personal, imagination and reality, often intertwine. This paper attempts to trace, along with the theme of exile, some common aspects shared by these writers. Of course, one can also bypass this French vs Czech debate by avoiding what Salman Rushdie calls 'the folly of trying to contain writers inside passports'.

Four of Kundera's novels, *The Joke*, *Laughable Loves*, *Life is Elsewhere* and *The Farewell Party* were written in former Czechoslovakia. Five others, *The Book of Laughter and Forgetting*, *The Unbearable Lightness* of Being, *Immortality*, *Slowness* and a play *Jacques and his Master* are written in France. Apart from fiction he has written two long essays, *The Art of the Novel* and *Testaments Betrayed*. His novel, *Laughable Loves*, 1969, deals with man-woman relations, the 'complex erotic games and stratagems' men and women practise on each other. Kundera shot to fame with *The Unbearable Lightness of Being*, 1984; a rather philosophical title for a novel (the influence of Heidegger is too obvious to be missed! Mark the German title: *Die unerträgliche Leichtigkeit des Seins*). This novel has been made into a successful movie. The novel, *Immortality*, 1991, in my view, his magnum opus, criss crosses different historical periods, exploring the love-hate relationship between Goethe and Bettina Brentano, with a parallel story running into the present. The common theme of immortality, which Kundera defines as the desire of human beings to leave something of themselves for posterity, holds the two stories together. His latest novel, *Slowness*, 1995, deals with the nostalgia for slowness as a way of life in our common past of the last century vs speed, a hallmark of the contemporary world intoxicated with technology. His book, *Testaments Betrayed*, 1993, is a sort of a continuation of his celebrated long essay, *The Art of the Novel*, which, in Kundera's own words, is a 'practitioner's confession'. *Testaments Betrayed* discusses, as the very title suggests, how the creative artist and his fragile art survive in the face of mighty assaults and grievous betrayals. In this context, he discusses Salman Rushdie, Franz Kafka, Hemingway, Stravinsky, Janacek and several others. Also included are several other themes such as the 'novel's mysterious kinship with music', artists in exile and problems of translation. No one interested in the history of European literature can afford to ignore these remarkable essays.

I have attempted to analyse in this paper a narrative called Lost Letters from *The Book of Laughter and Forgetting* written by Kundera in Czech in 1978, when communism in Czechoslovakia was at its zenith. This was three years after he fled from Czechoslovakia to France; it is his first novel in exile. The analysis makes use of several terms as used and explained by Kundera in his essays. The narrative has exile as one of its main themes. It also mirrors, in my view what may perhaps be termed as Kundera's post-modern version of existentialism. The term 'existentialism' has not been used here within the narrow confines of Christian existentialism derived from Kierkegaard nor the Sartrean existentialism focusing on the atheist philosophy of human freedom conceived in terms of individual responsibility. The term is being used here in a very general way, with its emphasis on the individual and the absurdity or the meaninglessness of human existence. Viewed in this context, all literature is to some extent existential in nature.

LOST LETTERS

The Book of Laughter and Forgetting comprises seven parts, seven being his ubiquitous favourite in respect of the architectonic division of chapters in most of his novels or essays (*The Joke, Laughable Loves, The Farewell Party, Immortality, The Art of the Novel* etc). The novel is divided into parts which are further developed into chapters. Each chapter is set off sharply from the other by sufficient space and a prominent number.

Part IV of the book, titled Lost Letters, is divided into twentythree chapters spread over thirtysix pages. Although the seven parts of the book are separate stories and lack unity of action, each part being complete in itself, Kundera insists on calling the book a novel. It is the thematic unity, according to him, that makes the seven narratives a single entity. Kundera explains the architectonic structure of the novel: In *The Book of Laughter and Forgetting*, the coherence of the whole is created *solely* by the unity of a few themes (and motifs), which are developed in variations. For Kundera, a novel appears to be a game without pre-set rules, where it is the artist who decides the rules of the game. He discards the conventional structure of the classical modern novel; at the same time he is conscious of the techniques he employs to construct the structure of his novels. The reader also goes along with him because he accepts the rules of the game. The structure and the mode of presentation of his novels create the impression of a light and lucid text, easy to read and grasp. Yet it is more often than not a camouflage for his well thought-out ideas.

Kundera, himself a writer in exile, explores in this narrative the inner world of Tamina, who escapes after the Prague Spring 1968, along with her husband, from the 'iron curtain' in Czechoslovakia only to find herself in a world quite alien to her. Her non-participation in conversation, mistaken by others as the unmistakable virtue of a good listener, is an important pointer in this direction. It is as if she keeps 'a golden ring' in her mouth and to prevent it from falling, she keeps her lips tightly sealed.

I picture the world growing up around Tamina like a circular wall, and I picture her as a small patch of grass down below. The only rose growing on that patch of grass is the memory of her husband.
Or I picture Tamina's present (which consists of serving coffee and lending an ear) as a raft drifting on the water, with her sitting on it and looking back, looking only back."[2]

On the one hand is the *lost homeland*, and, on the other, little, if any, hope of a *promised land*. This dialectics between the two leads to the more universal existential crisis, which appears to lie at the core of Kundera's writings. The death of Tamina's husband, also a Czech, leaves her shattered. She takes tranquilisers, but survives. The reader is told that for three years since this tragedy, Tamina has lived in silence. She decides to make the beautiful moments she and her husband spent together, the focal point of her existence. It is as if she has erected a memorial to her lost husband within herself. This is what keeps her going in life. But the inexorable irony of life is that, all her efforts notwithstanding, those cherished memories start fading away slowly. She struggles desperately to cling on to each and every detail, yet time is more powerful than her memory.

Every day she spends some time in a sort of spiritual exercise, trying to remember what he looked like in profile, then half profile, then quarter profile, going over the lines of his nose and chin, and every day she is horrified at new fuzzy spots where her memory hesitates about which way to go." (p. 84).

Tamina tries her utmost to put together the scattered memories, in order to reconstruct her dead husband who once meant so much to her and has now disappeared from her life. She tries to evoke his skin, its colour and all its minor blemishes, but all this is an exercise in futility. Whenever somebody sits across her in the bar, (she is a waitress in a shoddy café), she attempts to visualise her husband's face: darkening the complexion, adding freckles and warts, scaling down the ears and colouring the eyes blue. All this again is in vain. Her husband's image, a metaphor for the lost homeland, recedes slowly but surely till it almost disappears for good. The past becomes for her more and more inaccessible. In Homer's *Odyssey*, the hero Odysseus does not forget his home, Ithaca, even after an absence of nineteen years. He defends the memory of his country, his wife Penelope and friends, against the supernatural forces, such as the Lotus Eaters, the beautiful enchantress Calypso and the songs of the Sirens, which try hard to make him 'forget' them. He has to consistently think of the 'return'. But then he is helped by the Olympian Gods in his mission, whereas Kundera's narrative treats *Forgetting* at the level of a *natural* process, like eating and sleeping, where the time lapse itself is enough to banish or fade the memories of the past. In this realistic discourse, Tamina is not noble and godlike as Odysseus. She is simply an ordinary mortal, who cannot help *forgetting*.

At this point of time, the love letters she and her husband exchanged and eleven notebooks documenting the eleven golden years they spent together in Bohemia, loom up in importance. Tamina wants to make them her points of reference in order to recreate the past.

"And as her past begins to shrink, disappear, fall apart, Tamina begins shrinking and blurring." (p. 86).

The package of letters and notebooks becomes the raison d'être of Tamina's life. However, due to the fear of persecution, her relatives in Czechoslovakia cannot send it to her directly. Twice in the narrative her hopes of retrieving the letters are kindled, only to die soon.

The first occasion is in the form of a visitor, named Bibi, to the café where Tamina works. Bibi is planning to go with her husband and child on a vacation to Prague. Tamina breaks her silence and befriends her. Bibi wants to write a novel but does not know 'The Art of the Novel'. There is not a single book in her flat. Reading bores her to tears. Tamina helps her by introducing her to a writer who has so poor a name in literary circles that he himself is contemptuous of those who read his books. While Bibi and this writer exchange notes, Tamina makes expensive phone calls to her relatives in Czechoslovakia, at times even daring to call from Bibi's apartment without her knowledge. She finally succeeds in persuading her surly mother-in-law to keep her package ready so that her brother can collect it and deposit it with her father in Prague, from where Bibi will collect it. Her father cannot understand why she is so interested in some old letters. He would rather send Tamina her old fur coat which, in his perception, would be of more practical use to her. However, after all this effort on Tamina's part, Bibi changes her plans for a vacation in Prague, as she decides to leave her husband.

Then Tamina lets Hugo, a lover, enter her life, the first ever after her husband's death. Her sole purpose, however, is making free calls to Czechoslovakia from his apartment and using his projected visit to Prague to retrieve her notebooks. Hugo also desires to write a book. While Hugo makes love to her, Tamina thinks of her notebooks. As Hugo tries his utmost to impress her, Tamina concentrates hard on remembering where she spent the vacation every year with her husband. Even the chronology of the events fails her, frustrating her evermore. One day as they are sitting in a restaurant, Hugo announces that he has given up the idea of his visit to Prague, because he could no longer resist the publication of an article, condemning the totalitarian regimes in Eastern Europe. Tamina finds the whole thing too nauseating to bear. She goes to the ladies' room and vomits. As she vomits, she remembers the gentle lovemaking of her husband, juxtaposed against the unpleasant sexual encounters with Hugo. The past and the present are intertwined. She realises painfully that the memory of revulsion is stronger than the memory of tenderness. When she comes out, her mouth, still full of the foul smell, is firmly sealed and she stubbornly refuses to speak. This signifies the end of the affair. The reader feels the impact of the violence of the situation, the rape and murder of a person's dreams and desires.

Kundera explores, at one level, how history and politics affect the lives of individuals; he examines, at another level, in this narrative as well as in his other writings, the hollowness of human relationships. Why does Bibi decide after all to leave her husband? There seems to be no particular reason, except perhaps an existential one. And why does Tamina feel more irritation than love for her near and dear ones in Prague? Why, again, is she—a tall and beautiful, thirtythree year-old lady— more interested in the dead than in the living? Why does she not have a single relationship in her life? The reasons are again existential.

Kundera investigates human existence at the turn of the twentieth century, at the end of the modern era, a time characterised by mass media and 'graphomania'. Kundera digresses here from the main story to reflect directly on another theme of the narrative which appears to be more a critique of the French or European society in general. He talks in detail about *graphomania*.

A woman who writes her lover four letters a day is not a graphomaniac, she is simply a woman in love. But my friend who xeroxes his love letters so he can publish them someday— my friend is a graphomaniac. Graphomania is not a desire to write letters, diaries, or family chronicles (to write for oneself or one's immediate family); it is a desire to write books (to have a public of unknown readers). (pp. 91-92).

The ostriches running after Tamina and her lover in a zoo, opening and closing their beaks with an urgency, aggressiveness and belligerence of their own are metaphors for graphomaniacs, who want to talk about themselves. According to Kundera, graphomania blows up into a mass epidemic in an environment of affluence coupled with a general feeling of isolation of an individual in a society, wherein nothing concrete really happens at the external level, forcing people to withdraw into themselves. Kundera gives the example of France where the percentage of writers is twentyone times that in Israel, where significant social changes are a way of life. Kundera, in this narrative makes fun of intellectuals in a lighter vein. Bibi, Hugo and the writers harping on their childhood experiences on the radio and television are but variations of such intellectuals.

This brings us to another principal theme that appears to be close to Kundera's heart, the right of an individual to privacy. This theme is particularly crucial to East European writers who have experienced the might of the State. For Kundera it was like living in a 'glass house'. Tamina is horrified at the thought that her mother-in-law, her brother, her father or the omnipresent State would intrude into her private world, which is exclusively hers. She is paranoid about somebody reading her letters or notebooks, not because they contain something important, but because they are her own very personal experiences and reflections.

In his book *Testaments Betrayed*, 1993, Kundera argues:

Shame is one of the key notions of the Modern Era, the individualistic period that is imperceptibly receding from us these days; shame: an epidermal instinct to defend one's personal life; to require a curtain over the window; to insist that a letter addressed to A not be read by B. One of the elementary situations in the passage to adulthood, one of the prime conflicts with parents, is the claim to a drawer for letters and notebooks, the claim to a drawer with a key; we enter adulthood through the rebellion of shame."[3]

Further, ...private and public are two essentially different worlds and that respect for that difference is the indispensable condition, the sine qua non, for a man to live free; that the curtain separating these two worlds is not to be tampered with, and that curtain-rippers are criminals."[4]

Need one aver that the phone call to her mother-in-law leaves Tamina stunned, because she realises that her mother-in-law has read her love letters and notebooks? Tamina is not a writer, nor does she aspire to become one. In contrast to Bibi and Hugo, she has no urge to talk about herself. Her letters and notebooks are meant for her eyes only. They are her intimate discourse with herself. They tend to lose their significance if they are read by others.

Finally, Tamina realises that the 'package' is practically out of her reach. She finds the only goal she had set for herself—the procuring of the 'package'—so that she could build a new house with those memories to live in, inaccessible. The present is stripped of causality and the past is slipping out of her hands. According to Kundera, 'A name means continuity with the past and people without a past are people without a name'. Tamina is one such person. Having once crossed the geographical *border* of her country, she now withdraws into herself, thereby crossing the metaphysical *border*, beyond which life becomes meaningless, an empty signifier. This is indeed the real emigration. Not without reason does the last sentence of the narrative read:

She went on serving coffee and never made another call to Czechoslovakia. (p. 115)

The key word to Tamina's existence is *alienation*. Kundera depicts the alienation and lonesomeness of an individual in a world peopled by characters who do not understand one another. In his lucid style, marked by the realistic mode of presentation, Kundera's narrative is a statement on the frustrations and anxieties of an individual in the present world. It is a commentary on the helplessness experienced by an individual in the face of an anonymous, ubiquitous enemy who cannot even be identified. The narrative presents the psychic history of an individual as a series of violences done to her. Bibi and Hugo represent in this narrative windows that open fleetingly to a world of happiness and purpose. But these windows close before the protagonist can escape the confines of her existence. The narrative also seeks to examine the futility of language as a means of communication. For Tamina, language has lost its evocative power, her muteness signifies her innate distrust of verbal communication. Her muteness and aloofness can also be seen as a sulky protest against a world indifferent to her concerns. The narrative Lost Letters is not a political thought in the garb of literature, as its critical analysis shows. For Kundera, the greatest ideology is life itself. Relating it to a particular political system is thus a gross underestimation or lack of understanding of what Kundera stands for.

Kundera's mode of presentation has a peculiar blend of humour and irony, both constituting the nerve centres of his works. Irony in literature, says Goethe, is like a pinch of salt in the meal, little in quantity but vital to the taste. It is this 'irony' that lends sharpness to Kundera's writing. At the same time his writing has a liberal sprinkling of humour, an element often neglected and underrated by most critics. So vital is humour to Kundera that he highlights it even in the titles of his novels—*Laughable Loves*, *The Book of Laughter and Forgetting* and *The Joke*. He holds that, the novel is itself 'an art born of the laughter of God'. He seeks to investigate human existence through laughter, although the comic is at the same time inseparable from the tragic. Many Czech writers like Kafka, Hašek and Hrabal show inclination towards this 'dialogue' between humour and irony. Nowhere is the 'aesthetic kinship' more evident than in this respect. For these creative writers, the world is a stage that arouses laughter. In the case of Kafka, however, it is more of a chilling dialogue of the grotesque and the comic. For Kundera, two key themes appear to be sadness and loneliness. This is also true of the manner in which he explores the serious, sad and comic side of 'sex' to present the absurdity of a situation. He appears to declare: whether man or woman, each person is essentially alone in the world. His narratives are conspicuous by the absence of a lyrical sentimentality. He further shows the ability to transcend the gap between elite literature and mass culture. He is a typical post-structuralist writer who entertains. His books are read by what is called in German *Berufsleser* (those who read by virtue of their profession) and are also accepted into the mainstream. He is also a commercially successful novelist which places him closer to his predecessors like Hasek and Hrabal (Kafka, however, still remains an elite writer) and contemporaries like Umberto Eco and Salman Rushdie. He does not seek to free himself from the traditional past, for that would, as Eco aptly puts it, 'lead to silence', but he finds new ways of confronting the tradition—through the erotic, the comic, irony and scepticism.

TEXT AS A METAPHOR

In his writings, Kundera often refers to the motif of *Forgetting*. *Forgetting* may hence be counted as one of the vital concepts to the understanding of Kundera's universe. It also finds a mention in the dictionary of sixtythree words listed at the end of *The Art of the Novel*, 1986. This dictionary compiled by Kundera contains his 'key words', 'problem words' and 'words that he loves'. He borrows the term *Forgetting* from the philosopher Heidegger, and at the same time transforms and uses it as a novelist, who creates a world comprising of concrete situations and characters. The first example of its usage is in the first page of *The Art of the Novel*, where Kundera makes Heidegger a point of departure to arrive at his definition of 'novel'. In the book, *Being and Time* (*Sein und Zeit* in German), Heidegger laments 'the forgetting of being' in a world obsessed with technology, which has a logic and necessity of its own that surpasses human control. In the midst of this technological frenzy of production and consumption, of subordination and exploitation, man fails to recognise that he has completely obliterated his place in the world. Even the metaphysics before Husserl and Heidegger neglected man's concrete being, his 'world of life' or the *Lebenswelt*, reducing him to a mere thing. In Kundera's view, Husserl and his pupil Heidegger should have taken the great European art, the Novel, into consideration, for it is in the four centuries of the history of the European novel that this being, *forgotten* by science and philosophy, has constantly been the focus of attention.

> 'Indeed, all the great existential themes Heidegger analyzes in *Being and Time* — considering them to have been neglected by all earlier European philosophy— had been unveiled, displayed, illuminated by four centuries of the novel (...). The novel has accompanied man uninterruptedly and faithfully since the beginning of the Modern Era. It was then that the "passion to know", which Husserl considered the essence of European spirituality, seized the novel and led it to scrutinize man's concrete life and protect it against "the forgetting of being"; to hold "the world of life" under a permanent light."[5]

The Eurocentric bias is evident in Kundera's definition but that need not distract us from the universal significance of what he has to say about the novel.

In his novels, particularly *The Book of Laughter and Forgetting*, Kundera uses the motif of *Forgetting* in different situations. There is a character Mirek, who is ashamed of a woman he was involved with about twenty years ago because she is ugly and his friends often make fun of his taste in women by referring to her. He wants to somehow wipe out every trace of her existence from his past so that he can make his friends *forget* this embarrassing phase of his youth. The desire to forget certain sections of our past, the desire to rewrite one's own biography is, as Kundera calls it, an anthropological issue. This type of Forgetting is deliberate and conscious. Interestingly, Mirek and his friends are at the same time struggling not to be *forgotten* in a politically charged atmosphere just after the Russian occupation in 1968. The puppet government installed by the Russians was sending all dissident voices for manual labour in the country, at the conveyor belt of an out-of-the-way factory, or behind the steering wheel of a truck, where no one would hear them and they would be *forgotten*. The personal and the political, or the individual and the collective *Forgetting* are hence juxtaposed in this story and both appear to be equally important to the author. Mirek is as much involved in trying to rewrite history as the Communist Party or for that matter all political parties, all nations and all people. The ironic as also the self-ironic element of Kundera's writing comes through very well in this narrative.

In Part VI of this novel, Kundera coins the term 'organized forgetting'. He uses this term exclusively in the political context. Dictatorships organise mass *Forgetting* of the collective past of the people and conspire in manufacturing a past that suits their political ambitions. World history is littered with such examples. The erstwhile Soviet Union expected small nations like Latvia and Lithuania, that had forcefully been made part of it, to forget their past ethnic identities and rejoice in being parts of a collective whole. They were expected to Russianise themselves. Yugoslavia faced a similar experience, when Marshall Tito brought different ethnic groups together under one banner and expected them to *forget* their past ethnic differences. Wherever the Communists came to power, they tried to make people *forget* God and even Christmas. Kundera cites another example of a Czech Communist, who after he fell from grace, was so thoroughly erased from the history and hence from all official photographs that all that was left of him was his hat, which he had placed on the head of an important Communist Party leader on a cold winter day. Even in India, which is the world's largest democracy, one can see several examples of it. A poet of the stature of Mohammad Iqbal is being forgotten, because he is associated with pre-partition Muslim politics. But for his *Saare jahan se accha Hindustan hamara*, he is practically forgotten in present day India, where remembering Shivaji and Rani Jhansi is considered more important. Yet for the same political reasons, Iqbal is being officially promoted in Pakistan. Irrespective of the political system in a country, history books are being rewritten everywhere, even names of streets are being changed. This Forgetting is again deliberate and induced or organised. Ironically enough it is these very conditions that beget Remembering. Memory struggles to remember what the all-powerful State wants people to forget. 'The struggle of memory against forgetting in general becomes a struggle against power.' The Baltic states did not forget their past even after almost a century of distortions by the Communist rule, because their *Remembering* was a deliberate and conscious act. Even the Tibetans in exile are fighting a battle against forgetting organised by the mighty Chinese state, by the conscious act of *Remembering* and promoting of their culture. The protection of memory in this case becomes an element of national survival, and literature also contributes to it. That is why writers and politicians are natural rivals. Both vied for the same territory. The Novel becomes a means of confronting the official, politicians' version of truth.

In his novel, *Slowness*, Kundera deals with the theme of *Forgetting* in terms of the onslaught of multimedia. How quickly the images of starving children in Somalia are forgotten and replaced by some other event! In the lives of our grandparents and greatgrandparents, history and time moved slowly, so events could be easily remembered. Today's world of newspaper, television, computer, internet etc., glamorises tragedies, reducing them to trivialities. This makes Forgetting quick and easy, like fast food.

In times when history still moved slowly, events were few and far between and easily committed to memory. They formed a commonly accepted *backdrop* for thrilling scenes of adventure in private life. Nowadays, history moves at a brisk clip. A historical event, though soon forgotten, sparkles the morning after with the dew of novelty. No longer a backdrop, it is now the *adventure* itself, an adventure enacted before the backdrop of the commonly accepted banality of private life.[6]

It is particularly interesting how Kundera deals with *Forgetting* in his novel *Immortality*. According to him, immortality is the desire to remain, even after death, in the memory of posterity. In other words, immortality is defined in terms of *Forgetting*. That is why each one of us strives to project a carefully nurtured image of ourselves for others. Autobiographies are written with that purpose in mind. Yet these images are often forgotten in favour of a selected few sensational anecdotes which become immortal, acquiring thereby the status of myths. Kundera lashes out at critics who are so obsessed with digging out the personal lives of famous men that they almost forget the works of art created by them. He cites the example of the grand old man of German literature, Goethe. He recounts the famous tale of Goethe and Beethoven taking a walk together. As an aristocrat passed by in his carriage, Goethe is supposed to have stepped aside; he took off his hat and bowed respectfully like a humble servant whereas Beethoven is said to have acted as a rebel, striding forward without any regard for the blue blood. This episode (whose authenticity is doubted) is gleefully cited by many critics to prove Goethe's weakness for nobility. The episode is so fascinating for public memory that it has become immortal, as much or perhaps even more than Goethe's Faust! Another incident that Kundera narrates, revolves around Goethe's wife, Christiana, who may have otherwise been forgotten as the spouse of Goethe with little contribution of her own, were it not for the infamous episode between her and Goethe's beloved (?) Bettina Brentano. Bettina, a woman associated with the women's movement in the Romantic period in Germany, called Christiana, a woman with working class background, 'a fat, crazy sausage' all over Weimar. This was her vicious revenge on Goethe's wife who slapped her for daring to question the maestro's taste in art. *The crazy sausage* became an immortal remark and the immortal laughter still resounds down to our times.

A Forgetting, that is a natural and a gradual process, is crucial to the theme of exile and has been thematised in the narrative Lost Letters, analysed earlier. Most of Kundera's writings, at least the earlier ones, are influenced by his political and personal experiences within the orthodox Communist system in former Czechoslovakia, which ultimately forced him to leave his native land. But at the same time he creates, like any other creative writer, existential situations, to say things which can only be said within the genre of a novel. The story of Lost Letters can be read at the manifest structural level as the alienation and suffering caused by the Communist system, i.e., the alienation of a person forced to leave her/his homeland and settle elsewhere – in this case, Western Europe. This level of reading is historically and temporally conditioned. At this level, the text can function as a 'frozen image' of a particular historical time in Europe: it becomes its historiography. It contains in a condensed form both the synchronic and diachronic aspects of history. However, at the immanent level, the discourse enters the realm of universal significance and appeal if considered as a metaphor for alienation and forgetting. Then it can apply to any situation, anywhere in the world, where an individual living in the past and fighting a battle against memory, is completely alienated and is not able to find her/his place in the society. Tamina's experience is not necessarily the exclusive experience of an emigrant; there is something universal to this experience of *Forgetting*. It is the human condition that is being thematised here. Often we want to immortalise certain moments in life like falling in love, birth of a child etc. Photo cameras and video cameras are meant to serve that purpose. But however hard we may try, it is practically impossible to capture and preserve for ever the magic and warmth of those moments. Not just the beautiful and sublime, but also the most horrible incidents are subject to

Forgetting. What does the French Revolution mean to the French or the Partition to Indians? This Forgetting, in contrast to 'organised forgetting' is, as mentioned already, a gradual and a natural process. The past, hence, becomes 'lighter than feathers', never to return. Salman Rushdie points out in *Imaginary Homelands*:

the past is a country from which we have all emigrated, that its loss is part of our common humanity. (...) for the writer who is out-of-country and even out-of-language this loss is experienced in an intensified form. It is made more concrete for him by the physical fact of discontinuity, of his present being in a different place from his past, of his being 'elsewhere'."[7]

In his essay *Testaments Betrayed,* Kundera discusses the experience of exile—his own as well as of other artists such as Stravinsky, Nabokov and Gombrowicz. He deals with it at two levels—the artistic and the personal or existential problems of a literary emigrant. According to him,

the numerically equal blocks of a life-time are unequal in weight, depending on whether they comprise young or adult years. The adult years may be richer and more important for life and for creative activity both, but the subconscious, memory, language, all the understructures of creativity, are formed very early; for a doctor, that won't make problems, but for a novelist or a composer, leaving the place to which his imagination, his obsessions, and thus his fundamental themes are bound could make for a kind of ripping apart. He must mobilize all his powers, all his artist's wiles, to turn the disadvantages of that situation to benefits."[8]

For Kundera, the benefit has perhaps translated into access to world readership. His Czech predecessors like Hašek and Hrabal, writing in a minor language in a small country, appear to write primarily for the local Czech readers. Their provincial setting put them at a disadvantage that Kundera has overcome through exile. Paris has provided him the opportunity to gain access to the world stage of writers and publishers; at the same time the displacement has also enriched his vision of the world with fresh perspectives. Bilingualism may be counted as another gain. Kundera's novel, *Slowness*, is written in French. With this book, he joins the ranks of Nabokov and Beckett, who are among the few bilingual writers of the world.

Exile is, however, hard from the purely personal and existential angle. Most people generally think in terms of the pain of nostalgia; but what is worse is the pain of estrangement: the process whereby what was once intimate becomes foreign. Does the émigré experience that estrangement vis-à-vis the new country? No, the process here is inverse.

What was foreign becomes, little by little, familiar and beloved. According to Kundera, 'the shocking, stupefying form of strangeness occurs not with an unknown woman we are trying to pick up but with a woman who used to belong to us. Only returning to the native land after a long absence can reveal the substantial strangeness of the world and of existence'.

The narrative, Lost Letters, also sheds light on the probable reasons, why Kundera chose not to return to his native land even after 1989, when there was no longer a political compulsion to stay abroad. Tamina is an emigrant who is neither 'at home' *here*, i.e., in emigration nor *there* i.e., in her native country. The feeling of estrangement related to the motif of forgetting goes hand in hand with nostalgia and perhaps even overtakes it. The past can neither be retrieved nor reconstructed. It is simply lost. However, Kundera's emigration is not total. Several characters in his novels written in his adopted country, France, are Czech. Often the novel is set in Czechoslovakia, although the last two novels, *Immortality* and *Slowness* show a marked shift from the Czech setting towards the exploration of a past which is the common past of Europe. He betrays, however, even in these novels a sense of loss. For example, he remembers affectionately and at the same time sadly his mother-tongue in *Slowness*. The Czech scientist in the novel, upset by the wrong pronunciation of his name, goes out of the way to explain the Czech phonetic sounds to a rather indifferent French receptionist. He refers tenderly to the small marks, small V over some Czech consonants(C,Š), transforming them into the poetry of birds in flight, or the doves with wings outspread or even butterflies! The desire to look back is thus strongly manifest in *Slowness* although it does not appear to be unduly traumatic in the first reading. After a quarter of a century in Paris, chinks may have developed in the wall that leads to his native land, but the rupture or the break, if any, is not yet evident. Kundera's writing, as mentioned earlier, can be described as a kind of anti-lyrical writing, where he often makes fun of human relationships, ideologies, biographies etc. But it is at the level of his relationship with his native land that a kind of sentimental attachment develops. It is so subtle that one almost misses it. Only a close reading of Kundera reveals that the wounds of emigration are perhaps far too deep and intimate, rendered thus incommunicable. Kundera summarises the experience of exile in one short sentence, 'Some things we can only leave unsaid'.

NOTES

1. The Velvet Revolution in Czechoslovakia was absolutely peaceful, accomplished without any bloodshed. Hence it derives its name from the word 'Velvet'.
2. Milan Kundera, *The Book of Laughter and Forgetting*, translated from the Czech by Michael Henry Heim, Rupa & Co, Delhi, 1978, p. 83.
3. Ibid, *Testaments Betrayed*, translated by Linda Asher, Faber and Faber, England, 1993, pp. 259-260.
4. Ibid, p. 261.
5. Ibid, *The Art of the Novel*, translated by Linda Asher, Rupa & Co, Delhi, 1986, p. 5.
6. Ibid, *The Book of Laughter and Forgetting*, p. 8.
7. Salman Rushdie, *Imaginary Homelands,* Penguin, Great Britain, 1991, p. 12.
8. Milan Kundera, *Testaments Betrayed*, op. cit, p. 94.

MARIA ALZIRA SEIXO

Faces of Exile in Portuguese Literature

Exile as a human situation always implies a dramatic relation between two fundamental categories for the course of common existence: the *places* where human beings are located, as well as those into which they have moved by different ways of compulsion; and the *travel* that directed them from one place to another, developing a specific notion of *parallel time* that opposes the past and the present. This opposition normally means a consideration of *differences* existing between both temporal and spatial levels. However, the category of space is in this case more relevant in order to define the configurations of feelings, judgements and other orders of manifestation of sense that result from the expression of this specific situation in art or in literature.

In fact, the paradigmatic situation of exile supposes a separation from homeland and the consequent nostalgia of personal roots, produced mostly on a political or moral basis, with models like Ovidius, for the ancients, like Saint-John Perse, for the twentieth century, or Milan Kundera and Salman Rushdie, for contemporary literature. Nevertheless, exile may be faced nowadays, in literary expression, also as a poetical form, meaning a kind of ostracism that writers manifest in relation with a specific social status, since Romanticism, but underlining particularly the feeling of self relegation concerning the whole social ambience that nowadays involves human activity and sensibility. Beckett and the notions of absurd and void, as well as the contemporary controversy of postmodern parody, rewriting and loss of values may also be considered in that sense.

Portuguese literature has evolved in the same way as European literature in general, dealing with the theme of exile sometimes in a political sense, sometimes in a mere literary perspective. Amongst the classics (sixteenth century), Camões, the epic of *The Lusiads* (where the first maritime voyage of Vasco da Gama to India is the essential poetic subject), develops, in lyrical texts, the theme of human life considered as an exile for the soul separated from the happiness of Heavens (according to the biblical «topos» of Babel and Siam); with less erudition, but a much more impressive mark of the empirical experience coming from his perception of the eastern world, Fernao Mendes Pinto gives us in the *Peregrinaçao* (Peregrination) the sense of adventure felt by a common western human being caught by the exotic and strange practices of the Orient; and being victim of the misfortunes that made him suffer in jail and in other forms of captivity during his twenty year spent in India, Malaysia, China, Japan and so forth. Camões experienced poetically the expulsion of man from paradise (as Milton did), while Pinto underlines the euphoria as well as the distress of man reluctantly exploring unknown territories and observing fearfully different ways of life. In 18th century, during the Enlightenment two writers intimately related by similar conceptions of art and by personal affection, the Marquess of Alorna and the priest Filinto Elísio, consider their political positions and restrictions as an exclusion of common society, thus a form of exile. It is, however during Romanticism, in 19th century, that the idea of nationality and homeland become stronger, according to Herder's doctrine, underlining the notion of expatriation with pain and disturbance. Garrett, Herculano and Camilo Castelo-Branco are some good examples of this position, the first two authors in poetry and in fiction, the third in his several and very emotive novels. Garrett had to run away to England during the political quarrels that made possible the parliamentary regime in Portugal and, returning home, he wrote impressive verses in his poem significantly entitled *Camões* (1825), which is supposed to introduce romanticism officially in Portuguese literature:

> Saudade, gosto amargo de infelizes,
> delicioso pungir de acerbo espinho
> que me estás lacerando o íntimo peito.

> (Nostalgia, bitter taste for unfortunate,
> delightful piercing of steeled thorn
> that is deeply wounding my heart.)

Herculano also had to emigrate to England and France; and he develops in his poetry, namely in *Tristezas do Desterro* (Griefs of Banishment), 1838, a plaint for his homeland, in loneliness and sorrow, from a religious and social point of view:

> Berço do meu nascer, solo querido,
> Onde cresci e amei a fui ditoso,
> Onde a luz, onde o sol riem, tão meigos,
> Meu pobre Portugal, hei-de chorar-te!

(Cradle of my birth, my cherished ground,
Where I've grown up and I felt happy,
Where light and sun softly laugh,
My poor Portugal, I'll cry for you!)

After the sentimental and sensual perspective carried by Garrett, the philosophical mode adopted by Herculano enhances in the poem a larger social implication, pessimistic and even metaphysical, where man and earth coexist in the same entity of thinking, divided between death and life, shadow and light, dream and appearance:

Ai, que és tu, existência?! Um pesadelo,
Um sonho mau, de que se acorda em trevas,
Na vala dos cadáveres, em meio
Da única herança que pertence ao homem,
Um sudário e o perpétuo esquecimento.
(...)
E da pátria a saudade, em sonho triste,
Imóvel, do viver me tece a noite.

(What are you, existence?! A nightmare,
A bad dream, from which we wake up in darkness,
In the grave of the corpses, in the middle of
the unique heritage to man belonging,
a sudarium and eternal oblivion.
(....)
and a longing for homeland, melancholy,
Is weaving this night, which is my life.)

In fiction, we may observe in various novels written by Camilo Castelo-Branco, not exactly the experience of exile, but the composition of some characters that may represent it, either in a romantic or in a realistic way (the transition between these two aesthetics was experienced in Portuguese literature during the second half of the nineteenth century). The most common character to depend on this type of meaning is the expatriate. In his well-known novel *Amor de Perdição* (Love and Dishonour), exile in overseas represents the punishment for those who fall in forbidden and extreme love situations. On the other hand, the expatriate, going out of homeland and giving up complex circumstances in the universe of fiction, or, on the contrary, coming back in pain and misery or even rehabilitated, is a decisive element in the plot and determines the sense of the action: misery may become opulence, the conversions of characters and values may be accomplished and, as it happens in Balzac or in Dickens, or even later in Thomas Hardy (*Tess of the D'Ubervilles*, for instance), the conventions of the bourgeois systems contend with the tendencies of the heart. This may be observed in one of the best novels written by Camilo Castelo-Branco, *Livro de Consolação*, 1872 (The Book of Consolation).

In the twentieth century, exile becomes frequent in Portuguese society, especially during the dictatorship of Salazar (from the thirties until the April revolution, in 1974). On the other hand, compulsive voyages to the so-called Portuguese colonies in Africa and the phenomenon of emigration come together to create new situations of expatriation. They differ in principle from the situation of exile but have in common with it the same feelings of separation and nostalgia and, essentially, a similar perception of the otherness of space and of the doubleness of time. In a book published recently, entitled *Manual dos Inquisidores*, 1996 (Handbook for Inquisitors), António Lobo Antunes mixes all these levels of Portuguese civilization in the last decades and as a technical narrative device he constructs two orders of time (the parallel time that I was evoking in the beginning), the time of enunciation (complex in itself because it is constituted by several instances of memory) and the time of history (where he respects the exactitude of selected objects in the description of what happened in a defined space in remote past). And many poets had written before (as also later) about those topics and the complex situation they implied in Portuguese culture. Let us remember a poem where Manual Alegre, during the sixties, exiled in Paris for political reasons, followed the traces of Portuguese emigrants in the streets of Paris, *Portugal em Paris*, 1967 (Portugal in Paris):

Solitário
por entre a gente eu vi o meu país.
Era um perfil
de sal
e abril.
Era um puro país azul e proletário.
Anónimo passava. E era Portugal
que passava por entre a gentre e solitário
na ruas de Paris.

Vi minha pátria derramada
na gare de Austerlitz. Eram cestos
e cestos pelo chão. Pedaços
do meu país.
Restos.
Braços
Minha pátria sem nada
sem nada
despejada nas ruas de Paris.

(Lonely
amongst people I saw my country.
That was a profile
of salt
and april.
That was a pure blue country, proletarian.
It was passing by, anonymous. And it was Portugal
that was passing by amongst people, lonely,
in the streets of Paris.

I saw my homeland
in the Gare d' Austerlitz. There were baskets
and baskets by the ground. Pieces
of my country.
Scraps.
Arms.
My homeland with nothing
with nothing
poured out in the streets of Paris.)

It is this conscience of division (a particular element of western modernity, as is commonly shared by scholars) that creates the most intense feeling of exile, in my view, in contemporary Portuguese literature. The division of the self may consist in the possibility of a choice between two ways of life; and this choice may be stimulated by external circumstances (political or other) or by intimate reasons of dissatisfaction or even literary modes of sensibility. In the end of the nineteenth century, the need of escape and exotic appeals, related with the aesthetics of symbolism, originate voyages of writers and the adoption of new countries by them. Venceslau de Morais (1854-1929) went to Japan, where he lived until his death, got married and adopted all the particularities of Japanese tradition. This form of exile converts external compulsion into a kind of internal one, cultural and psychological, where free choice leads to the nostalgia of the past, not exactly because it was good (it was not) but because it is past – and lost. What is more, Morais becomes sensitive to small details in Portuguese culture that he never really appreciated, but which with distance and absence emerged in his memories; for instance the 'caldo verde', a traditional soup with cabbages which he tried to reproduce with other plants to celebrate Christmas far away from his homeland, as he describes in a short story (*O' Yonè e Ko-Haru*).

Exile may be faced therefore as a division felt by the conscience of the writer, concerning space or time, in a feeling of expatriation that can be voluntary even if not desired. This division doesn't necessarily have negative consequences, from a moral point of view. In emigration, or even in other forms of voyage that make writers move away from their countries (political forms that do not consist only in disagreements with governments, but let us say, the needs of diplomatic functions), the division of the self may exist, but it is enriched by the multiple knowledge of different ways of being. The very notion of otherness becoming much too heavy for the individual, it reinforces in fact the yearning to reconstruct identity. That is why for some of these writers, staying far from homeland, the sense and the taste for origins, traditions, memories of childhood and roots was stronger. In the twentieth century, we may consider two examples of these two tendencies; the case of *Jorge de Sena* and the case of *José Rodrigues Miguéis*. Both lived in the United States and elsewhere, for the most part of their lives, but we may argue that Sena was closer and more related to the Portuguese culture and to the Portuguese contemporary events although he was living abroad. Miguéis, without forgetting peculiarities of his homeland, which he described constantly in detail and with soft irony, realized a cultural and affectionate articulation with the countries where he was living. In his short-story *Léah*, 1958, he deals with his difficult understanding of a young woman, in Belgium, due to her free manners and spontaneous nature, opposite to his own shy and conventional behaviour (and to that of the young Potuguese ladies...), in a very special love and death story. In other narratives, namely in the volume *Onde a Noite se Acaba*, 1938 (Where Night is Over), we find a similar way of facing cultural differences in a constant dialogue that maintains individual specification but at the same time is always trying to incorporate the manifestations of the other. On the contrary, Jorge de Sena is continually trying to preserve the individuality of his own culture, not exactly dealing with the theme of exile or expatriation, but developing the meaning of Portuguese patrimony (in History, in Literature, in Art), in what we should call its permanent paraphrase, in homage, parody or violent direct attacks. His last book, a posthumous novel entitled *Sinais de Fogo*, 1979 (Signs of Fire), faces more directly the theme of expatriation and the political and personal reasons that motivate it.

However, several generations experienced this division of the self as the very division of the Portuguese land - in immigration, in the colonial war, or even in the permanence they have chosen in staying in Portugal during the dictatorship, and fighting in silence or in resistance. Journals of poetry were created in order to signify a way of parallel and poetic communication, opposing symbols and artistic intentions to the distress and impossibility of everyday life. Particularly meaningful is *Noticias do Bloqueo*, 1957, directed by Egito Gonçalves and Daniel Filipe, from the title of a poem of Egito Gonçalves (News from the Blockade). In fact, the notion of exile is assumed by those who, living in Portugal, feel this place unlike their homeland, as we may observe in the title of a book written by Daniel Filipe, *Pátria, lugar de exílio* (Homeland, Place of Exile). The lyrical voice par excellence of this tendency is *Sophia de Mello Beyner Andresen*, one of our more famous writers. All her work is bound to the sea, to voyages, to the search of identity found and lost by the maritime discoveries, which nowadays need rewriting, implying dialogue and critical consideration. Sea and land were to Sophia places of two levels of time, a time to rejoice for goods given by nature and shaped by culture and a time to deplore the waste and destruction resulting from political oppression and censorship. All the poetry of Sophia Mello Breyner is conducted by the idea of freedom in nature and civilization and thus the notion of exile is naturally embedded in the consideration of a blocked country even for those who live in it.

Quando a pátria que temos não a temos
Perdida no silêncio e na renúcia
Até a voz do mar se torna exílio
E a luz que nos rodeia é como grades

(When our homeland is not a homeland
Lost in the silence and in renunciation
Even the voice of the sea becomes exile
And light surrounding us is like a jail)

Staying in a lost country where the feeling of homeland cannot exist is like making a journey hoping to return home, a return to childhood and to the freedom of thought and the discovery of meaning - and return here coincides entirely with arrival:

Eu regressarei ao poema como à pàtria à casa
Como à antiga infânia que perdi por descuido
Para gritar obstinada a substância de tudo

(I will come back to the poem to homeland I'll return home
As to ancient childhood which I lost carelessly
To firmly shout the substance of everything)

Home thus coincides entirely with homeland and the word recovers its entire sense of territory on earth, space where the human being keeps his life in affection and tranquillity, constituting the sense of identity.

A casa que eu amei oi destroçade
A morte caminha no sossego do jardim
A vida sussurrada na folhagem
Subitamente quebrou-se não é minha

(My beloved home was wasted
Death walks in the peaceful garden
Life whispered by the movement of leaves
Suddenly is broken it is not mine)

Recovering life is recovering home and homeland - for Portuguese people, it was a revolution, that is freedom and time to live; in that sense, Sophia tells us that recovery is like a discovery, which means a restart for understanding others and reconstructing the idea of truth.

Revolução isto é: descobrimento
Mundo recomeçado a partir da praira pura
Como poema a partir da página em branco
- Catarsis emergir verdade exposta
Tempo terreste a perguntar seu rosto

(Revolution is this: discovery
World restarted from a pure seaside
Like the poem starting from the white page
- Catharsis emerge exposed truth
An earthy time demanding for its face.)

Sophia integrates time in space by the configurations of homeland in the ethical course of existence and by abolishing the need of exile, restituting to the voyage the sense of a positive displacement for knowledge, for the practice of freedom and for the understanding of other ways of life.

ALBERTO CARVALHO

Travel and Metaphors of Exile in African Literature in Portuguese

Leurs chants étaient si purs et si beaux qu'en les entendant les vents et les eaux suspendirent leur course, la lune et les constellations, fascinées, tressaillirent. Et six mois s'écoluèerent ainsi sans que personne s'en aperçût. Depuis lors, on appelle cette nuit 'la nuit de Brahmâ.

Jean Herbert, *La geste de Krishna*, p. 251

Their songs were so pure and so beautiful that air and water suspended movement while listening to it, the moon and the starry constellations remained stupefied in fascination. And six months passed by without anyone being aware of it. Since then, that night is called 'The night of the Brahmâ.*

Krishna Leela(SL)

LITERATURE AND HISTORIOGRAPHY

One of the more common aspects of literature written with tradition instilled by time, and of recognised prestige, consists of forming a series that benefits from a status of reasonable autonomy with regard to the other fields of human activity into which reality is broken down and diversified. This means to say that this attribute of autonomy also expresses the cultural importance enjoyed by literary creativity of a particular sector of society as a whole, considered in its organic completeness in the light of the advanced stage of development in which it currently stands. Over and above the complementariness that governs the various sectors of social life, it is the individuality of literature that justifies its working and the diverse displays of verbalised content. And these, as a rule, are viewed from the point of view of the human interest of the messages that sustain them and, thus appraised in keeping with their own internal attributes, also constitute grounds for the development of the whole diversity of studies the object of which is literary matters.

We can therefore include within the limits of this specific field, extended to its various forms, languages and substances, the most diverse understandings that literary work arouses, in this case the theme dedicated to "exile" which will include in its simplest expression the problem of existence and of social inclusion and exclusion. All the senses of the literary end up by referring, in keeping with differing angles and paths, to contents directed by an axiology that, in all likelihood, can always be related to the order of the real world or of the possible world. Its imaginative rounds that allow it to be conceived as fiction means that, very often, the need for direct legitimation provided by empirical reality can be dispensed with.

At a wider level, the study of the aesthetic and poetic co-ordinates of the works and of their genealogical descent is the logical result of this gnoseological process. Seen thus, the works gain the status of objects of knowledge that shape literary studies, finally destined to enter into the field of cultural communication. But, as Eva Kushner points out in her essay 'Historic Articulation of Literature', integration of literary knowledge into the vaster set of other knowledge does not comply with simple procedures, but rather several problems of a nature as methodological as epistemological. The essayist therefore sustains the advantage, in such studies, of progressively articulating literature with the time axis of its historiography and, then, the latter with the more general history of the nations.

The pondered attitude in this case, is a virtue of method to avoid the risk of dissolving literary specificness within social and political contexts for obvious reasons. In one sense, the human interest of the contents of the texts works as a factor of identification preventing total separation between the literary and social life. In the other sense, and for that too, it would also be absolutely damaging to the individuality of the works if such identification were reduced to a documentary function of history and, particularly, of its political paths.

HISTORY AND LITERATURE

If we admit that the principles set forth take their validity from the possibilities of general application, their usefulness is especially pertinent in the case of the literature of the five Portuguese-speaking countries of Africa, the Cape Verde islands, Guinea-Bissau, São Tomé e Prícipe, Angola and Mozambique. In reality, their differing levels of evolution should be interpreted in accordance with the historic developments of the respective countries as spaces organised by the process of colonisation. In this particular aspect three structural factors are of prime importance: the schooling of the population by religious missionaries and by the administrative power; the growth of the urban populations and of the mercantile economy; and the institution of the press. Although we are dealing with national literature of very remarkable differences, it would not be incorrect to admit that the ones of Cape Verde, Angola and Mozambique, in aspects as diverse as thematic, the specifications of genre and the distribution in time, brings together all that is most representative that distinguishes this sector within the Portuguese-speaking space.

Strictly speaking, just as the European literature of the early nineteenth century, which was viewed as a support to the socio-cultural conscience of the emerging nations, so too the role played by writing launched within the space of Portuguese colonisation by the official press during the 1840s was historic. As from the middle of the nineteenth century, literary writing in Cape Verde and in Angola, particularly poerty, responded to the need to constitute an awareness provided with its own territory. Then, as from the beginning of the twentieth century, in those countries and in Mozambique as well, it was journalistic writing that took over the deepening of this awareness at the level of social, political and economic values, driven by interests different to those of metropolitan Portugal or even opposed thereto.

But one should take into account the fact that these consciences represented by documentary and literary writing express, in their differing manners, two distinct types of creative dynamics of the colonising enterprise. In the Cape Verde Archipelago (and in São Tomé e Príncipe, too), the peopling of the territories, starting from the previous total absence of population, led to the formation of a strictly Creole society. On the African continent, in the areas of Angola and Mozambique (and also in Guinea-Bissau) the system employed was not one of peopling but of colonisation.

The process of socio-historic formation of the communities was therefore in keeping with the logic of occupation of coastal spaces at the expense of economic, diplomatic, religious and military contacts, in encounters both pacific and bellic with the local ethnic groups truly rich in history and in traditional oral cultures.

We must therefore value their cultural and literary practices through recourse to various nuances of a particular hermeneutics. In the milieu of the essays of the West and North, in Europe, one can admit a dominance of an axiological framework of literary creativity that particularly enhances the sociological order of the communities that specially value the individuality of the authors. In the literature of the countries located on the African continent, however, the orders of representation and of the meaning of the literary texts can rarely dispense with the anthropological order of reading. This is, indeed, the more productive means of access to the meanings arising from circumstances and processes that seem to us to be essential. Both for contextual reasons of an active African ancestry or for cultural osmosis leading to intertextual absorption, either conscious or unconscious, of the orally-recorded genres by contemporary written works, the substances of the communitarian traditions must never be neglected.

And it is in this particular aspect that one should distinguish the special case of the literature of Cape Verde. The Creole evolution of its cultural base left scant traces of African influence; and for this reason the anthropological meaning of literary reading should specially value the existential dimension of the themes that almost always include the problem of the territory and of its Atlantic insularity. From this derives the nature of the typical imagery of the Creole ethnicity of Cape Verde, in which oceanic solitude stands out as does the geography of semi-tropical drought, similar to that of the Brazilian North-east, the very intense economic migration and the yearning for the absent fatherland.

In turn, the literature in general of the continental countries, particularly that of Angola and Mozambique, organises its representations around highly syncretic themes. Its characteristics can be explained by the type of colonisation undertaken by a country of little power such as Portugal, different from other models that were set up just in the second half of the nineteenth century and operated particularly under administrative sovereignty (France) or mercantile sovereignty (England).

Developed over several centuries, the Portuguese colonial process allowed the elaboration of a historic dimension marked by slow material adaptation in economic and agricultural activities and in settling populations, ending up by creating a vast network of human ties and of profound social experiences.

On the other hand, through mutually acculturative contacts, the African Black and the Portuguese gave rise to the appearance of the culture of the mestiço populations. The acquisitions made by each ethnic group from the heritage of the other, of objective and subjective value, led to the appearance of an urban syncretic culture, clearly to be seen in the folklore of Angola. With the Africanisation of the Portuguese, the values of European civilisation were socialised, and so too the adaptation of the Portuguese language, particularly in the coastal regions of Angola and Mozambique. In turn, the adaptation of the native people to urban civilisation opened up the way to their mestiço intellectual training applied directly to writing and to literature.

SPACE, TRAVEL AND METAPHORS OF EXILE

The centripetal force of the African land is the motivation of spatial centring, guiding in a convergent manner the writing of authors marked by opposing basic cultures. We would sum up the historiography of Angola by saying that, in a first stage, one of the great textual paradigms cultivated by poets of Portuguese origin is exactly what is ordered by the themes of attraction and adaptation of the European individual who emigrated voluntarily to the natural space of the African Black. In turn the literary production of mestiço or African Black authors opens up, as it were, to a twofold movement of spatial addresses, some more cosmopolitan addressed to other cultures in other spaces, and others given life by ethnic centring.

Right in the middle of the nineteenth century, in Angola, in an edition by the Government Press, in Luanda in 1849, the mestiço José da Silva Maia Ferreira published a book entitled *Spontaneities of My Soul - To the Women of Africa,* which is exemplary in this regard. Revealing a knowledge of contemporary Portuguese, Brazilian, French and English authors, in addition to the Greek and Latin classic, the epigraphs and poetic content, the set of the book's fifty-four poems fit in completely with the programme of European aesthetics of that time. Right in the period of birth of this literature, and at the same time in Cape Verde, adoption of the foreign Romantic canon revealed at least two meanings to which special attention must be given.

For this African author, access to poetry originating from another culture seems to be a form of desire of universality. The cultural experience thus established opens up the way to inter-subjective relations that break with the isolation, as a metaphor of exile, in which space itself runs the risk of being confined. Furthermore, and as in other areas in which it was cultivated, the Romantic canon also constitutes an artistic instrument of recognition in the service of ideology and of the spirit of the nation that begins to take birth in Angola and Cape Verde.

In practice, the biography of the author is a model in keeping with such an interpretation of the work. Exiled in Rio de Janerio for political reasons, his poetry of this period constitutes, in fact, a form of inter-textual cosmopolitan dialogue with the Brazilian Romantics. But the lyrical expression of his experiences also serve as a means of ethnic self-recognition invested, in a direct manner, in themes that ennoble the value of African origin, lending meaning to a nativist ideology, also common to the Romantic-cosmopolitan authors of Cape Verde of that time.

And it is also in this same sense that it is represented in the works of Portuguese authors of the second half of the nineteenth century such as Cândido Furtado, Eduardo Neves in poetry and Alfredo Troni in narrative. The lyricism of sensual colouring addressed to the African woman, seductive despite being black; and the interesting description of the black traditions are some of their more well-known literary forms. Though set apart from their cultural background by administrative missions, by emigration or by birth in Africa, their presence in the space of others is not expressed in problematic forms of uprooting. Instead of the nostalgia that could be caused by territorial exile, or of the conservation of their cultural values in an untouched state, the works bear witness, rather, to a constant and total tie to African land.

The periodological interest of this theme of the ethnically Portuguese authors, which reading without adequate information could confound with a superficial fascination with the exotic, was to gain its true meaning half a century later, in the 1940s. At that time, the poetry of the Portuguese poet Tomás Vieira da Cruz gave updated continuity to the previous local integrating vision, though through an admiring lyricism of total reality.

His poems, that clearly capture the popular taste of Angola, constitute a model of suggestions of which advantage was taken by authors who, now, work in to the appearance of committed modernity in the process of national awareness.

With the development of this literary period, that lasted until the acquisition of national sovereignty during the 1970s, the realistic aesthetic orientation of political commitment is common to all the African literature in Portuguese. Wherever authors driven by ideological commitment are to be found, whether citizens of Cape Verde exiled for economic reasons or whether from any one of the five countries, studying in Portugal or politically exiled in Paris, Algiers or Conakry, or incarcerated in the prisons of Portugal's New State (such as Luandino Vieira and António Jacinto, of Angola, or José Craveirinha, Luís Bernardo Honwana and Rui Nogar, of Mozamique), the same motive of militancy inspires them all. The meaning of the themes in poetry and narrative therefore obey the tropism of ethnic return to and centring on themes of patriotic praise, denunciation of colonialism and songs of heroes in battle.

Equally common is the influence exercised by the internationalist component of the Black movement active in Europe and in the Americas, although with differing shades of interpretation. Following adaptation to the reality of Portuguese colonisation, the French-speaking Negro movement could be found in the motives that inspired the activists of the Atlantic area of Africa, Francisco Tenreiro (of São Tomé e Príncipe), Amilcar Cabral (of Cape Verde and Guinea-Bissau) and Mário de Andrade (of Angola). But more than at the level of literary creation, their example was of particular service to the process of re-Africanisation of the nationalist conscience of the intellectuals. Perhaps due to the proximity and influence of the English-speaking countries to the South and along the coasts of the Indian Ocean, the influences in Mozambique were even more mediated.

They can be found in one of the first nationalist writers of this period, Noémia de Sousa, through the implication of the musical discourse of the protest of the American Blacks in their very vigorous poetry of denunciation and revolt.

None of these processes can be properly understood without taking into account the process, referred to above, of the themes of local integration in the poems of Portuguese authors. The fact that it is necessary to distinguish between Portuguese colonialism and the socially Africanised Portuguese-based communities is a measure of their character of documental truth. At literary level, objective proof is evident when it is seen that an appreciable number of the nationalist poets of Angola (about 30%) and of Mozambique (about 40%) was born in Portugal or descended directly from Portuguese.

But at literary level, the interest of the question is owed less to the integrating disposition of the Portuguese in African space than to the centripetal power of their ethnic cultures, as reflected in the vaster structure of the narrative works.

Dating from the fifties, the novel *Portagem,* by the Mozambican Orlando Mendes, is a narrative that puts into practice the thesis of nationalist conscience radicalised by the absolute antagonism between the Whites and the Blacks. In this context, which leaves no socially acceptable room for the mestiço, the web of the work is organised as the dramatic path trodden by João Xilim, the son of a white settler and of a Black Woman, who rejects his status as a mestiço. From the point of view of the topic of space and of its aggregating force, the essence of the tale consists in the frustrated attempts at voluntary exile by the central character. Whether his decision to sail off as a seaman to escape the truth of his mestiço identity, in one case, or that of emigrating to the mines of South Africa, to escape from a frustrated marriage, in the other, the departures can be but temporary. The end to the experiences corresponds to recognition that the being and the being's identity must be authenticated by a return to the place of ethnic ancestry. The better to respond to the demand of the political times of the novel, this process is completed in an action of protest in which João Xilim publicly expresses acceptance of his Black condition by rejection of his mestiço status.

Along the same line is the 1990 novel *Patriots* by the Angolan Sousa Jamba who lived in exile in Zambia between 1976 and 1984. It may be that the subject of the novel is based on the fictionalisation of his own experiences, despite the organisation of the work in the third person singular. Once again, the place of exile is reached at the end of a journey to a nearby territory that does not take the leading character far from his place of origin. In addition to being temporary, the adaptation of the group of refugees who are suspicious of the customs of the host country is also critical. That is, although African and neighbours, the Zambians and the Angolans are different in their historic national conscience, as distinct as was the English and the Portuguese colonisation. And this without prejudice to the esteem in which the protagonist, Hosi Mbueti, confesses he holds English literature. Two vectors are predominant in the story of the character and of his knowledge of reality, aggregating the essence of the messages of the work. In the first place, the ethnic motivation of the return to the fatherland to take part in the military combat as a member of UNITA, the political party of the character's region of origin, is not open to debate. Secondly, the direct experience of the war between MPLA, UNITA and FNLA shows that ethnicity merely constitutes a label that hides ideological differences in the struggle for power in a country that identifies with them all.

Simplifying and summarising the complexity of this problem, the literary representation of exile in the literature of Cape Verde can now be defined as an intermediate case, for the attenuated repercussion of the thematic examples of the Portuguese authors on the one hand and of the Angolan and Mozambican, on the other. In the first place, the ethnicity of the Cape Verde author truly possesses a singular substance of a conscience that is totally identified with the founding territory of the islands, and with a history that began around 1460. From the modernity of its literature therefore emerges a form of realism that faces the problem of being a Creole within a framework of contradictory existence. It is modelled by the insularity, the landscape, the drought, the tedium of work, the roots in the land and the dream of other places, and it is conditioned by the dilemma of remaining in the economy of scarcity on the islands or of emigrating from a desire to improve living conditions. The majority of the more important themes are in keeping with this historic reality, as a rule based on three paradigms of an existentialist framework. In one the predominant theme is one of insularity, of the land conceived as a space of isolation-exile, an obstacle to establishing intellectual relations with authors of other cultures. Thus it is with the poet Jorge Barbosa, the principal representative of this poetic current, in which there are frequent works that exploit the desire for evasion and for dialogue with the 'other', particularly with the Brazilian poets of whom Manuel Bandeira is the leading representative.

At the opposite end to this poetic experience is the Diaspora that assumes the forms of physical uprooting. The desire for 'evasion', generated by the awareness of insularity, and the desire for 'return', generated by the experience of orphanhood away from the fatherland, obey the same principle of contradiction caused by existential insufficiency. Therefore, the theme of 'return' of the authors in Diaspora, very well presented by Orlanda Amarilis, constitutes, as a rule, a cultural restatement of loyalty to one's roots and, in particular, confirmation of the personality of the Creole, of the being that reflects the harmonised synthesis of two or more cultures.

Another way of expressing this Creole synthesis as an emigrant consists of putting it into practice in the reality of life in concrete, omitting it, however, at the level of literary creation. Of the work of several authors, that of Manuel Lopes is especially significant, in poetry dedicated to the themes of the relation with the sea and in the narrative that poses the problem of man's setting down roots in the land. In both these genres, the thematic dominants that bring those of Cape Verde into a debate between the scarcity of their resources and the riches of the world of the "other" always consist of the refusal to depart, in contradiction with the reality experienced by the emigrant author.

To sum up: Everything takes place, in this real case of Diaspora, as though literary writing constituted a path of recollective redemption of an absent fatherland.

NOTES

* The epigraph has been translated from French by Sharmistha Lahiri.

1. Alcântara, Osvaldo (Pseud. de Baltasar Lopes), *Cântico da Manhã Futura,* Praia, Banco de Cabo Verde, 1985.
2. Amarilis, Orlanda, *Cais-de-Sodré té Salamanca,* Coimbra, Centelha, 1974.
3. *ilhéu dos pássors,* Lisbon, Plátano, s.d. (1982).
4. Andrade, Mário de, "Contribution des hommes de culture à l évolution de la conscience politique en Angola", in *Mélanges - Présence Africaine, 1947-1967,* Paris, Présence Africaine, s.d.
5. Anón., *Mantenhas para quem luta! A nova poesia de Guné-Bissau,* Bissau, Conselho Nacional de Cultura, 1977.
6. *Memento primeiros da construção* .. Bissau, Conselho Nacional de Cultura, 1978.
7. Barbosa, Jorge, *Jorge Babosa- Poesias I,* Praia (Cape Verde), Instituto Caoverdiano do Livro e do Disco, 1989.
8. Bessière, Jean, "Literatura e Representāç", in *Teoria Literária,* Lisbon, Publicações Dom Quixote, 1995.
9. Bremond, Claude, "La logique des possibles narratifs", in *Communications* N°8, Paris, Seul, 1966.
10. Carvalho, Alberto, "Evasionismo, confiuração existencial da insularidate

caboverdiana" , in *Coscienza Nazionale Nelle Letterature Africane di Lingua Portohese,* Roma, Bulzoni Editore, 1995.

11. Espírito-Santo, Aldã, *Antologia Poética de São Tomé e Príncipe,* São Tomé, Arquivo Histórico, 1978.
12. Ferreira, José da Silva Maia, *Espontaneidades da Minha Alma -às senhoras africanas,* Lisbon, Edições 70, 1980.
13. Ferreira, Manuel, *No Reino de Caliban, Antologia panorâmica da poesia africana de expressão portuguesa,* I, II, III, Lisbon, Plátano, s.d.
14. Frelimo (Org.), *Poesia de Combate,* Maputo, Departamento do Trabalho Ideolóio da Frelimo, 1977.
15. Gonçalves, António Aurélio, "Bases para uma Cultura Caboverdiana", in Rodrigues Matias (Coord.), *Diário da Viagem Presidencial às Provínias Ultramarinas de Guiné e Cabo Verde em 1955,* Lisbon, Agência Geral do Ultramar, 1956.
16. Jamba, Sousa, *Pariotas,* Lisbon, Cotovia, 1991.
17. Kushner, Eva, "Articulação da História da Literatura", in *Teoria Literária,* Lisbon, Publiações Dom Quixote, 1995.
18. Lopes, Baltasar, *Cabo Verde Visto por Gilberto Freyre,* Praia (Cape Verde), Imprensa Nacional, 1956.
19. Lopes, Manuel, *Poemas de quem ficou,* Angra do Heoísmo, Ed. de Autor-Tip. da "Livraria Editora Andrade", 1949.
20. *Crioulo e outros poemas,* Lisbon, Ed. de Autor- Gráfica Silva, 1964.
21. *Chuva Brava,* Lisbon, Edições 70, 1982.
22. Macherey, Pierre, *Pour une Théorie de la Production Littéraire,* Paris, Maspero, 1974.
23. Martins, Heitor, "Evasionismo como consciencialização. O caso de *Chiquinho* de Baltasar Lopes", in *Brotéria,* Vol. 119, Nº , Lisbon, Jul./ 1984.
24. Mendes, Orlando, *Portagem,* Lisbon, Edições 70, 1981.
25. Ngijol, Pierre, "La critique littéraire dans la littératture traditionnelle orale, in *Le Critique Africain et son Peuple comme producteur de civilisation,* Col. de Yaoundé, 16-20 Avril 1973, Paris, Présence Africaine, 1977.
26. Oliveria, Mário António F., "Para uma perspective crioula da Literatura Angolana, O "Reposiório de Coisas Angolenses" de J.D. Corderio da Mata", in *Reler Africa,* Instituto de Antropologia-Universidade de Coimbra, 1990.
27. "O Primeio Livro de Poemas Publicado na África Portuguesa", in *Reler África,* Idem.
28. Pacheco, Carlos, *José da Silva Maia Ferreira-o Homem e a sua Época,* Luanda, União dos Escritores Angolanos, 1990.
29. *O Nativismo na Poesia de José da Silva Maia Ferreira,* Évora, Editorial Pendor, 1996.
30. Senghor, Léopold, Sédar, "L'espirt de la civilisation ou les lois de la culture négro-africaine", in *Le ler Congrès International des Écrivains et Artistes Noirs,* Paris-Sorbonne, 19-22 Septembre 1956, *Présence Africaine,* Nº. 8-9-10, Juin-Nov./1956.
31. Tenreiro, Francisco, *Cabo Verde e São Tomé e príncipe - esquema de uma evolução conjunta,* Sep. do Boletim *Cabo Verde,* Praia (Cape Verde), 1956.
32. Troni, Alfredo, *Nga Mutúri,* Lisbon, Edições 70, 1991.

FERNANDO CRISTÓVÃO

Two Exiles in the Contemporaneous Brazil

The theme of exile is common to all literatures in the course of time, for the basic reason that all of them keep up with real life, where situations of tension and exclusion are always present. Such situations occur both in the small universe of the individual and in that, more vast, of collective life. Because exile isn't only the compulsory deviation from that reality to which the individual is connected as part of his personality, but also the banishment from the Country to which one belongs and where one enjoys living, with the interdiction of coming back. Today, we bear in mind the exiles of Joyce, Pound, T.S. Eliot, St. John Perse, among others. But to these exiles of deeply cultural and existential nature, we can add the exiles originated by political or ideological banishment.

The most notable works in this field are those of Solzhenitsyn, Kundera, Arrais as well as those of many other dissidents. As far as Brazilian literature is concerned, besides the romantic and symbolic exiles we find, nowadays, new patterns of political exile and cultural exiles. To illustrate this assertion we have chosen two novels: *O Amor de Pedro por João* (The Love of Pedro for João), by Tabajara Ruas, published in 1982, and *O Mar Nunca Transborda* (The Sea never Overflows), by Ana Maria Machado, published in 1995.

Tabajara Ruas, who had already dealt with a similar subject in his novel *A Região Submersa* (The Submerged Region), an edition made in Portugal, places the action of the novel in the seventies, featuring that decade stigmatised by a military dictatorship through the perfect image of a social climate of repression and fear that led many to take exile voluntarily or to be compulsively expelled to foreign countries.

The second part of the sixties and the first half of the seventies, were, in Brazil, the time of political, social and labour unrest, aroused by the ideological affront and incited by the revolutionary ideas and movements.

Actually, since Fidel de Castro assumed power in Cuba, in 1958, the revolutionary ferments of the Left gave rise in all the countries of Latin America to movements that required a social revolution with the establishment of socialist and communist governments.

Che Guevara extended and deepened the ideals of Castro and his revolutionary apostolate, starting in October 1965, when he left to go and fight in other fronts, and thus strengthened other revolutionary movements in several countries. Having entered Bolivia in a clandestine way in 1966, Che organises the guerrilla in this country and exerts his influence in those of the other neighbouring countries. Quite as Bolivia, also Peru and Chile are agitated by the MIR (Movement of the Revolutionary Left), Venezuela by FALN (Military Force for the National Liberation), Uruguay by the Tupamaros, Colombia by FARC (Colombian Revolutionary Force) and ELN (National Liberation Army) joined by Father Camilo Torres, Argentina by ERP (People's Revolutionary Army), of trotskrist tendency and the Montoneros, leftist peronists, already in the 70's. In what concerns Brazil, the urban guerrilla emerges from 1968 on, headed by Carlos Marighela, who had broken off with the Communist Party because of its refusal to taking up arms and subsequently created the ALN (National Liberation League).

In this way, with either more or less intensity, the whole Latin America was agitated by the leftist revolutionary movements, even those countries that have not known organised guerrilla, since all of them felt the ideological and social commotion, of communist pattern, that emphasised the distribution of wealth and the resulting social disparities. At the same time there was an explosion of anti-American feelings, of the ideological fight against capitalism and colonialism, of a repudiation of the colonialist past, by requiring a historical and cultural revision of the cultural origins of the Latin-American nationalities.

We must keep in mind that the sixties. were deeply stirred by important student movements, not only in the United States, with protests against the Vietnam war, as it happened in 1964 at the Berkeley University, but also in France, in May 1968, pressing on the cultural evolution, in times already marked by woman emancipation, sexual freedom and the generalised yearning for "giving power to imagination". In Brazil, the great inspiration for the revolution comes, naturally, from Castro and Che. In Tabajara's novel those elemental references are followed by another one, that is responsible for the greatest part of the evocations and actions of the novel: the events that occurred in Chile with Allende and the military rebellion that discharged him in 1973. And also, as a permanent background, the memory of the events and of the social climate deriving from the military rebellion of 1964, in Brazil, that sent away the Vice-President João Goulart. The army consolidated its power right away, mainly through the promulgation of 'institutional Acts', of which the AI-l, the AI-2 and the AI-5 were of particular importance, in so far as they suspended the parliamentary immunities, abolished political rights, suppressed the other Parties, regulated the right to strike and carried out a violent repression towards all the 'subversive' individuals.

The evocations and actions of the novel take place in this context. Moreover, the very fact that the novel has been written abroad (in Copenhagen), as it happened also with the previous one *A Região Submersa* (in Buenos Aires and Copenhagen), also reveals the climate of insecurity that predominated, even during the first stages of the political 'overture' introduced by President Geisel in 1974. It permitted the returning to Brazil of hundreds of exiles, but this process would only succeed completely in 1985, with the election of Tancredo Neves and the triumph of democracy.

O Amor de Pedro Por João features, in an exemplary way, the greatness of the revolutionary dream and its dissipating like smoke. In order to express it, the novel was elaborated in a chaotic and unexpected way, where the narrative passages and the dialogues of the characters are mixed up in time and in space, accordingly expressing love, hatred, fear, terror, despair, joy.

There is no integrating action, no narrative structure of conformity, only fragments, like in a puzzle. It is up to the reader to organise or just receive those data and meditate on them, just as it happens with the disintegration of a star, when it gets dispersed by falling to pieces, before the amazement and the terror of the watchers. In such fragments, where the narrator, whatever he does, is unable to hide his liking for the guerrillas, the impersonation of the characters is implacable in what concerns the description of their grandeur, distresses and ridicules.

Thus, *O Amor de Pedro por João* is an epic of tragic ending and of a collective hero: Pedro, João, Marcelo, Mara, Hermes, Dorival, Josias, the Pig and others have entangled their lives in a common ideal but they permanently go their different ways, because fiasco has dispersed them and because the feelings they nourish for each other, of love, rivalry, mistrust, sympathy, go different ways as well. Forced exile will bring them together temporarily, to fall apart right after. What bound the group together and gave consistency to each one of its elements was the revolutionary action. First in Brazil and afterwards in Chile. Actually it is in a nostalgic way that João recalls, in a critical moment, the Brazilian dream of '68:

> that at last, the time had come for the so much expected and definitive Revolution. That they had got arms. That it was that historical moment they had

looked forward to for so long. That the governor and the people were sticking together. That we should advance towards Brasilia, give Jango the power, to urge the instauration of a democratic republic (pp. 62-63).

However, it didn't become reality. Instead, in reply to the actions of commotion and guerrilla that had begun that same year, the military government of Castelo Branco unleashed the intense repression in the year of the death of Marighela, resorting to torture, cessation of rights, various kinds of terror, that caused the withdrawal of many people to exile abroad, both labourers and intellectuals. But a new hope emerged in the skyline for the revolutionists: in Chile, in September 1970 Salvador Allende was elected President and was establishing a socialist government in his country. All the hopes of the revolutionists were now directed to him, hoping that a new wind, favourable to the left, would blow from Chile. Volunteers of the revolutions of the surrounding countries converged to Chile. However, such as in Brazil, as also in Chile the army took steps to obstruct the way to the new revolution. Thus, the Brazilian group, taking refuge in the Argentine Embassy of Santiago do Chile, has no alternative but to follow through the most dramatic episodes of the conflict.

The narrator describes the protagonists of that "suspense" in chapter nine, in the following manner:

> The inhabitants of the Embassy were already beginning to operate in groups. These groups differed in degree and quality, in number and need, in nationality and ideology. There was the group of the Uruguayans, the Argentines, of the Ecuadorians, of the Brazilians and the Chileans. But also that of the intellectuals, the sportsmen, the depressed, the pregnant, the vehement, the serious people and the bohemians. Each one of these groups was not influenced either by the nationality or by the ideological solidarity, but rather by the natural tendency (p. 192).

The resistance of Allende is followed with passion. His own victory would be the victory of all the revolutionists, and his defeat would be, no doubt, the consummation of failure, not only that of the guerrilla but of all the revolutionaries, the very end, with disillusionment and exile.

The narrative technique of Tabajara is perfect, especially to give rise to the climax of expectancy.

As it happens in mystery or terror fiction, in which something crucial is expected to happen, or when the conclusion is uncertain, Tabajara Ruas develops short scenes of fast movement, interested by slow narrative sequences. Not so much in the manner of the Hitchcock model of cinema, since in spite of the suspense the public knows that some explanation is already foreseen for the end, but rather in the manner of the radio or of the television, in the live and direct reports. In this way the reader is in permanent suspense, especially in the scenes concerning Allende's resistance. For instance, when Dorival, Ana, Marcelo and the German hear the President declaring that he will not surrender. That suspense becomes more intense and is extended by the actions of the characters, foreseeing the worst:

What we must do is very simple. To buy enough provisions, in case we must stay here very long, to keep an ear on the radio and on the phone, to burn at once any compromising document and try to be aware of what happens in the surroundings. Since this place is close to la Moneda..." And further the narrator synthesises: "The town was mad and nobody knew. Its face softened, cheerful faces could be seen coming out from the hippodromes, laughter in the cinemas, vehement rootings in the National Stadium. The town (the beast) disguised the surprise attack that was being prepared on the sly, with every muscle. Each building hid a menace. Each corner a snare. And all its inhabitants were prisoners of the huge trap. (p. 33)

Presentations-narrations like these punctuate the whole novel and remind us of another novel in which the technique of repetition and amplification of the events reaches the maximum perfection, *Em Câmara Lenta,* by Renato Tapajós[2], published in 1977:

a group of guerrillas is caught by the police which interrogates and arrests them and tortures Marta ("she") to her physical annihilation and death. The images of the scene are repeated and amplified several times, as if in a *replay* in which the *zoom* gives gigantic proportions to the details visualised afterwards, very slowly, till the end, when a great plongée recreates the complete scene, because "time is over, the gestures will continue to be made, repeated and improved. As in slow motion" (p. 16).

In counterpoint to the dignifying presentation of Allende and his myth, Ruas describes the scenes of torture with realism and candour, mainly that of Ana Maria kidnapped by the army and taken to join her husband, desanguinated due to the brutalities he had been subject to. She will also be tortured and raped in the presence of her son.

Scenes like that, due to the contradiction and hypocrisy that they reveal, are utilised by the narrator to confront and affront both the ideologies in question, the one of the army and that of the revolutionaries. The one of Power is presented in a rhetoric and artificial way, that of the guerrilla in a passionate way, even because they don't need long speeches to say what they believe in, as their subjection to torture is, by itself, a testimony of the authenticity of their convictions. During the interrogation of Josias or Ana Maria the torturers speak "from head of the family to head of the family", or, "for everybody's sake", they invoke the safeguard of God, of the Fatherland and of the National Security. Vale asks:

> Madam, you love your country, don't you? Do you know what Communism is, Dona Ana Maria? Are you aware of the danger it means? Tell me something: do you want your Fatherland to become a satellite of Russia? You have heard about the iron curtain, haven't you? Have you ever thought of your people, your habits, your mode of life, dominated by the Communists? Have you ever thought? All your joy will finish, dona Ana Maria. This will become a sad country, with no law (p. 132).

To those torturers who justify themselves by saying they just perform orders, Sajé will reply:

> You are a puppet. I do not respect you (...). I'm a man. I do what I want (...) I don't recognise anybody as being superior to me. I stopped being a puppet for the rest of my life (p. 241).

One who described the contradictions and arbitrarinesses of the "doctrine of the National Security" in a more vehement and complete way, was António Callado in *Quarup*[3] of 1967, a work that, without any doubt, served as a reference to Ruas, even because it represented one of the most important moments of contemporary Brazilian fiction and, no doubt, the most violent and dramatic libel against military dictatorship.

As a matter of fact, it can be asserted in a certain way that *O Amor de Pedro por João* is a recapitulation of the fight, on the part of the writers, against that same dictatorship, recovering previous moments of fiction writing.

Actually, if Ruas' book intends above all to dramatize the dissipation of a dream that ends with the exile of its protagonists, it also refers to other behaviours and intents towards the revolution. For instance, by stigmatising, through the words of João Guiné, those who identify themselves with the revolution only by making use of inconsequential words and a lot of cowardice:

> Revolution is something natural to males and poor people, not to those well brought up and well spoken little boys nor to those "bacanas" either pretending to be saints or speaking obscene words in every sentence they say, as if that would make them become more independent or equal to the males (p. 92).

With this same caricature of the "well brought up and well-spoken little boys" Antonio Callado has also distinguished himself by making a demolishing portrait of the so-called Brazilian "festive left", in Bar D. Juan, in 1970, one which among whiskeys, women and the smoke of cigarettes made imaginary revolutions and demeaned themselves in cowardice and in rhetoric. Another feature emerges from Ruas' novel as he completes the social and cultural framing of the revolutionists' action - that of the participation of groups connected with the Church. Besides several allusions, the most remarkable case is that of the origin of one of the leading protagonists of the action, a true inspiring muse or "passionaria" of the guerrilla, loved by Marcelo but who loved Herrnes, Mara. Before joining the guerrilla Marta was a nun, till two years ago she had lived in a Benedictine Convent for ten years. Precisely during the age of convictions and steadiness, from the age of eighteen to that of twentyeight. Therefore, her participation in the guerrilla movement had a symbolic meaning, precisely because a large number of members of the Church, priests and laics, integrated the vanguard of the resistance to the dictatorship as well as the leadership of the social movements both in the urban centres of the big industrial towns and in the inland, among the "no-land people" and the "posseiros". Father Camilo Torres had become, since 1965, a true symbol of those who had left the exercise of the Orders to join the revolutionary combat; and the Archbishop of Recife, D. Helder Câmara, personified in an exemplary way the posture of the Brazilian Church, mainly since 1967, when the "Manifesto of the Bishops of the Third World" was published. The CELAM (Episcopal Council of Latin America) reached the point of ratifying, openly, "a certain right of the oppressed countries to insurrection". And this occurred both in theoretical and practical fields, for in the continuity of the political theology of Metz and Harvey Cox, it emerged that in Latin America the 'theology of liberation' of Gutierrez and, above all, of the Brazilian Franciscan Leonardo Boff, provided the outlines of thought for the action of the militants from the base communities and others. Even before Ruas, Antonio Callado had created a symbolic figure of this fiction, Father Nando de Quarup who, from stage to stage, passed from pacifism and a few theocratic ideas to the factual militancy of the guerrilla. Moreover, were not some of the best novelists of the time (Callado e Carlos Heitor Cony) themselves also former seminarists? Mara is a synthesis character, even because she doesn't reject her past, on the contrary, she takes some unconformism out of it, recalling that time with nostalgia:

> I even miss my cell. There I had real peace. A perfect silence, a perfect solitude. I wouldn't feel the want of absolutely nothing (p. 194).

The fact is that the social problems in Brazil and the revolutionary dynamic have reached everybody, and didn't allow anyone having a minimum sense of responsibility to be left out.

That is the orientation of the novel *Pessach: a Travessia*, by Cony[4], of 1967, the same year of *Quarup*.

When the protagonist, Paulo, (he himself also an ex-priest, like Nando) a successful writer, celebrates his fortieth birthday, in peace and quietness, he is visited by Silvio who comes to make an invitation that at the same time is a point-blank summons to join the Revolution:

There are only two attitudes (...) I come to offer my way, which can be our way: a simple, small and dangerous word: fight.

Paulo at last got involved, reluctantly, and joined the guerrilla. It is of that same militancy that in Ruas' novel Josias wishes to persuade his son Luís, whose apathy or cowardice he feels ashamed of. But Luís replies mentioning the evolution of time and his refusal of a life even worse:

The fear we felt... I don't want my own children to be frightened as Sejé and myself were when we were kids. Nor do I want them to be designated at school, by the other kids, as the Communist's children (...) You must understand that times have changed. It's no longer the same thing. Of course the boss is still the boss and the employee is the employee, but the country itself is no longer that backwardness it was, you see? (p. 58).

Luís' generation is not that of the seventies, nor the problems are the same, in view of which that situation is also revealed in the novel-story book *A Festa,* by Ivan Ângelo[5] where in that sort of fiction organised like an inquiry or a report, some of the characters adopt the same attitude as Luís, after the 'party' of the military coup d'état.

Crushed by the evolution of the movement for the Brazilian revolution, the guerrilla in particular and the revolutionists in general are compelled to leave their fatherlands, the natural and the historical one where they were born and that of their leftist ideological option, Marxist or not, on their way to exile.

They wanted to contribute to the improvement of the standard of living and even in that they were betrayed by the evolution of economy, by "an extraordinary economical development with considerably low inflation rates (...) and by the great expansion of foreign trade"[6], that occurred exactly in the seventies, more precisely from '69 to '73, under the so-called "miracle" of the minister Delfim. Defeated combatants, they are now surprised their own ingenuousness and altruism. What they wanted was not exactly democracy, rather the collapse of capitalism and of the bourgeoisie as a spell to achieve social justice. On their way to exile they felt sad, frustrated and betrayed in the generosity with which they put everything in risk, including their own life, aiming at the gigantic task of changing the world.

While *O Amor de Pedro por João* narrates the process that is going to culminate in a political exile, Ana Machado's novel *O Mar nunca Transborda* questions a cultural exile that already exists, about to be overcome, that of the exiles without exile who, while abroad, make the discovery of their own fatherland and dream of their imminent returning home. In 1995, the historical and socio-political frame in which the novel is inserted is very different from the seventies and from the former novel.

The problems of Brazil and of the rest of the world have progressed since then. From 1985 on, Brazil begins to live in democracy and with it the different options are debated and confronted within the Institutions, in the political parties, in several basic organisations. In the precise moment of these transformations, they must abide by the Constitution and the deliberations of the legitimate majority.

On the other hand, as it happened in the United States of America and in Europe, the student movements here began to fight other causes; differently from the ideals of May '68, they tended to identify themselves more and more with revindications of better quality in teaching, law and professional jobs. As to the working-class movements, more and more the trade unions took control over them in a context of contestation or adhesion, regulated by agreements.

However, the revolutionary inheritance and the dreams of non-conformism went on in many of those who did not adapt themselves to democratic rules and without political reasons deliberately took the way to exile and just for economical reasons they emigrated to foreign countries, not accepting Brazil as it is in reality. And, all of them were always longing for their homeland.

Ana Machado goes to equationate these questions using a story with a very simple plot:

Liana and Tito live and work in London, in the branch-office of a Brazilian mass-media network. They feel perfectly adapted to the English way of life but are longing for Brazil. Above all Liana, who doesn't forget the Manguezal, the family property where she grew up and towards which there are urbanisation projects with which she does not agree. Divided between the comfort of London and the real Brazil, Liana follows the advice of a friend and wishes to find an illusion to Manguezal which may conciliate tradition with economical advantages. Through this banal story, the author puts in debate the problem of cultural roots, making of Manguezal a true metaphor of Brazil and showing the modes in which Liana, Tito, Silvia and others position themselves in relation to their country, accepting or rejecting it.

Among all of them, Liana and her companion Tito represents two personifications of opposite attitudes of adhesion and rejection. Both feel exiled but the reactions are different and exemplar. Indeed, Liana in spite of the happiness she felt in London, and the love of Tito, she could not help realising: "The more she felt well and happy she knew all the time she was out of her ground" (p. 87). She considered herself and her work" a drift boat in a cultural exile".

Consequently she took advantage of all free moments such as bus distance, in the town, letters to of the family and friends, the polemic talks with Tito to clarify her inner world and reflect about her identity. In these meditations, the evocation of the evolutive history of Brazil has an important place, since the first Portuguese caravel had arrived there. As to the technical process of that evocation-reflection, the author chose to make the counterpoint between the history of Brazil from the beginning and her own daily story in London, through a kind of artifice, alternating, in frame-chapters, the several stages of the two historical ways, putting in italics the first story and in Normal the second one.

This kind of counterpoint between past and present continues a textual tradition which deals with privileged antecedents such as *A Ilustre Casa de Ramires,* of Eça de Queirós (1900) and *Caetés,* of Graciliano Ramos (1953), directly inspired by the former and both of them known well by the author.

Between *O Mar Nunca Transborda and Caetés* also occurs another parallelism: both vindicate the Indian legacy as their anthropological and cultural patrimony. The same happens to João Valério, of *Caetés,* who explained his behaviour through the Indian blood he carries in his veins. Liana, as well, is only able to explain herself through both European and Indian and African tradition.

But the similarities do not finish here. They extended to stylistic and structural elements too, inherited from the classical culture, very common in the XVI and XVII centuries in this kind of works, constellated around archetypal characters or even personifications which assume the two antithetic poles of a controversy.

Thus, in *Diálogos das Grandezas do Brasil,* of Ambrósio Brandão (1618), Alviano defends the European authenticity and superiority and Brandónio defends the great worth of "Braziliality". In Canaan, of Graça Aranha (1900), Lentz guarantees the European superiority through German imperialism; and Wilkan is favourable to a miscegenation and to a diffuse integration into the cosmos. In *O Mar Nunca transborda,* Tito decides for himself the comfort and superiority of the European and London life. Liana surrenders to the truth of Brazil, such as it really is, to miscegenation, to the history written by three ethnic groups and many peoples.

For Tito, Brazil has no future and the present is also abominable.

For that reason he reviews some of its wounds: violence, murdering by military police, the "street children" in front of Candelária Church, in Rio; misery and primitivism of many rural populations; the precariousness of employment, the corruption of the political class; the incompetence. He declares that, despite the nostalgia

sometimes I think that Brazil is no good, is no good at anything, never. I can't find a way out (...) Brazil is still a country where life has no worth at all, a country where people are only a number, a merchandise. An element to sum up, to subtract, to multiply, to divide (...) a country of slaves (...) no one thinks that, in Brazil, the way to secure a better life is to work and to receive a worthy payment (cc. 97-101).

In frontal opposition to the cultural itinerary he says;

in those past matters, I do not go far, no I don't.

And because in his veins also runs black blood, such as that of the supporters of the black movement, he finishes by saying that, if he wants to assume coherently his past, this will demand from his the return to Africa:

I get out to the "senzala", I'll take the slave-boat back and I'll have change country. I'll have change even continent (...) I have nothing to do with that Brazilian history about which you speak so loudly (p. 173).

Tito's exile reveals in this way a profound drama, because of his not accepting the past Brazilian historical evolution and the integration of his forefathers in the "melting pot" of a country that has its origins in the fusion of several ethnical groups and nations, because he doesn't accept his own integration in the social culture of the present Brazil and because he also acknowledges himself to be an alien in relation to the European continent.

Tito strives against contradiction and insurmountable impulses and his axis of coherence lies almost exclusively in negations: he rejects Brazil and rejects Europe, but lacks the courage to go back to Africa because he also rejects its lack of economical guarantees and comfort.

Exiled and alienated by his own will and by weakness, he becomes more and more bitter, and only the London comfort and Liana's love are able to illude decisions that, one day, he will be forced to take.

Not at all does he repeat the thesis defended by Paulo Prado, in 1928, in *Retrato do Brasil,* who sees in Portuguese colonisation only a negative reality:

in a radiant land live a sad people. That melancholy was legated to them by the discoverers, who have revealed it to the world and have colonised it.[7]

To this thesis Liana opposes a cultural itinerary which took her to opposite conclusions, the same ones that Gilberto Freyre has theoretically developed in *Casa Grande e Senzala* (1933) and in all his works, showing that :

the crossing of races unifies men who are separated by racial myths. The crossing of races brings together societies that were divided into unfriendly groups by racial mysticism. The crossing of races reorganises nations compromised in their unity and democratic destinies by social superstitions.[8]

In the beginning of her reflections Liana felt very confused and hesitant. She agrees and disagrees with Tito's proposals. But the Brazilian evolutive history took her to love and to make a compromise with her cultural roots, because she found the true Brazil only in the ethnical and cultural diversity.

We must add that Liana's historical reflection is reliable and very well informed even because in such a theme, where the "fictional" depends so deliberately on reality, the fable must not obey exclusively to verisimilitude proper of the novel, but come close as much as possible to whatever historians and sociologists in this matter take for granted.

For that reason the author could not restrain herself and decided to precede the fictional text by a prologue "to the reader" in order to inform him of those authors and texts she bases her book on.[9] An unnecessary explanation or even useless in fiction, but it aims above all at the less informed of the readers. This explanation contributes to emphasise the character of thesis defended by the novel.

To that discovery we have to add the decisive importance of language as a factor of integration and identity.

One day, in the London subway, she met an Arab and a Japanese who talked Portuguese with a very heavy accent of Rio, she agreed with what had been told to her once by a Brazilian diplomat about the theft of passports:

The individual may be black, white, Indian or yellow, everyone passes for Brazilian. A passport of ours can be used by a Japanese, an Hungarian, a Hollander, a Nigerian, a Greek, a Turk, people of any country or race. All that turns into Brazilian.

And she finishes, answering mentally to Tito:

he spoke Portuguese, he loved Brazil, he turned into Brazilian (...) we may have many problems, including prejudices, injustice and a social and criminal inequality (...) but we do not underline the difference as usual in other countries (pp. 189-190).

It was also important in Liana's itinerary the contribution of her friends, above all of Iona and Silvia, who encouraged her. Silvia explained her what 'saudade' can comprise:

after all, our land has a very strong weight. It's all the rememberings, the childhood, the history.., think that, besides the friends, it is a mixture of the landscape with culture, music, humour, language and past. Then it turns into 'saudade' (p.172).

Iona, who had a great influence over her, reminded her that if it is proper of men to create labyrinths,

it is proper of women to discover the way out and Liana had to get rid of hers (p. 195).

Finally Liana decided to do that. The epigraph of the novel, extracted from the Bible, Book of Ecclesiasts 1, 4-7, says:

a generation passes, another comes; but the land always remains. The sun rises, the sun sets; it hurries to come back to its place to rise again. The wind blows to the south, blows to the north and turns around doing the same circles. All the rivers run to the sea and the sea never overflows.

Swept away by that tide and by that wind and the little daily things being reduced to minor dimensions, Liana follows Iona's advice and travels back to Brazil in order to take a decision about Manguezal and, consequently, to end with her situation of culturally exiled without real reasons for that.

Revisiting the Manguezal/Brazil of her childhood, she will take a "miscegenous" resolution: neither sell the Manguezal to the real estate agents nor let it be abandoned. Instead of that she will opt for a solution of compromise with Zé Alfredo (as to the land) and with Bruno as to future working projects.

A solution of compromise even for the conciliation of opposite ideals: that of a vague distributive socialism, legacy of her grand-father, propitious to an agrarian reform and to social initiatives; and that of solidarity with brothers and brothers-in-law who, in order to support financially worthwhile projects, wish to make the land fruitful.

In this manner the story of Liana comes to an end. Like this also ends the last chapter of the history of Brazil she has imagined:

From time to time appeared new societies among brothers, cousins, brothers-in-law in order to carry on specific projects — a rice-field, a new flock, a plantation of pineapple, some joined construction. By the old tradition of the grand-grand-fathers. (p. 218)

The strength of the sea of culture mingled with the water of the rivers from all the generations, it put together good wills without overflowing nor getting out of its space.

BIBLIOGRAPHY

1. Tabajara Ruas, *O Amor de Pedro por João,* Porto Alegre, L e PM, 1982; Ana Maria Machado, *O Mar Nunca Transborda,* Rio, Nova Fronteira, 1995.
2. Renato Tapajós, *Em Câmara Lenta,* São Paulo, Alfa-Omega, 1977.
3. António Callado, *Quarup,* 8th edition, rio, Civilização Brasileira, 1977.
4. Carlos Heitor Cony, *Pessach: A Travessia,* 2nd Edition, Rio Civilização Brasileira.
5. Ivan Ângelo, *A Festa,* 2nd edition, S. Paulo, Vertente, 1976.
6. Boris Fsusto, *O Refime Militar, 1964-1985* in História do Brasil, S. Paulo, Ed. da Universidade.
7. Paulo Prado, *Retratos do Brasil,* São Paulo, Dupart Mayençau, 1928, p. 9.
8. Gilberto Freyre, *O Brasil em face das Áfricas Negra e Mestiças,* Lisbon, 1963, p. 18.
9. Ana Machado menciona, para além de outros documentos, as obras de Sérgio Buarque de Holanda, Guilherme Santos Neves, José António de Carvalho, Vilma Paraíso Ferreira de Almeida.

ANA PAULA LABORINHO

Camilo Pessanha and the Poetry of Exile

SYMBOLISM AND THE ISSUE OF POETRY

Camilo Pessanha (1867-1926) is an uncommon figure both in terms of his poetry and the poetic dimension that his life acquired during his voluntary exile in the Far East. He is the author of only one book which, left to him, would never have been published. Several of his poems never came to be written: he would compose them mentally, committing them to memory and recite them to friends who would then write them down.

In 1920, when he was already fiftythree years old, a close friend poet collected thirty poems that comprised the first edition of *Clepsidra,* which means time and water. Only after the author's death two editions appeared containing a larger selection of poems collected during various poetry recitals.

In a certain sense, Camilo Pessanha is the author of a book that he didn't write as he is not responsible for much of what it contains. However, it is still considered a fundamental work of Portuguese literature.

This unique figure of the early twentieth century Portuguese poetry, considered Portugal's major symbolist poet, had an eventful life, which made a decisive impact on his personality.

Camilo Pessanha was born in Coimbra, a university city particularly active in literary movements of the time, where he graduated in law, in the year 1891 and published his first poems, short stories and chronicles in newspapers and journals.

However, he didn't participate in the controversies surrounding the different literary movements that co-existed and fought at that time and refused to integrate into any one of them. Yet his style of writing leans towards Symbolism, even if his work is distinct from the other Portuguese symbolists. In fact, although he is considered by critics Portugal's major symbolist, he is also said to be "a strange symbolist" (Jorge de Sena, *Estudos de Literatura Portuguesa III,* 1988).

His poetry is mostly considered with particular interest among the critics, for his troubled life and, overall, for his stay in the Far East that created a *vision of the world* of which his poetry had become the expression.

This traditional literary criticism views Symbolism as the literary expression of decadence, defined as the existential rejection of positivism, technology, materialism and social conventions. Although his criticism established an aesthetic distinction between the decadent movement, which is marked by a strong subjectivity and Symbolism as a major poetic issue, both are understood to be the result of the end-of-the-century crisis in the romantic fashion. This conception of poetry could recover a metaphysical dimension of the universe and could decode the mystery of existence, thus serving to translate the mysterious network of correspondences that exist between man and the universe, expressed by the symbol that is used to suggest instead of describe the reality.

Anyway, this synthesis of the symbolist program is intrinsic in matters of language (the function of poetry, the symbol as searching of meaning and the theory of suggestion). However, it is rooted in an understanding that language is a way of transmitting a previously constructed conception of the world and forgets the essential issue of the nature of the poetic discourse.

This is a mechanical and somewhat crude way of considering literary problems because it reduces Symbolism to a simplistic form: the disillusionment of man in the face of scientific progress. The result is also a simplistic interpretation: the containment of man within his own sensibilities to the point he could reach a morbid and pathological state bordering on alienation. However, if the concept of crisis can be useful, it is too wide an explanation of the poetic revolution roused by Symbolism.

In fact, the cultural crisis at the end of the nineteenth century was the result of the rise of modern literature as an aesthetic and socially autonomous movement. But the particular contribution of Symbolism to modernity was its query about the identity of literary discourse considering the answer as important as the query. In this sense, poetry becomes the experience of crisis as it explores and deepens, in and through language, its very mode of existence.

It is within this framework that the poetic evolution of Camilo Pessanha and its reflection on the *issue of poetry* can be understood. We would like to demonstrate that the Orient as a place of exile does not only represent the source of a hallucinating and mythical experience for the poet, but also, and above all, it provides him a distance essential to his conception of the poetry.

"UM ORIENTE A ORIENTE DO ORIENTE" (FERNANDO PESSOA)

However, Symbolism is not just a question of poetry; and we must also consider the poet's desire to use his poetry as a way of leaving his mark on the world: thus his poetry becomes more than the written word; it becomes a model of life.

This could explain Camilo Pessanha's decision to remove himself to the Far East corresponding to the idea that poetry requires a distinct element of existential organisation that could only be found through the creation of a geographical gulf by exiling himself to the far end of the world. The decision to settle in Macau is more than a change of place, it represents a displacement of his values and feelings by the encounter with a fictitious world.

In one of his few essays, Camilo Pessanha explains the role of biography in poetic creation: instead of the facts, he thinks the most important is the legend, i.e., what remains as mythical tradition. According to this view, what the author really lived is entirely irrelevant since it is external to his work.

For this reason, it is a pointless exercise to attempt to identify in his poetry traces of his long stay in Macau where he arrived in 1894 and lived until his death in 1926.

Macau was at that time a fantastic and a contradictory world where Chinese culture, with all its fascination, co-existed with the more or less conventional values of the Portuguese society mainly formed by the civil servants. Camilo Pessanha came to Macau to teach at a local middle school, a job for which he had applied from Portugal. After two years, he obtained the post of judge and, despite his inconvenient way of life, he was nominated, in 1923, as government advisor on Chinese affairs.

Despite respect for his juridical knowledge and wide culture, the contemporary testimonies show him as a pathological person, unable to adapt to the society, looking for a shocking behaviour, living openly with his Chinese concubine and destroyed by opium. However, he was also esteemed for his knowledge of Chinese culture and Chinese people. Therefore, people related to him with respect and fear and named him the 'living dead' (*pune-lio-iane-mean*). Consequently, the poet himself became the interest of a fictitious discourse, encompassing narrative and painting that, in various ways, gave central importance to his life. Indeed, Orient was essential to his poetry and above all to his reflection upon the issue of poetry. Macau awoke within him a deep interest in Chinese civilisation, he became a sinologist, studying Chinese philosophy, art, literature and law as revealed by his letters to family and friends and his notes compiled under the title *Critical Sketch on Chinese Civilisation*

(1912). Besides this, he dedicated himself to learning Chinese language, which would then give him access to the inner secrets of the Chinese way of life. In a letter to a friend he says: "I have already learnt a lot of Chinese: I can read, speak and even write a little." His knowledge of Chinese characters encouraged him to translate Chinese poetry, an experience that certainly contributed to some formal characteristics within his poetry.

In a letter to another friend, he states that he is

> engaged in concluding the almost completed translation into prose of an extremely beautiful book of elegies from the Ming Dynasty — a unique and minuscule work that I would like to put into print or, at least, complete as a measure of my gratitude to those who have been concerned with the imperfection of my soul...of my life (8/3/12).

The translation was enriched by a large number of explanations and by an introduction that reveals the author's deep knowledge of Chinese literature.

According to his own words, he attempted to preserve, wherever possible, the rhythm, musicality and the prosodic elements inherent to the Chinese language, an extremely difficult task that gave him, in his own words,

> hours of such calm spiritual bliss that I had never imagined possible (*O Progresso,* Macau, 13th September, 1914).

Camilo Pessanha considered Chinese language "the most beautiful and suggestive of all literary languages, whether living or dead" and studied its prosody, "of high oratorical and poetic value", admired the aesthetic majesty of its ideograms and "its great power to evoke visual imagery" which, in his opinion, surpassed that of its etymological orthography.

This contact with Chinese culture certainly contributed to his reflection upon the ambiguity of poetry: the gap between one superficial and immediate meaning and another one symbolic and erudite.

In his comments on Chinese poetry, he mentions also the apparent contradiction between the impression of language, "which in literary Chinese is a fundamental quality, the words lacking any real significance" and the epigraphic conciseness achieved by the suppression of words indicating logical relationships, a device that creates, as he says:

> more vivid impression on the mind of the reader (and this intensity of suggestion is one of the untranslatable charms of Chinese poetry) – without the least indication of a mutual logical dependence, the concrete ideas adopted by the

author are presented as poetic symbols.

Those are the devices that we find in Camilo Pessanha's poetry explained in his theoretical texts written in Macau.

EXILE AND THE EFFECT OF DISTANCE

However, the oriental experience has left no visible thematic traces upon his work with the exception of a few poems. There is no trace of exoticism at least understood as a re-creation of a distinct and far distant place that provokes feelings of strangeness and a new emotion within the European traveller searching for an alternative to his tedium.

The orientalism of Pessanha is not the one that goes deeper: it is an aesthetic experience intensified by his knowledge of the Chinese culture. Chinese tradition establishes a link between writing and divination, which strengthens the metaphysical issue of symbolist poetry. Furthermore, the Chinese system of writing and the system of characters that supports it, regulates several significant practices such as, besides poetry, calligraphy, painting and mythology. Thus, language is not understood as a denotative system that 'describes' the world, but a representation that organises the link between things according to significance - in much the same way as metaphor in western poetry.

Through exile, the necessary distance for reflective thought is created, but the knowledge of Chinese poetry also allows Pessanha to achieve a better understanding of his own and identical devices for producing meaning of other formal devices such as the disarticulation of syntax, the elision of linking words and personal pronouns which recreates a subjectivity through the relationship between living beings and things (this is the case of the poem "Chinese Guitar" which recreates, besides the music, the feminine hand of the musician that plays, but is never named).

We note also the identical understanding of poetry as an art of suggestion, which makes its plural meaning rooted in ambiguity, demanding participation and a nimble mind from its reader. The concept of the sign-symbol as an aesthetic object providing a plural meaning draws these two poetic strains together. If the Chinese calligraphy reveals immediately his aesthetic dimension by the pictorial draw of the character, in western poetry the aesthetic dimension is more intellectualised due to the abstract nature of the language.

In Pessanha and in Chinese poetry a powerful musicality and imagery are also essential means of expression to achieve the aesthetic dimension.

In both cases, these are ways to reach the inner and mysterious essence of reality through language.

In conclusion, the voluntary exile represents for Camilo Pessanha a necessary condition of his poetry, creating by the strangeness, a space for the reflection on the identity of literary discourse which is a distinctive trait of modernity.

POEMS OF CAMILO PESSANHA

1.

Violoncelo	Violoncello
Chorai urcadas Do violoncelo! Convulsionadas. Pontes aladas De Pesadelo ...	Cry, bows Of the violoncello! Convulsed, Winged bridges From nightmares ...
De que esvoaçam Brancos, os arcos ... Por baixo passam, Se despedaçam, No rio, os barcos.	From which flicker, White bows ... The boars on the river, Pass underneath, And are wrecked.
Fundas, soluçam Caudais de choro ... Que ruínas (ouçam)! Se se debruçam, Que sorvedouro! ...	Deep, they shed A flood of tears ... What shipwrecks (listen)! If you lean forward, What a maelstrom!..
Trémulos astros ... Solidões lacustres ... - Lemos e mastros ... E os alabastros Dos balaústres!	Flickering stars ... Lake retreats ... -Rudders and masts ... And the alabaster Of the rails!
Urnas quebradas! Blocos de gelo ... -Chorai arcadas, Despedaçadas. Do violoncelo.	Broken urns! Blocks of ice ... -Cry, bows, Broken bows, Of the violoncello.

2.

Viola Chinesa	Chinese Guitar
Ao longo da viola morosa	To the sound of the morose guitar
Vai adormecendo a parlenda	The idle talk subsides
Sem que amadornado eu atenda	And I, feeling drowsy, pay no attention
A lenga-lenga fastidiosa. .	To the tiresome rigmarole.
Sem que o meu coração se prenda,	My heart remains untouched,
Enquanto nasal, minuciosa,	As the nasal, circumstantial,
Ao longo da viola morosa,	Chatter subsides,
Vai adormecendo a parlenda.	To the sound of the morose guitar.
Mas que cicatriz melindrosa	But what sensitive scar
Há nele que essa viola ofenda	Does it have that the guitar troubles it
E faz que as asitas distenda	And makes it spread its wings
Numa agitação dolorosa?	In painful agitation?
Ao longo da viola, morosa...	To the sound of the morose guitar!...

BIBLIOGRAPHY

1. António Falcão R. Oliveira (1979). *O Simbolismo de Camilo Pessanha,* Lisbon, Ática.
2. Teresa Coelho Lopes (1979). *Clepsidra de Camilo Pessanha* (*Textos Escolhidos*), Lisbon, Seara Nova, Textos Literários.
3. Esther de Lemos (1981). *A Clepsidra de Camilo Pessanha, Notas e Reflexões,* Lisbon, Editorial Verbo.
4. Barbara Spaggiari (1982). *O Simbolismo na Obra de Camilo Pessanha,* Lisbon, ICLP.
5. Isbal Pascoal (1987). (Introdução). *Clepsidra*, Lisbon, Ulisseia.
6. Gustavo Rubim (1993). *A Experiência da Alucinação. Camilo Pessanha e a Questão da Poesia*, Lisbon, Caminho.

MARGIT KÖVES

Sunday Circle on Mondays: Exile in Vienna

In August 1919, after the fall of the Workers Republic in Hungary, the Hungarian Communist Party went underground. Many of its prominent members and active sympathisers decided to emigrate before the retaliation of the conservative 'white terror' began. One of the most obvious choices was Vienna, a four hours distance from the Hungarian capital Budapest. Vienna was also a transit point for Hungarians to Germany and Paris with a relatively easy access to Switzerland, Prague, Slovakia, Russia and Transylvania. Many members of the Sunday Circle, the most outstanding intellectual group in Hungary, left after the revolution of 1919 to meet again in Vienna.

The organizers of the Sunday Circle were Georg Lukács, the philosopher and Béla Balázs, the writer who later became known as a theoretician of films. The Sunday Circle started its meetings regularly at Balázs' place after 1915 where Lukács and Balázs discussed their ideas before publication. The Sunday Circle included people of various political persuasions, from bourgeois radicals to socialists and anarchists who went through transitions and moved apart politically during the First World War and the at the time of the 1918 and 1919 Revolutions. Though members of the Sunday Circle, like Arnold Hauser and Karl Polányi did not have to go underground like Lukács, who was deputy minister of culture at the time of the Workers Republic or Balázs who worked in the ministry of culture, they left Hungary to be able to study further (like Hauser and Antal in Italy, Fogarasi in Prague, Mannheim in Germany). Those who were in Vienna met on Mondays. The change from Sundays to Mondays registers the distance in time and place which the move from Budapest to Vienna meant for the exiles indicating the dislocation of time and space for the émigré. Time had become a central category in Lukács' and Balázs' work and they used it in similar but not overlapping meaning and different contexts in the early years of their exile. Many of Lukács' and Balázs' aesthetic ideas grew out of their discussions, in response to each other's work. It was only later towards the end of their exile in Vienna and in Moscow that they grew completely apart.[1]

Exile in Vienna was a philosophical turning point for Lukács. In the first two decades of the century Lukács and Balázs invented 'Soul', a metaphysical concept to link the separation between the world of experience and the intelligible world. The dualism between the knowing and acting man has been the subject of philosophy from Descartes to the Encyclopedists and Diderot and was further emphasized by Kant's separation of the world into phenomena and noumena. Man, the world confronting him and the meaning he is trying to find in the world is the subject of existentialist philosophy.[2] Lukács and Balázs were trying to understand the place of Man within the world through Soul and its temporal aspects. Soul, the problematic of Man as a separate entity, was connected to Time. Lukács widened this combination in the direction of ethics and politics and Balázs took up the question of Soul and Time in various areas of aesthetics.

After the October Revolution in Russia and the upheavals in Hungary, Germany, Austria, Poland and Bulgaria, Lukács and Balázs found themselves in Vienna in an atmosphere of the anticipation of World revolution interchanging with the fear of military takeover. Austria was a place of transit from Hungary to East and West Europe and many Hungarian exiles stayed on legally or illegally depending on the status of their passport. The Vienna city administration which was in the hands of the Social Democratic Party was ready to connive at the presence of Hungarian political émigrés. The Austrian Government took a different view. It depended on the support of the Church and the military and semi-military forces called Heimwehr and it was prepared to persecute political émigrés. The tension between the city administration and the rightist Government and the presence of the *Heimwehr* meant that a military takeover in Austria was also a dreaded possibility for the exiles. If that happened, Lukács, who was wanted in some cases of political killings and Balázs would have been extradited.

In the 1920s among the émigrés from Poland and Southern-Europe the most numerous were the Hungarians. Lukács participated in the establishment of the international journal *Communism* which became the center of ultra left tendencies and a meeting point for Dutch, Italian, French and Polish communists with ultra left sympathies. Lukács, as he described this phase of his activities, was working under two opposed tendencies. Theoretically and in terms of the international working class movement he was a representative of an ultra-left line projecting the imminence of revolution in Europe, if not world revolution. This attitude included a total break with bourgeois institutions and mode of life. The tactical need to maintain these institutions were discarded referring to the need of developing class consciousness. While Lukács represented ultra-left positions in the international communist movement in the Hungarian Communist Party he worked for the possibility of communists working within the Social Democratic Party as the only real perspective for progressive working class movement in Hungary in the 1920s. Both Lukács and Balázs opposed the line of Béla Kun who was the leader of the Hungarian Communist Party and also the head of the Workers Council. Lukács, Balázs and Landler criticized Kun's projects on the basis of Kun's lack of acquaintance with the Hungarian reality.[3] The division between Lukács' international stand against his praxis-oriented Hungarian party line became obvious from 1921.[4]

During his exile in Vienna Balázs was commissioned to write new books, rewriting his earlier pieces and had the opportunity of translating his tales, short stories and plays into German.[5] He also wrote a series of articles for the *Rote Fahne* (the organ of the German Communist Party, published in Berlin) and reviews on films and books for *Der Tag* (a newly published paper, in Vienna). Balázs held lectures about aesthetics, poetry and drama in many places, for example in study classes organized for promoting workers' education. He wrote scripts and corrected scripts written for films by others. This work gave him an insight into the medium, the economy and the effect of films.[6]

The emigration meant for Balázs displacement, scarcity of space and harassment from the police. The two opposite impulses of Balázs' life, the wish 'to be alone' and the desire 'to merge in a community' were reinforced in Vienna. This sense of harassment is conveyed in one of the notes from his diary:

> one cannot stay alone even for half an hour, people love us and visit us. Four or five of them every day. I sit in cafés.[7]

The lack of space motivated Balázs to rethink his earlier ideas about 'loneliness'. Speaking about his early childhood, Balázs emphasized the experience of standing apart, alone, as an important impulse to creativity.[8] In a poem, *My sweet Fellow-traveller* written before his exile to Vienna, transcendent homelessness is coupled with a sense of being hounded by time. It addresses his fellow-traveller:

> We are expelled every day into a new day./We will never reach home my sweet fellow-traveler.

In the poem *Argirus* a spatial metaphor 'cave' stands for passing time, hours are 'figures without a face and footprint'.[9]

In the first quarter of the century philosophy and literature presented a new concept of time: Kierkegaard's theory of choice as an ethical step, a decision taken at the right moment, Bergson's *Time and Freedom*, novels, like Joyce's *Portrait of an Artist as a Young Man* and Thomas Mann's *Magic Mountain* were structured around time. In these novels two concepts of time function. One, a given parameter of life, symmetrical in past and present and unchangable, predetermined future. If this was the only scope of time, it would be as if man acted under compulsion.The other concept of time which has a dominant place in these novels is subjective time, the time of inwardness. It gives scope to ambiguities, alternatives and choices. In the course of choices one of multiple actualities is realized. Human freedom and ethics, where alternatives exist and real choices can be made, can only be consistent with this notion of time.

Balázs and Lukács refer to a dual concept of time in the context of Soul. In their work Soul is a symbol with multiple meanings. It has references to Plato's philosophy, to St. Francis of Assissi, Meister Eckehardt and it is enriched with metaphors taken over from theosophy by Balázs and Lukács. Soul and the related metaphors were useful to break out of the language of conventional philosophy and bring in new correlations with the new terms. Central to the evolution of these terms were the language of orientalism and theosophy that implied inner sight and inner hearing. This singled out an area to counter positivism and brought in metaphors to help to articulate the problem Lukács and Balázs struggled with to express that the phenomenon is multisided and that it stands "in a not mechanical relationship with the great substances".[10]

Soul, a term which started being used by Balázs in 1906, is the substance which enables human beings to communicate with each other and serves to build up a community with others.[11] As Lukács wrote to Paul Ernst, a playwright : "The only important thing is the way from Soul to Soul. All else is an instrument."[12] In an essay about modern Hungarian poetry Lukács ,points out that love without ethical content "becomes alliance for a joint lie to cheat a third person,". He points out the trivialization of the use of this word 'love' by going to words linked to 'love' and says 'goodness' means "to forgive oneself an untruth and forgive it to others, since one never knows when one would need the other person" and knowledge of others is "acceptance that everybody tells lies when it is in his interest".[13]

Metaphors of journey and landscape figure in many of Lukács' essays and Balázs' early writings and time is conceptualized in terms of space. This prepares the description of subjective time, against the general concept of time. Indian mythology, Radha, Krishna, the figure of Buddha extend the conceptual system in a new direction. The most clear-cut examples of how Lukács used these concepts are in the Phillipe-essay and in the Metaphysics of Tragedy in the *Soul and Forms*. In the description of the development of the tragic hero in the age of modernity, spatial terms referring to landscape lead from aesthetics to ethics. Comparing the mystical experience with the experience of the tragic hero whose "selfhood overleaps everything merely individual" Lukács depicts the experience in a spatial metaphor of a peak with "past, present and future" united. This aesthetic experience is shifted and transformed into ethics when in Lukács' words the problem of the hero is,

the longing to transform the narrow peak of his existence into a wide plain with the path of his life winding across it.[14]

Balázs' notion of Soul was applied to his theory of ideal community, an attempt of a non-verbal transcendence of the difference between subject and object. Soul as the monad of subjectivity is determining as well as determined in a two way mutual exchange with the world. The communion of Souls could compensate for alienation, but these are possible in human relationships only for instants. Loneliness is not only a spatial, but also a temporal concept. The suspension of loneliness, the union of Souls is only possible for brief intervals, the present moves into the past or is ahead of us as future. The metaphysics of Soul was linked with Balázs' interest in tales. Tales are according to him 'myths of Soul' similarly to ancient tales myths of nature.[15] Many of Balázs' tales are recreations of Hindu and Chinese themes and Balázs created the prototype of modern parables in Hungarian prose as he inverted rules of time and space. These tales which are in many ways similar to the tales of Oscar Wilde and in some other ways to the parables of Franz Kafka, were translated into German and published again in Vienna.[16]

In *The Theory of the Novel* Lukács used this double concept of time in his analysis of the nineteenth century novel. The hero of the novel lives in two frameworks of time, one objective time, which corresponds to the notion of 'real', 'uninterrupted flow of time', 'deterministic' and one corresponding to Bergson's notion of 'duration' - 'subjective' time. This subjective time is the memory of past 'life-experiences' recalled later and 'irradiated' by hope. This 'subjective' time with its utopian content instills the challenge of reality. Thus the concept of time turns into an ethical problem namely that of the action. Bakhtin's idea of the hero in the polyphonic novel of Dostoevsky, the consciousness which belongs to every human life[17], to some extent corresponds to Lukács' notion of the agency of the protagonist. The final pages of *The Theory of the Novel* in reference to the novels of Dostoevsky describe the 'pure-soul-reality' which transcends the duality of man, as a social being and his inwardness. *The Theory of the Novel* is the introduction of what Lukács planned to be his book on Dostoevsky which finally did not materialize.[18] He took down a number of notes in preparation of that book which show how Lukács' thoughts about ethics relied in this phase on his understanding of Russian literature. In these notes he separated two systems of ethics. Ethics I is an equivalent of law, as it has been practised by jurisdiction for thousands of years lifting man out of barbarism. Lukács rejects the absolute primacy of these institutions. Ethics II, Lukács calls the imperatives of the Soul. Lukács calls those who belong to this system "gnostics of the deed" underlining the element of agency in their character. His examples for this ethic are protagonists of Dostoevsky's novels, Myshkin in *Idiot* and Alyosha in *Brothers Karamazov* who are not good in the conventional sense , but seeing the needs of people around them simply become the others. In a letter to Paul Ernst he writes about the possible conflict between the two systems, duties to institutions and duty to the Soul. He mentions Judith, the protagonist of Hebbel's tragedy *Judith* who can save her people, the Jews, only by killing Holofernes, suspending elementary commands of morality.[19]

While Lukács analyzed isolation as a product of the social situation, Balázs perceived it as an element of inwardness which increased his sensibility to respond to others, sometimes perhaps in other than linguistic ways. The 'loneliness' Balázs upholds is a state which prepares the creative moment that can be shared by the ideal readers of a work. It is an experience, which excludes bourgeois ubiquity shared only by those who reject and ignore that world. In the essay *About Lyrical Sensibility*, published during his exile in Vienna, Balázs elaborated the concept of time in reception and in creativity.[20] Some of his ideas go back to his earlier essay, which was also his doctoral dissertation *Aesthetics of Death* "art or poetry are immobile in the dimension of time. It takes you out of the current of time. Here you can stop by and have a feeling of the present."[21] The audience of the poems presupposes a spiritual community in which there is a common experience of a special perception of time and metaphysical loneliness. So loneliness is also a concept of time. According to Balázs, the past and future belong to ordinary life and the present belongs to art and is expressed by the work of art.

If people function in a deterministic world then creativity is nothing else than discovery. If time contains possibilities then creative talent is a product of individuality. The essay *About Poetic Sensibility* takes up the problem of creativity as the coordination of soul, now renamed by Balázs as soul-consciousness and time. According to Balázs, lyrical sensibility, with the awareness of transcendental homelessness, is a product of modernity and loneliness. Modernity and loneliness become the source of tragic heroism and a wish for redemption. This wish for redemption can be satisfied in the experience of community, in the union with other Souls, in friendship or love. This union can be only temporary because the Soul can find its substance only temporarily. So the Soul is redeemed from time to time to return to homelessness. Creativity has the potential of redemption in a similar way. The Soul provides the opportunity to form a world view free of alienation. Lukács subscribed to this paradigm in his early works and suggested that the work of art provides an illusion of freedom as a contrast to life.

Balázs' acquaintance with Indian literature and his readings in Indian culture and theosophy equipped him with the possibility to use metaphors referring to the timelessness of Indian culture as of Nature. The memory of the erstwhile unity with nature and poetry is what enables the modern poet to create. His Indian tales and the novel about his childhood *Dreaming Youth* also describe this erstwhile unity. The child has got hold of the present and he does not live in alienation. Childhood, dream and imagination are spheres where a different dimension of time operates. Indian culture figures in Balázs's writings as the direct opposite of modern sensibility with its keymotives: desire, loneliness and the moment.

The awareness of the time factor in film was the key to Balázs' success as a theoretician of films. The 1920s was the time of the silent film and Balázs after a number of film reviews wrote a book on film theory "The Visible Man" which was one among the first books on film theory. The lack of language in silent films was understood by Balázs as a factor promoting the internationalism of films. His book deals with such aspects of film as the technical possibilities of duration of the film and the economics of cinema halls. Balázs underlines the importance of the visible moment of reality despite the simplicity and kitsch of the storyline. He also recorded the various possibilities of movement of the camera, aspects of time, light and various ways of receiving it. He was the first person to describe montage and this was due to his understanding of the temporal dimension of the films.[22]

The question of praxis, the contradiction between his theoretical stand and his position in the politics of the Hungarian Communist Party and the anticipation of World Revolution motivated Lukács to write the articles of *History and Class Consciousness*. It expressed the expectation of redemption from bourgeois society and from the possibility of the bureaucratization of the communist movement. Lukács ascribed to proletarian consciousness the inherent ability for revolutionary action, a mission to be fulfilled at a preordained time. The overlap of theory and praxis in *History and Class Consciousness* coincided with the special moments in history.[23] Lukács' analysis of the interconnection of revolutionary agency and special moments of time corresponds with the role subjective time plays in his ethics. His interest from aesthetics to ethics and politics preserved that specific notion of time.

In *The Specificity of the Aesthetic*, written forty years after *The History and Class Consciousness* Lukács defined 'quasi-time', the visible moment of the work of art and 'quasi-space' in music and literature as the factor which may reveal the genesis of the work of art. Without this element the work of art becomes a 'fetish', an object alienated from time and history. Artistic mimesis is the possibility to counter the division of space and time and contribute to the defetishization of the work of art.[24] This judgement after many decades does not alter the fact that Lukács' and Balázs' interest in the Soul, subjectivity and the examination of its temporal aspects led them to relate to reality in totality, in contrast to positivism. They set out from an idealist point of view to examine the concepts of Soul and Time and became radicalized in the process. The metaphors of journey and time which they used to express this relationship opened the possibility to place man within the world, part of a completely new set of problems and relations.

NOTES

1. Georg Lukács, *Record of a life*, ed. by István Eörsi, London, 1971, pp.45-69; Béla Balázs, Napló 1903-1922 [Diary 1903-1922] ed. by Anna Fábri, Budapest, 1982; Ferenc Fehér, Balázs Béla és Lukács György szövetsége a forradalomig [The Alliance of Béla Balázs and György Lukács to the Revolution] in: *A Budapesti Iskola, Tanulmányok Lukács Györgyről*, Ferenc Feher & Agnes Heller, Budapest, 1995, pp.9-67.
2. See also, Lucien Goldmann, *Lukács and Heidegger, Towards a New Philosophy*, London, 1977 pp. 1-24.
3. This is a point of separation between theory and understanding of the world beside being one of the cheerless examples of the history of the Hungarian Communist Party. The clash became evident for Lukács when after the fall of the Workers Republic Kun decided to leave Lukács and Korvin, another prominent and well-known member of the Communist Party to organize the Communist underground. Lukács escaped to Vienna after his place of hiding was discovered but Korvin was caught and executed.

4. Georg Lukács, *History and Class Consciousness*, London , 1971 pp. IX-XXXIX.
5. Béla Balázs, *Napló* op.cit.; Béla Balázs, *Mantel der Träume*, München, 1922.
6. Béla Balázs, *Schriften zum Film*, ed. by Wolfgang Gersch, vol. I-II Berlin.
7. Béla Balázs, *Napló*, op.cit. p.294.
8. Béla Balázs, *Álmodó ifjúság* [Dreaming Youth], Budapest, 1976, p. 44.
9. Béla Balázs, *Tristan Hajóján* [On the Ship of Tristan], Gyoma, 1917.
10. Béla Balázs, *Napló* vol.II pp. 90-195; Georg Lukács, *Record of a Life*, p.150.
11. Béla Balázs, *Napló* vol.I p.56.
12. Georg Lukács, *Briefwechsel* 1902-1917, ed. by Éva Karádi and Éva Fekete, Stuttgart, 1982, p.352.
13. Georg Lukács, *Uj Magyar Líra* in: *Ifjúkori Müvek* [Works of the Young Lukács], Budapest 1977 pp.247-263.
14. Georg Lukács, *The Bourgeois Way of Life and Art for Art's Sake*; The Metaphysics of Tragedy, both in: *Soul and Form*, London, 1974, pp.55-79 and 152-174.
15. Béla Balázs, *A lírai érzékenységröl* [About lyrical Sensitivity], in: *Válogatott Cikkek és Tanulmányok* ed. by Magda K. Nagy, Budapest, 1968, pp. 123-170.
16. Béla Balázs, *Der Mantel der Träume* op.cit. Many of Balázs tales are recreations of Hindu and Chinese themes.
17. Mikhail Bakhtin, *Problems of Dostoevsky's Poetics*, ed. by Caryl Emerson, Minnesota, 1984, pp.78-100.
18. Georg Lukács, *The Theory of the Novel*, London, 1978, pp.112-131.
19. Georg Lukács, *Dostojewski, Notizen und Entwürfe*, ed by J.C.Nyíri, Budapest, 1985; Georg Lukács, *Levelezése* 1902-1917, Budapest, pp.594-598.
20. Béla Balázs, *Lírai érzékenységröl* ...op.cit.
21. Béla Balázs, *Halálesztétika* [The Aesthetics of Death], Budapest, pp.45-49.
22. Béla Balázs, *Der sichtbare Mensch*, Wien, 1924.
23. Georg Lukács, *History and Class Consciousness*..op.cit.
24. Georg Lukács, *Az esztétikum sajátossága*, Budapest, 1969, vol. I, pp.127-164 and vol. II, p. 318; p. 372-373.

MANFRED STASSEN

Neither Here nor There : Reflections on German-German Exile

My topic is in need of explanation - apologies in advance because it is otherwise a minefield for misunderstandings and pretext for ideological skirmishes :

(i) How can a German dare to speak of German-German exile when it was the Germans who inflicted unprecedented suffering on those of their own and others whom they exiled from Germany to foreign, often inhospitable countries, with alien languagues and cultures?

(ii) How can a West-German dare to speak of (former) West-Germany as "exile territory" for people, especially writers, from former East Germany, the GDR ? - when, obviously, the East Germans had nothing better to do than to join the West Germans the minute they got a chance to do so ? And when, previously, every "refugee" automatically got a West German passport ?

To avoid some of these misunderstandings, permit me to clarify:

1. EXILE

(i) In Greek and Roman times; and still throughout the 19th century in Europe, a form of severe punishment for alleged offenses against the State, frequently a seemingly benevolent substitute for capital punishment.

(ii) Self-selected or imposed physical severance from a (political or cultural) entity to which one rightfully belongs, with which one identifies and which is sorely missed during the intensely alienating experience of living in a foreign country.

(iii) Creation of a protective, intellectual space, fortified by a fence of self-selected or imposed silence, amidst a hostile political/cultural environment (inner exile); frequently considered to be a form of dissent and/or resistance, sometimes nothing more than an euphemism for tacit complicity and cowardice.

This paper will focus on an example of the former : inner exile as dissidence and resistance and subsequent exile as an artistic challenge and failure; Heidegger is an example of the latter : So-called inner exile as "Ge-Schweige", as "idle silence", in the face of the Nazi dictatorship and the Holocaust.

One has to be aware of the inflation of the concept : Respect for the suffering of the masses of true exiles forbids its usage in instances where the conditions of the displaced persons are rather comfortable or smoothed over by amenities of all kinds : status, money, privilege, and a certain political "untouchability" that comes with notoriety.

2. THE GERMAN CONDITION (IN THE FORTY YEARS SUCCEEDING WORLD WAR II, 1949-89)

(i) The philosopher Alexander Kluge has said : The closer you look at a concept, the more distantly it stares back at you : Germany. Germany - "ein schwieriges Vaterlan"[1]

(ii) The division staatsnation - Kulturnation one that has existed since the Middle Ages, despite the attempts at unity in 1871 (Bismarck's Prussian solution), 1919 (Weimar Republic) and 1933 (Thousand Year Reich).

(iii) For intellectuals, Germany is the country in which "we live like strangers in our own house" ("In diesem Lande leben wir wie Fremdlinge im eigenen Haus" - cf. Hoelderlin, "Hyperion : "So kam ich unter die Deutschen"[2]) or, in the language of the Nazis :

"Hinweg mit diesem Wort, dem boesen,
Mit seinem juedisch grellen Schein !
Wie kann ein Mann von deutschem Wesen
Ein Intellektueller sein !?"[3]

To be a Jewish intellectual in Germany was bad news, indeed, at any time in the German past !

After the German-German divide, in the aftermath of World war II, which was a divide along the irreconcilable ideological lines of capitalism and socialism and additional, typically German dilemma ensued :

To be a socialist (Jewish) intellectual criticising conditions in the West, was tantamount to treason, punishable by exile ("Wenn es Ihnen hier nicht passt, dann gehen Sie doch in den Osten !"[4] a typical "Tot-Schlag-Wort" used to silence any critique of the post-war West German regime).

Conversely, to be a socialist (Jewish) dissident in the East (criticising really existing socialism from a Marxist point of view), was considered counter-revolutionary disloyalty and playing into the hans of the class enemy, punishable by "Berufsverbot" (ban on government employment)

3. A GERMAN CASE ("EIN DEUTSCHER FALL")

WOLF BIERMANN

Born in 1936 in Hamburg (later West-Germany), of a communist Jewish father - later murdered by the Nazis at Auschwitz) - and a communist working class mother, wolf Bierthan emigrated to East Germany in 1953 which he considered to be the better Germany to have emerged from the Nazi disaster, because of its thorough cleansing of the country's fascist legacy. He also honestly believed that, by getting personally and artistically involved, the ideals of a democratic socialism, for which Rosa Luxemburg and others had died, could be realised in the GDR this credo was : "No socialism without democracy, no democracy without socialism !" He traced his poetic lineage to Francois Villon, an outcast French poet of the late Middle Ages, to Heinrich Heine, himself a quasi exiled Jewish 19th century author from Hamburg/Duesseldorf, friend of Karl Marx, and living in Paris. (To be Jewish and a Francophile was even worse news in Germany !).

The communist regime of East Germany supported this reverse "Republikfluenchtling"[5] enthusiastically when he sang against American atrocities in Vietnam and Mississippi and in favour of the communist brigades in the Spanish Civil War; but when he turned his critical gifts against the GDR itself, attacking bureaucratic inertia, complacency and dogmatism, he was confronted with strong opposition, including a "Berufsverbot" from 1966 onwards : forced "inner exile".

Sitting in a two-room apartment on Chaussestrasse 130 in East Berlin, he produced hundreds of powerful and witty songs, critical of the "really existing socialism" in the GDR and published them in the West by having them smuggled out. But they were exclusively written for his fellow socialists in the GDR to whom they were smuggled back and who copied them by hand in the clandestine press operation known as "samisdat" across the socialist camp.

When the régime somewhat surprisingly allowed him to accept an invitation of the West German metal workers' trade union to give a concert in Cologne in 1976, it used the occasion to refuse his re-entry into East Germany : A "de facto" expulsion from the "paradise of workers and farmers" and a forced re-patriation with his origins in the capitalist West. This decision triggered a massive exodus, legal and illegal, of the artistic and intellectual elite from East Germany and was, in essence, the starting point of the creation of popular based critical dissent in the GDR and the beginning of its eventual demise a little over a decade later. Biermann characterised his own fate thus :

"Ich hab' ihn am eigenen Leibe
Gemacht, den brutalen Test :
Freiwillig von Western nach Osten,
Gezwungen von Ost nach West."[6]

Heinrich Boell who greeted him in Cologne and gave him initial shelter from the West German right-wing Springer Press and the politicians who wanted to co-opt Biermann as a critic of the East German regime, told him : "Jetzt bist du ein "In-die-Heimat Vertriebener !"[7]

4. GERMAN-GERMAN EXILE

Biermann did not exactly endear himself with the West-German establishment when he declared in his first poem written in the West, entitled "Deutsches Miserere (Das Bloch-Lied)" :

"Und als ich von Deutschland nach Deutschland
Gekommen bin in das Exil
Da hat sich fuer mich geaendert
So wenig, ach ! Und soviel."[8]

On the one hand, so little change, his exile was almost a "Heimins-Reich-Fall" : The language, the culture, the history are the same, the German mentality and the unmistakable German national character are detectable on either side of the divide. And they are nothing to be proud of :

"Und wie die einen heissen
So sehen die anderen aus !
Die einen sind mir ein Schrecken,
Aber die andern sind mir ein Graus."[9]

And yet, on the other hand, so much change : Had he been sent to Bulgaria, a fellow socialist country, he would have had to learn a new language, but he would have remained within the socialist frame of reference and the socialist horizon of aspirations. But in "falling" into West Germany, he had to learn a different political system, that of capitalism, in which there are no utopian aspirations left, because of the ubiquitous hegemony of the ideology of profit :

"Und im Osten bleibt dir die Luft weg
Im Buerokratenmuff,
Aber der Western ist ein Nepplokal,
Ein kalt gekachelter Puff."[10]

To have been forced to trade the cosy, if inefficient and frequently suffocating ambience of socialism for the cold and calculating efficiency of capitalism, is like stepping from a murky Turkish bath into the tiled parlor of a Western night-club, or the antiseptic "Eros-Center", the VIP-bordello of West German Frankfurt am Main (which, because of its 400 banks, we refer to as "Mainhattan").

To have been forced out of the first and only German socialist state, is to have been deprived of one's involvement, one's commitment for the creation of a better world. The cause was lost overnight and the West German language, even though linguistically and historically the same, was inadequate to word the experience of dissidence under socialism : It is tantamount to having been marginalized, silenced, poetically liquidated.

Even if the Germans on the one side of the divide were not much different from the ones on the other, Biermann felt that, rather than to have escaped a dismal condition in the East by being catapulted into the freedom of the West, he had actually wound up in a greater bind than he had been in before : The puddles of water caused by the constant Eastern rain pouring down on him in East Berlin, in the West has turned into a cesspool of liquid manure:

"Hier fallen sie auf den Ruecken,
Dort kriechen sie auf dem Bauche.
Und ich bin gekommen
Ach ! 'kommen bin ich
Vom Regen in die Jauche."[11]

Exile here is the feeling of irrelevance and of a forced aphasia, speechlessness. This aphasia is not to be confused with the irritations of Thomas Mann, Adorno and Brecht in their hated California exile in Santa Monica - because they had problems with English and the American culture - but it is the inner impotence to word one's political cause, because one has been ostracized from the reality that gave rise to its expression, as well as from the audience with whom one no longer shares the experience.

Biermann had been the conscience of the socialist alternative on German soil, the confessor for a congregation of believers in the true Marxist faith, a thorn in the thighs of the traitors of that socialism, the

Soviet marionettes in the GDR government. Now, his pulpit, and his confessional, had been forcefully taken away. The petit-bourgeois East German "Mief" may not have smelt very good, but it did not have the repellent pungency of the stink of money (for a convinced socialist, "pecunia olet" - that is why "Traufe" becomes "Jauche", and, in my English rendition, "fire" becomes "pyre").

The sudden freedom to write about anything under the sun in any imaginable way - a luxury that the capitalist West affords the writer - turned out not to be a liberation but a much more severe from of censorship than that exercised by the cultural gurus of the Central Committee in the communist prison-house of the GDR: the Western ideology of "anything goes" in the arts, condemns the politically committed writer to compete in the cacophony of voices and the information pollution of the Western media and condemns him to total irrelevance.

Biermann saw the danger of wailing self-pity (cf. "Miserere") in the perception of his situation in West Germany as one in exile:

"Was ist das : Exil ?
Ich will dir zuviel
Nicht klagen
Will lieber sagen :
... Heimat ist ja da
Mein Freund, wo ich dich find
Und wo Genossen sind...."[12]

But who are the "Genossen" in the West and what is their favorite past-time ?

"Und ein Linker nennt den andern
Verraeter ! und recht ! und schlecht !
Sie schlagen sich in die Fressen
Mit MAO und MARX und BRECHT.[13]

But, on the other hand, Hamburg was home to Biermann, "Heimat", a "biotop" with reminiscences of childhood, of his first political socialisation in a communist working class environment among the Hanseatic dockers, of the greasy sandwiches of his communist grandmother. So, in the end, Biermann is neither here nor there, in the double sense of the phrase, irrelevant and displaced : (cf. "And when we reached the shore")

"Was wird bloss aus unsren Traeumen

In diesem zerrissenen Land
...
Und was wird mit unsern Freunden.
Und was noch aus dir, aus mir -
Ich moechte am liebsten weg sein
Und bleibe am liebsten hier."[14]

5. THE PRUSSIAN ICARUS

While still in the GDR, which we used to refer to as the People's. Republic of Prussia, Biermann had premonitions about his eventual failure, his "fall" as a partisan between two fronts, the inner exile in the country with which he identified and the virtual exile in the country of his origin (which, ironically, was, and now again is, the same country !). He wrote "to himself" the ballad of the Prussian Ikarus.

It has always been the case that our imagination is more stimulated by the ill fate of Ikarus - the dare-devil son who disregards his father's advice and flies too close to the sun and crashes into the ocean - rather than by the success of his father Daedalus - who invented the artificial wings that allow him to escape the Kretan labyrinth across the Aegean Sea.

The fortuitous and somewhat facetious photograph of Biermann in front of the Prussian Eagle on a cast iron bridge in Berlin that outlasted the state of Prussia as well as the Third Reich, suggests that the wings of the eagle - pointing downwards - grow out of Biermann's shoulders. This optical illusion led to his entirely serious self-identification with the mythological Ikarus.

The correspondences between the situation of Ikarus being held prisoner in the Kretan labyrinth surrounded by the ocean, and Biermann living in the "island" that is the GDR fenced in by barbed wire and defended by the leaden bullets from the rifles of the border police, are obvious. Being fenced in has become second nature to him, the barbed wire (Biermann's first collection of poems was called *The Wire Harp - Die Drahtharfe*) has carved deep furrows into his brain. This is the legacy of the spirit that is represented in the poem by the Prussian eagle.

Biermann has the premonition that this hated bird will one day pick him up by its claws and drop him somewhere which, for him, is nowhere : "ou-topos" in the negative sense, exile : i.e. turn him into a modern Icarus.

If I had to live in the West, he said before his expulsion from the GDR, I know that I would not be able to write another line.

He wrote many more lines since his "exile" in the West, with one of which he took back his early, angry apostrophy of West Germany as a cesspool.

Today, Biermann's experience is nothing more than a historical episode. Neither country that he could not leave and not live in at the same time, exists any more. His poetic inspiration and extraordinary virtuosity with the German language did not survive his exile into the West, his bark remains, but it has lost its bite and its particularly East German timbre. German unification under exclusively Western political premises - and not, as he had hoped till the end, under that of a "third way" of democratic socialism - has rendered him fully obsolete and, even as a prophet, a hushed voice in the capitalist desert that has no new kingdom to announce, a rich and famous failure, a crashed German Ikarus, ein deutscher "Fall" and a friend.

When Biermann physically dies, he will be buried in the Dorotheenstaedter Friedhof, a cemetary originally reserved for the exiled Huguenots from France. It lies in the Eastern part of Berlin, near the Chausseestrasse where Biermann began his flight towards the sun, against all good advice, but following in the footsteps of his communist father, murdered by the Nazis. There, he will be in the company of Hegel and Brecht, among many other philosophers and poets; and I will say about him what he said about them :

> "Wie nah sind uns manche Tote, doch
> Wie tot sind uns manche, die leban."[15]

NOTES

Translation from German by Shaswati Majumdar

1. "a difficult fatherland"
2. "Thus I came amongst the Germans"
3. "Away with this word, the evil one, with its Jewish flashy appearance! How can a man with a German soul be an intellectual !?"
4. "If you don't like it here, why don't you go to the East!"
5. illegal emigrant
6. "I have carried it out on my own body, the brutal test: voluntarily from West to East, forced from East to West."
7. "Now you have been exiled into your homeland."
8. "And when I came from Germany to Germany into exile, what had changed for me was so little, and yet so much."
9. And what those here are called, is how those there look! Those here I find

horrible, but those there I find terrible."

10. And in the East the air is claustrophobic with the musty smell of bureaucrats, but the West is a clip-joint, a brothel with cold tiles."
11. "Here they fall on the back, there they crawl on the stomach. And I have come, oh! I have come from the frying pan into the fire."
12. "What is it: exile? I don't want to complain to you too much: home is there, my friend, where I find you and where comrades are ..."
13. "And one leftist calls the other traitor! They hit each other in the faces with MAO and MARX and BRECHT."
14. "O what will become of our dreams,
    In this land torn asunder
    ...
    And what will become of our friends
    And what of you, of me -
    More than anything I want to go
    And most of all I want to stay"
15. "How close to us are some of the dead, but how dead are some, who live."

SHASWATI MAZUMDAR

Brecht's "Fugitives in Conversation"

When on 30 January 1933 the national socialists formally took over power in Germany with the installation of Adolf Hitler as Chancellor of the Reich, few writers thought immediately of emigrating. Most thought that a fanatic like Hitler would not be able to last beyond a few months. Some who were more uncertain kept packing and unpacking their suitcases without being able to decide what to do. Only a very few perceived that an unprecedented brutal regime had taken over and decided not to sleep in their own homes any longer.

Brecht too probably thought in much the same way as most other writers. And this despite the fact that his wife, the actress Helene Weigel, was a Jew and had already been warned by a friend in October 1932 that she should leave the country. Literary activity seemed to be going on as usual including sharp political attacks on the new regime for which some writers later paid with their lives. However, it took less than a month to bring a dramatic turn of events.

On 27 February Brecht was in hospital in Berlin recuperating from an appendicitis operation when he received a call from Vienna from his close friend and collaborator, the composer Hanns Eisler. The same night the Reichstag building was set mysteriously on fire. The police allegedly caught a man in the act who for unexplained reasons had little on him except, strangely enough, a Communist Party membership card. For the Nazis this was a pretext to announce a crackdown on communists, social democrats and their sympathisers. The day after the Reichstag fire Eisler received a call from Berlin. An unknown voice told Eisler that Brecht was safe for the time being and that on no account should Eisler return to Germany. Brecht left Germany the same day with his wife and son.

Emigration took Brecht during the course of the first year through Prague, Vienna, Zurich and other places in Switzerland and Paris. In December of the same year he arrived in Skovbostrand near Svendborg in Denmark which became his place of refuge till 1939 when he shifted first to Sweden, then to Finland. "For we went, changing countries oftener than our shoes" said the writer in his poem *To Those Born Later*. Two years later he again moved on, this time to Santa Monica, a locality in Hollywood, California where he stayed till 1947 when shortly after an interrogation by the Committee on Un-American Activities he returned to Europe. He spent the last two years of exile in Zurich, thereafter settling down in East Berlin where, provided with his own theatre, he put into practice the dramatic theories he had developed.

While Brecht is popularly known the world over as a playwright, it is also not unknown that he was a poet, particularly since his poems come in handy in all kinds of political campaigns. What is perhaps less well-known is his not inconsiderable prose writing—novels, short stories, aphoristic texts and the particular text with which this paper deals, a collection of conversations. Most of Brecht's literary prose was written in exile: *The Threepenny Novel*, the novel fragment *Die Geschäfte des Herrn Julius Cäsar* (*The Business Affairs of Mr. Julius Caesar*), the elaborate plans for the *Tui-Roman* (*Tui-Novel*), in which Tui refers to intellectuals of which word it is a deliberate, inverted and abbreviated construction, half of all the short stories, the *Me-ti. Buch der Wendungen* (*Me-ti. Book of Turns*) on contemporary political, social, cultural figures, events and ideas in which Me-ti refers to a 5th century Chinese philosopher and "turns" might be understood both in the sense of 'turn of events' and 'turn of phrase', the *Geschichten vom Herrn Keuner* (*Stories of Mr. Keuner*) in which Keuner is Keiner[1] which in German means no-one, or no-one in particular, a wise, thinking person who represents and demonstrates in practice an unconventional but practical wisdom and the *Flüchtlingsgespräche* which I have translated as "Fugitives in Conversation".

This is not to say that while in exile Brecht definitively turned to prose writing for he wrote innumerable poems and nine plays including most of his best known ones. But a playwright also needed a stage. In a conversation with the cultural theorist Walter Benjamin, Brecht once said:

> They have not only taken away my house, my fish pond and my car, they have also robbed me of my stage and my audience. From my location I cannot admit that Shakespeare was fundamentally a greater talent. But he too could not have written for storing away. Besides, he had his figures in front of him. The people whom he depicted were running around him.

Being cut off from the German readers and theatregoers, exile writers were often compelled to turn to prose and in particular to the novel as the most widely accepted and most easily translatable form. Financial considerations, i.e., the need to earn their livelihood, naturally also played an important role. Brecht, who on several occasions in his life claimed to have written the one or the other text merely for making money, did not have much financial luck with most of his prose writings, since they were either written over long periods of time or left in fragment form with the idea of completing them at some later date. However, the experience of exile and the antifascist struggle provided the material and intellectual resources for varied experiments with prose writing.

It was in Finland that Brecht took up an old idea:

I was reading Diderot's *Jacques the Fatalist* when a new possibility occurred to me to put into effect the old Ziffel-plan... I wrote two small chapters by way of experiment and called the whole thing *Flüchtlingsgespräche* (Fugitives in Conversation, SM).

The *Flüchtlingsgespräche* consists entirely of a series of conversations between two persons, the middle-class intellectual and physicist Ziffel and the worker Kalle who has come through an experience in a concentration camp. Both Ziffel and Kalle are emigrants. Since they are condemned to wait, they are overtaken by an urge to talk. The pleasure of chatting dominates both of them and the opportunity is offered by their common exile in a place where no one else understands German.

The old Ziffel-plan that Brecht referred to was to be a description of a journey around Germany. Ziffel was to undertake this journey encouraged by the new "energetic leadership" of his country and also because he had always wanted to continue his studies on human progress and civilization. However, the old plan was completely changed. Instead of undertaking a journey around Germany, Ziffel finds himself confined to one place, Helsingfors in Finland, with Kalle as his only company. Ziffel and Kalle meet by chance in a railway station restaurant at a time when "The fury of war had devoured half of Europe, but it was still young and pretty and considering how it could make another leap over to America". The conversation partners are both highly individualistic figures and exchange their views on issues mundane and profound, political and philosophical, scientific and social, literary and linguistic. They discuss the virtues of their own land and those of the different lands of their exile: the excessive love of order, the principle of school education in Germany that taught the young how to advance in life through fraud, pretence, cliches, flattery, subservience, the readiness to betray your own kind to those above etc.; Switzerland's historic love of liberty, surrounded as it was by powers that would love to conquer something; the inordinate French patriotism, almost as if their country were their beloved; the misplaced conviction of the Danes that their humour would keep fascism at bay; the Swedes who were charitable except in cases that were professionally disadvantageous; Lapland and self-control, which meant being able to keep one's mouth shut and so on.

In his autobiographical notings in 1941, Brecht describes the *Flüchtlingsgespräche* as a small satirical book (in a manner most easily comparable to Voltaire's *Candide*), in which a fugitive flees from one country to the next since everywhere too many virtues are demanded. In one country to eat three times a day one needs an energy with which earlier empires could be conquered, in the other one has to help the regime to conquer the whole world so that it can continue to rule, in the third one needs too great a love of freedom since the lack of freedom is so great etc., etc. The fugitive is in search of a country in which one can live tolerably with average virtues and a few modest vices.[2]

"The world", as Ziffel mournfully tells Kalle,

has become an abode for heroes, where should we go? For some time it appeared as if the world could become livable, a sigh of relief went through humanity. Life became easier. There came the weaving loom, the steam engine, the car, the aeroplane, surgery, electricity, the radio, the pyramid and man could be lazier, more cowardly, oversensitive, pleasure-seeking, in short happier. . . . But what has become of this hopeful development? The world is once again full of the craziest demands and challenges. We need a world in which one can manage with a minimum of intelligence, courage, patriotism, self-respect, sense of justice etc., and what do we have? I tell you, I am fed up of being virtuous because nothing works, sacrificing because an unnecessary scarcity prevails, as hardworking as a bee because organisation is lacking, brave because my regime wants to embroil me in wars. Kalle, man, friend, I am fed up of all virtues and refuse to be a hero.

In *Life of Galileo* after Galileo recants in fear of the Inquisition, a student expresses his despair with the words: "Unhappy the land that has no heroes!" Galileo quips back: "No, unhappy the land that has need of heroes!"

The different social backgrounds of the two characters in the *Flüchtlingsgespräche* are constantly at play, in their manners, in their attitudes to the world around them, in their self-perception and in their understanding of the issues under discussion. Going to work on the project soon after the completion of the play *Mr. Puntila and His Man Matti*, Brecht still had the tone of the conversations between the landowner Puntila and his chauffeur Matti in mind. In his frequent bouts of drunkenness, the otherwise surly and self-centred landlord becomes halfway human and fraternizes with his chauffeur on equal terms, yearning for his friendship and advice. In the *Flüchtlingsgespräche* Ziffel is described as big and fat with white hands, while Kalle is of a stocky stature with the hands of a metal worker. Ziffel introduces himself by raising his 180 pounds of flesh and bones to a standing position, bowing and saying: "My name is Ziffel, physicist." Kalle, wondering at first whether he too should stand up and then controlling himself, remains sitting and mutters: "Call me Kalle, that'll do." Almost every meeting ends with the two taking leave of one another and going their own ways, each to his (assigned) place. The highly educated Ziffel who till he went into emigration had been engaged in research on the newest developments in atomic theory, expresses his wish to write his memoirs and persuades the worker Kalle to listen to some excerpts. Kalle, patient with the self-preoccupation of his conversation partner but also respectful of the written word and a bit curious, readily agrees. Having at last found a reader, Ziffel warms to the act of writing and looks forward with impatience to his meetings with Kalle, immediately demoralised if the latter does not turn up. Ziffel asserts that he is an unremarkable man with unremarkable views and holds forth on the intolerable domination of the memoir market by the remarkable views of remarkable men. Kalle concedes this point adding that this was part of the general tyranny prevailing and wondering why any man, x, y or z, should not be allowed to express his views in detail and listened to politely. Ziffel, deeply offended at being called any man, x, y or z, points out the great differences among the unremarkable, some possessing in special measure such characteristics as courage, talent, selflessness and others who in special measure do not possess them. Counting himself in the latter category, Ziffel insists on being an exceptional phenomenon.

In his readings from his memoirs, written with Kalle in mind as the reader, Ziffel explains the reasons that made him give up his privileged job as a physicist researching on atomic theory in an institute in Germany. After having spent around ten years of peaceful existence at the institute, blissfully disinterested in the application of the discoveries in physics to modern life including the armaments industry, having acquired a decent education through considerable financial investment and being thereafter well-provided financially, socially and culturally, the physicist Ziffel was caught unawares by the precipitate, shocking rise in unemployment and general increase in poverty around him and most disturbed by the fact that no-one seemed to have any explanation as to the causes for such terrible degradation. He suddenly realised that life in the centres of civilisation and the economy which man had built up had become so complicated that to understand them superhumans were required. The Heisenberg uncertainty factor in modern physics provided him an interesting analogy for the peculiar problems facing any attempt to investigate the causes of the current social misery. It had been noticed that the extra strong magnifying lenses necessary to observe the smallest particles of matter led to increase in heat levels and destructive processes or revolutions in the atomic world. The act of observing thus itself set on fire that which it wanted to observe. As in the microcosmic world, the investigation of the social world also set off revolutionary processes. As no superhumans were available who could overcome this problem, others who offered to radically simplify the economy and make it manageable found favour. The What'shisnameagain (i.e., Hitler) appeared opportunely on the scene with promises of a great epoch ahead. Soon he won the confidence of the Reich President, a General who had lost the First World War, and was installed in position to prepare the second. Ziffel who had already experienced one great epoch in his youth hastily left the country.

The conceptions of causality and determinism prevalent at the time greatly preoccupied Brecht. His readings on the subject included Max Planck and Werner Heisenberg. In an unfinished play planned on Einstein, a worker after hearing a lecture by the famous scientist insists on knowing whether the new theory had enough regularity to make prediction and planning possible. Entering into dispute with Einstein, the worker says:

> Your theory is an insurrection, and for insurrections one needs a good causality.[3]

While the causality and determinism of the modern, technologically advanced society of his times had drawn Brecht's attention even in the twenties, in the works of exile he attempted to expand the field of human action as far as possible. The many discussions on how to radically change society, but above all the experiences of the antifascist struggle made Brecht come to the conclusion that the independent movements of the individual had not been fully and finally determined. The urgency of this struggle also called for certain shifts in perspective. Whereas in his earlier writings, Brecht had focused on the individual and his experiences as the consequence of objective social processes, his interest shifted now to the possibilities for this individual to intervene in the social processes. Like the physicists who were resistant to far too rigid conceptions of causality, Brecht too turned against any extreme determinism that could lead to fatalism in the struggle against fascism:

> the formulation of the problem as determinism or indeterminism is completely hopeless. If everything that happens is determined, then the chain of determinations are unending and we cannot see unending chains clearly. Thus a complete and final determination of everything is impossible. However, the physicists' idea of probable causality allows for certain statements even in the case of irregular and complex happenings.[4]

Brecht was fascinated by the way physicists worked with probability calculations where hitherto existing conceptions of causality could not be established. The Heisenberg uncertainty relation (according to which there is no clear demarcation between the action of the subject and the reaction of the object) with which the physicists of his day looked at micro level physical phenomena could also be seen at work when trying to study the individual in society.

While defending the theory of causality on the one hand but rejecting over narrow conceptions of it and working on the possibilities of the struggle against fascism and a radical reordering of society, Brecht was nevertheless sceptical of the mere will to change:

Think of how difficult it is for people to decide on insurrection! It is a risky venture for them, new paths have to be cleared and trodden and along with the rulers their ideas also always rule. For the masses, insurrection is unnatural rather than natural and however terrible the situation may be from which only insurrection can free them, the thought of it requires as much effort as a new view of the universe does for the scientists.[5]

This notion of a kind of bond linking the ordinary worker trying to overthrow his material and ideological bondage and the scientist whose radical discoveries call for an overturning of prevailing conceptions of the universe finds direct expression in the conversations between the physicist Ziffel and the worker Kalle and lies at the heart of the conceptual idea of the *Flüchtlingsgespräche*.

Exile changed the social conditions of the emigrant writers' lives and so too of Brecht's. Isolated from most of his earlier social contacts and friends as also to a great extent from the German language, conversations with other exiles—often merely passing through – frequently became the only source of information and orientation about happenings in Germany and in the political struggle against fascism. The conception of conversation as a vehicle of information and varied experiences and as a mode of engaging with ideas is surely not unrelated to Brecht's aesthetic theories of an open-ended art form that invites the critical engagement of the recipient. But the dependence on stimulating conversation while in exile must have added an impetus to the choice of this form for an entire literary work.

Brecht's choice of a satirical style can also be located in the conditions and demands of exile. Though several well-known writers adopted satirical means to critique Hitler and the fascists, other writers and critics of the period objected to the use of satire, arguing that one could not combine the genocidal horrors of fascism with laughter. Even Chaplin, whose film *The Great Dictator* hit the cinema halls in the autumn of 1940 later admitted:

Had I known of the horrors in the German concentration camps, I would not have been able to make *The Great Dictator*, I would not have been able to make fun of the murderous madness of the Nazis.

Reacting to such criticism of satire in his notes to *The Resistible Rise of Arturo* Ui, a satirical play on the rise of the Nazis, Brecht wrote:

The great political criminals must definitely be exposed, and especially to ridicule.

The satirical attitude of putting the object of observation at a distance went well with Brecht's concept of a scientifically distanced reader thinking about the pros and cons of the observed situation and of the possibilities for intervention even as he reads. Confronted by the widespread demoralisation afflicting most exiles that could soon lead to self-destructive resignation—several exiles committed suicide in despair - the resolve to stick to a concept that aimed at activating the critical faculties of the reader could only have been strengthened.

However, it is not as if Brecht always used satire, nor that he chose satire as the preferred mode for all his exile writings. But the satirical mode lent itself aptly to the literary representation of the chosen situation: two fugitives from a mighty, demonic regime, isolated, cut off from home, family, friends and language, improbable companions thrown together by history, seeking each other out for want of anything better to do and warming to each other's company through their common distaste for the demonic regime at home, though from dissimilar viewpoints and with dissimilar experiences, and reflecting in conversation on the varied stuff that life is made of. More precisely, the satirical mode lent itself aptly to the dialectic of discussion, of criticism and self-criticism, through which the middle class intellectual and the worker - might one say Brecht's bourgeois Self and proletarian Other - attempt to arrive at a common understanding of fascism, of the possibilities of defeating it and erecting in its place a society that neither had any need for such strenuous virtues as heroism, patriotism, a thirst for freedom, goodness, selflessness, nor for a care-two-hoots attitude to one's homeland, a slavish mentality, brutality and egoism.

Kalle at one point ruefully confesses:

Sometimes, don't take it amiss, I get on my own nerves, that in a time like this I am sitting around and making wisecracks.

Ziffel consoles him:

Firstly I could reply that both of us are not well fed enough to be really serious, particularly with two motorized German divisions in the country and no visas. Secondly, seriousness as a standard of living is a bit discredited at the moment; for the most serious thing that ever happened is Hitler and his lot. He belongs to the serious murderers, murder is something very serious. No superficial nature, the Poles will certify that. In contrast, the Buddha was a humourist. And thirdly, we don't need to behave in a dignified manner, we aren't butchers. You can always express a good thing in a funny way as well.

The hilarity that liberates the oppressive and threatened condition of the two fugitives emanates from several factors built into the text: the unlikely companionship of the middle class intellectual and the worker, their invariably courteous, polite and even formal manner of interaction and its combination with the growing warmth and friendship, the meandering of their conversations from the everyday—for instance, beer, cigars and coffee—to the world historical—for instance, the Hegelian dialectic — and the equal solemnity with which all these subjects are treated, the depiction of phenomena that threatened their very existence in playful or ridiculing terms (Hitler is the What'shisnameagain, Mussolini is the Thingthere, the war is still young and pretty and considering how to make another leap over to America) and the coupling of the elegant, unagitated movement of the text with its subversive content.

The combination of criticism of fascism and self-criticism of the antifascist forces in exile is also inherent to the strategy of the text. Talking about the concept of goodness, Ziffel remembers how after the First World War a book came out with the sensational title "Man is good":

I was alarmed and felt relieved when a critic wrote: 'man is good, the calf appetizing'." For Brecht, being good was not good enough, it was also necessary for those who were good to work out how to be victorious: ". . .this goodness was beaten, defeated, hindered and was therefore a weak goodness, a bad, indefensible, unreliable goodness; for one cannot concede the flaws of goodness like one accepts the wetness of rain. To say that the good were not defeated because they were good but because they were weak, for that courage is necessary.

When Kalle, encouraged by Ziffel's repeated expressions of dislike for all virtues and recalling how the poor people were brought up to be virtuous and good, points out that the word "good" has an unpleasant flavour, Ziffel signals agreement with an example from colloquial American English:

The Americans have a word for a good human being, that is 'sucker', pronounced sugger, best spitted out of one corner of the mouth. It means one who has been hoodwinked, taken in, that which a confident trickster looks out for when he is hungry.

The two conversationalists also focus their reflections on linguistic mystifications, so for instance on the German word "Volk". When Ziffel comes to the defence of democracy, explaining that it literally means the rule of the people, Volksherrschaft, Kalle retorts:

The word 'Volk' is a strange word, have you noticed that? Its meaning is completely different towards the outside and towards the inside. Towards the outside, towards other peoples, the big industrialists, Junkers, high-level bureaucrats, generals, bishops etc., naturally belong to the German people (Volk), to no other. But towards the inside, where it is a question of domination, you will always hear these gentlemen talk of the people (Volk) as of 'the masses' or 'the common people'; they themselves do not belong to it.

Troubled by such inconsistencies as also by news of the landing of two motorized Nazi divisions in Finland, the two friends turn to lighter conversation and decide to lay the foundations for a new script, like the Chinese picture script, that would remove such stupendous inaccuracies. To give one example of this simultaneously playful and serious activity, the picture for TEACHING in the new script would be a blackboard, only to be used with the year (date) written in one corner. A blank blackboard without the year on it would stand for ETERNAL TRUTH and the same sign would be used for INTELLECTUAL FRAUD.

To conclude, the *Flüchtlingsgespräche* is a work, or rather a text[6], that reflects the conditions of exile both in form and content, but it is also another experiment with the Brechtian aesthetics that discards any morally educative role for literature and art in favour of strategies that present different facets of life with their varied colours, complexities, problems, threats and dangers, distanced through appropriate literary techniques to afford a better view to the reader and to thus encourage his/her active critical intervention.

NOTES

1. Hanns Eisler: Fragen Sie mehr über Brecht...
2. Bertolt Brecht, Tagebücher 1920-1922. Autobiographische Aufzeichnungen 1920-1954. Hrsg. von Herta Ramthun. Frankfurt am Main 1978, S. 229
3. Werner Mittenzwei, Der Dialektiker Brecht oder Die Kunst den "Me-ti" zu lesen / Verführt durch den Beweis. Der Einfluß naturwissenschaftlichen Denkens auf Brechts poetische Konzeption; in: ibid, Kampf der Richtungen. Strömungen und Tendenzen der internationalen Dramatik. Leipzig 1978, S 76/S. 203
4. Brecht: Arbeitsjournal.
5. Die Dialektik auf dem Theater.
6. Both in the sense of the distinction made by Roland Barthes between work and text and in the sense of it having remained a fragment.

STEFANO FOSSATI

Notes on *Fontamara*

In this article, I would like to suggest certain keys to a reading of *Fontamara*, the novel by Ignazio Silone, which is considered by some critics to be one of the most important products of 20th Century literature. However, not all the critics of Italian literature give it the merit it deserves. These discrepancies in the critic's judgement are due to the fact that although Silone plays an important role in the history of literature, politics and Christianity, it is always a detached, isolated role, outside the usual categories that we use for character analysis.

In the first part, I would like to show how the novel developed within the wider context of the artistic and intellectual work produced by Italians living in exile during Fascism.

In the second part, I will try to throw light on the aspects of the novel, which, in my opinion, can be traced back to the particular experience of living in exile knowing well that it is not possible to draw mathematical equations between the lines of life and creativity.

Ignazio Silone (pseudonym of Secondino Tranquilli) was born in 1900 in Pescina dei Marsi, an impoverished village in Southern Italy. In 1915 he lost his mother in an earthquake which destroyed the whole village. His father had died just a few months earlier. He had begun Grammar School but was forced to leave. At a very early age, he began to be active in politics, working to organize the agricultural labourers of his region and during the First World War he became the director of the socialist, pacifist weekly *Avanguardia*. At the Livorno Congress of 1921, he joined the Italian Communist Party and became leader of the Youth Federation. After the advent of Fascism, he worked with Antonio Gramsci, one of the founders of the Italian Communist Party, as a clandestine activist. When his brother was arrested, he sought refuge abroad, where he continued his antifascist activities, settling in Switzerland after travelling extensively. With Togliatti, he represented the Italian Communists in Moscow several times in the Komintern meetings, but around 1930 he left the Communist party as a result of Stalin's policies. This caused him a deep crisis, making him question communist ideology. His original Christian and libertarian aspiration began to re-emerge. Even after leaving the Communist movement, Silone was still regarded as one of the most important antifascist representatives in exile. It was during this time that he matured as a writer. His first novel, *Fontamara*, was published in German in Zurich in 1933.

Let's now take a step backward and try to put the politics and writing of Silone into the greater context of the political activists and intellectuals in exile during Fascism[1].

The advent of Fascist dictatorship in Italy in the 1920's hadn't caused a great emigration of intellectuals, writers, artists and philosophers, in contrast to the true Diaspora of German language and culture in the rest of the free world, provoked by the Nazi take-over of power in Germany and Austria. The first people to emigrate from Italy, in the early 1920's, were workers. Between 1925-1927 this migration became mixed up with and super-imposed by a haemorrhage of politically active people from parties, unions and opposition groups outlawed by the regime. These consisted of unknown militants as well as leaders of international stature.

This structural characteristic of Italian emigration continued to set it apart from that of central Europe which mainly consisted of German speaking people of Jewish origin, up to the mid 1930's.

However, running parallel to the political and propagandist activities, which was the sector most important for the exiled Italian intellectuals, an emigrant literature began to mature and gradually take hold, because it was through living in exile itself that revealed several writers to themselves and then consequently to others and to international acclaim. We can say that the particular experience of living abroad in exile brought people to writing, both in essay form and in novels.

There were intellectual resources which formerly in Italy had been directed towards political work.

Just to give a couple of examples, Angelo Tasca, an ex-communist militant and journalist, came to the fore as a history expert when Gallimard published his now classic study of the rise of Fascism, in Paris in 1938. And still in Paris Emilio Lussu wrote and published his *Marcia su Roma* (*March on Rome*) and *Un anno sull'altipiano* (*A year on the plateau*). These books by "new" writers were translated into several languages, enjoyed good circulation and made their mark. Gaetano Salvemini, whose reputation as a historian was already consolidated in pre-fascist Italy, suddenly acquired a much larger international readership for his books on Fascism, when he was forced into exile and relocated in Harvard University. Silone, too, came to join this category of writers, showing a talent for writing critical essays, short stories and novels. His was a double exile, away from his home country because of his opposition to Fascism, but also excluded from his second home, which for many years of his life as a militant revolutionary had been the Communist Party.

It was relatively easy for the exiled to get an article published because there were a lot of local and Italian periodicals and newspapers that had either been re-launched abroad by different anti-Fascist parties or founded because they were linked to movements born abroad. However, to get a full volume published was far from easy. The first obstacle to overcome was that of the language. Italian had long ceased to be recognised as an international language and so, to get into the distribution network of their host countries, the authors had either to express themselves in a foreign language and/or put their texts into the hands of translators or revisers.

The majority of the writers in exile, Carlo Rosselli, Nitti, Tasca and others, chose to use French as the medium for promoting the circulation of their works in Europe. As far as Silone was concerned, he published nearly all his work, written in his 15 years of exile in Switzerland, in German and collaborated with various political and cultural magazines run by German emigrants.

In particular, he formed a solid business relationship and friendship with Emil Oprecht, bookseller and later an editor from Zurich. In 1933 Oprecht founded the *Europa Verlag* and became a focal point for anti-fascist and anti-nazi propaganda between the two wars.

The German editions became the representative form of several of Silone's works because the Italian originals were lost. Also sometimes the Italian editions were published very late.

The Italian emigrants managed to create a network of publishing houses who were prepared to publish their books. In this way, anti-fascist works were read around the world, but often was ignored by the Italian public, not only, as is obvious, in Italy, but also by Italians living abroad. The majority of the latter were poor and ill-educated and could not understand the foreign language editions of the works. Neither did they constitute a readership big enough to activate a market for the books in Italian. So it was unviable for a commercial editor to launch a series in Italian. Meanwhile, it was illegal to bring any anti-fascist publication into Italy and distribute it. This law covered periodicals and books and it meant that in Italy they could only be published and circulated underground. In this regard, Silone says in *Memoriale dal carcere* (*Memorial from Prison*):

> The circulation of my books in Italy came about without my involvement. Usually they are read and circulated in the English, French and German editions,

which until 1939 were distributed freely, but I know that typed and printed copies of the original Italian versions can be found. They have been produced on the initiative of people completely unknown to me.[2]

A few years later, he said of his first novel, *Fontamara*:

If it has been round the world, no one can deny that it walked on its own legs.[3]

It is true that the Fascist authorities also banned various foreign language editions of Silone's books, that is, they were included in the list entitled *Elenco generale delle pubblicazioni sovversive e antinazionali edite all' Estero sottoposte a divieto d'introduzione e circolazione nel regno*, 1936 ("General list of subversive literature published abroad and prohibited in the kingdom").[4] This list, updated and distributed by the Ministry of Internal Affairs, indicated which titles, pamphlets and books published abroad should be confiscated. Italian and foreign authors and their works were listed side by side. Thus in the list of 1936 we can find *The history of the Russian Revolution* by Trotsky alongside Silone's *Fontamara*, an Italian edition which appeared in Paris. In the Swiss section for the same year, his essay, *Der Fascismus. Seine Entstehung und seine Entwicklung* (*Fascism, its origin and development*) and the novel, *Brot und Wein* (Bread and Wine) were included.

It was beyond any economic logic and any consideration of market demands to publish mother tongue editions of books by Italian writers in exile. In other words, it was a question of an autonomous initiative taken by Italian anti-fascism itself, if they were prepared to invest in the cultural sector. Obviously, initiatives of this kind were limited, partly because non-communist emigrants struggled to find resources for their own organisation's literature and survival. As a consequence, Italian works published were mainly concerned with political themes, ranging from the fight against Fascism to the prospects of the Italian society. We are talking about publishing taken on by different political parties and anti-Fascist groups and therefore, characterised by a definite orientation towards political activity. Obviously, there are significant exceptions. For example, Giorgio Amendola, an Italian communist leader, remembers that he was able to publish the very aberrant novel *Un anno sull'altipiano* by Emilio Lussu in 1938, in Paris. This was for the *Edizioni Italiane di Cultura* (Italian Cultural Editions) which was an organ of the Communist Party and was connected to an editing house financed by the Third International Association of Communists. The publishing plan, discussed every year with leaders from Moscow, was hinged on propaganda and the circulation of the Central Committee reports and Stalin and Dimitrov's speeches. However, Amendola printed this book despite the limit of the budget assigned to him by using different printers prepared to work on credit, in the hope, later proven true, that inflation would have cancelled out the deficit.[5] However, this was an extremely isolated case. It was only in the second half of the 1930's that the policy of strict control over publishing and cultural life, adopted by the Fascists, made it clear to the exiles that one aspect of the fight against Fascism was opposition to the cultural conformism and provincialism that was conditioning artistic, literary, historical and philosophical work in Italy.

Silone had already been following this route for a few years on his own. There were various elements that helped to stimulate in him the search for new cultural horizons and a revision of his socialism and Christianity. Among these, the most important were the decision to abstain from politics once he left the Communist party; his destiny as an Italian writer known only outside his own country and his contact with Zurich's society, which had a wealth of cultural activity.

Silone is an unusual case in Italian literature because his narrative is a vehicle for the Christian message as well as his socialist commitment.

He is a self taught intellectual and in his books he continually refers to the task of expressing the drama of an individual who is confronted with the hypercritical forms of political propaganda, but at the same time maintains steadfastly his faith in evangelical values and in the cult of freedom.

The fight against all types of dictatorship which Silone's characters (his alter-ego) carry out in the name of ethics and inner freedom, creates "positive" individuals. This personality trait is certainly new to Italian writing from that of the first half of the twentieth century. The novels written by Svevo, Pirandello and Tozzi are full of ambiguous, indecisive characters who are seeking their own identity. On one hand this positive trait of Silone's characters redeems them morally (or religiously). On the other hand it condemns them to defeat, to the imitation of Christ because society is fundamentally corrupt. Silone remained convinced of this, long after the war period and his terrible experiences in exile, reproposing it, to various extent, throughout his life in all his novels and essays.

According to a famous Italian critic Piero Citati, in the foundation of Silone's world there is a painful fracture between the individual and society which continually obstructs every effort made to repair it.[6] The central theme in Silone's world is isolation. Isolation not only of the individual in society, but also the isolation of the different social groups which are rigidly organised into a hierarchy. This is confirmed by the impenetrable linguistic levels: the working and the middle class, as we will see, never manage to truly understand each other, not even in small daily transactions. Finally, there is the isolation of the individual faced with his own conscience.

In *Fontamara*, his first novel, all these themes are already clearly evident. Silone wrote *Fontamara* in Switzerland when he was thirty years old. Psychologically and economically, his conditions were extreme. He was in exile, penniless, alone and unknown, because he was using a false name to avoid detection by the Fascist police. He was seriously ill. According to his doctors, he didn't have long to live, so he wrote anxiously and in a hurry.

Initially, it was difficult to get the novel published because, as we have already explained, most texts published were of a political nature.

In 1932, following the involvement of the Swiss novelist, Jakob Wassermann, the novel was translated into German. Originally they thought about publishing it in a serial form, in the *Frankfuerter Zeitung* and negotiated with the publisher Fischer of Berlin, but Hitler's rise to power made it impossible. So it was printed in Switzerland, translated into German by Nettie Sutro, financed by private individuals and given to the bookseller Oprecht of Zurich for distribution.

The novel had immediate success, not only in German speaking Switzerland, but also throughout the world due to the Diaspora of political refugees who passed through Switzerland in transit from Germany and other countries of Central Europe.

However, despite his international reputation, Silone had to print the Italian original in Paris, in 1934, at his own cost.

Fontamara tells the story of a village of the same name in the foothills of the Abruzzo region. Its agricultural economy had been destroyed due to the climatic changes caused by the drainage of the lake, the Fucino. Meanwhile the lowlands had benefitted enormously but these lands were not given as compensation to the peasants who had suffered but were colonised by the powerful local families. Although the name of the village was fictitious, the circumstances of the story were true. The problems related to the drainage of lake Fucino were factual. Also factual were the more extensive problems of the big landowners in Southern Italy and a badly needed agricultural reform.

The village, which for years had been immersed in dire poverty was inhabited by the *cafoni*: Silone used this term, which literally means 'peasants', knowing that in the 'civilised' world it was used as an insult.

The life, in the village, is monotonous. It follows the natural sequence of the seasons, until, one day, a wheeler-dealer, supported by Fascist government officials, decides to change the course of a little stream. The water from this stream is vital for the already sparse agriculture of Fontamara. This injustice gives rise to a process of conscience-searching among the *cafoni* of Fontamara. They are inspired by the example of the protagonist, Berardo Viola, an exceptionally strong and courageous *cafoni* who is imprisoned, tortured and finally killed by the Fascists. They decide to organise themselves, forming an elementary protest group. However, the fascists react drastically in a bloody manner.

I would like to concentrate on two aspects of the novel which seem to be particularly significant as far as our theme is concerned: the impact of the conditions of exile on creativity. The first is the characterisation of the places in which the action take place. The second is the function that language, or rather languages of different social groups, has within the society.

There are perhaps two elements which have a dramatic effect on the situation of the person in exile. First the separation from his former world which forces the refugee to experiment with the newness and the hostility of an external space; secondly, the language difference. As far as the external 'space' is concerned, we can say that in Fontamara, three types of 'space' exist. First the village, isolated, severe, extremely impoverished and natural; secondly the fertile basin of the Fucino, the promised land, which the people of Fontamara first catch a glimpse of and thirdly the hostile civilised world, where words are always translated into laws and laws sanction exploitation.

The spatial limits which the novelist imposes on the action are very rigid and this accentuates the impression of gloomy pessimism throughout the book and it gives the idea that one can only save oneself through one's inner conscience and not in the external world.

At the beginning of the novel, the description of Fontamara reveals a desolate author, as if the dry, lifeless landscape were a pregnant metaphor of his destiny. In this case, the description assumes a fundamental importance because it conditions the narrative aspect of the work.

Let's look at some of the typical features of the village:

> Fontamara is an "old and unknown village of impoverished peasants"[7]; "stagnant since time immemorial", "a place marked on no map", where life is "enclosed in an immobile circle, soldered by the unrelenting grip of the mountains and the passing of time. Welded into a natural unchanging circle, like a kind of life sentence.[8]

Note that the circle is soldered by "time" too. That is, Fontamara doesn't live in the linear time of history, like the city with all its transformations, but in a cyclic time, which is eternal.

Another descriptive passage:

> The same sky, circumscribed by the amphitheatre created by the mountains which close the territory like a gateless wall.

The contrast between the natural cyclic time and the historic, linear time, is constantly present from the very beginning of the book:

In the plains, it is known, many things change, at least apparently, but in Fontamara nothing changes.[9]

The people of Fontamara view the transformations of the plains from a distance as if it is a spectacle that has nothing to do with them. Here we've introduced the second spatial element: "the plains" where there is the fertile land the people of Fontamara long for. They come into contact with it when they are taken by the Fascist authorities to supplement the audience of an official event. The description, at this point, takes on a strongly subjective angle. I quote:

Suddenly, in front of us, we saw the vast basin of the Fucino, coloured golden by the mature corn, divided into giant rows. We caught our breath. Fucino took on a new aspect, that of the promised land.[10]

Between these two extremes, we can say that the 'space' of the civilised, official and bureaucratic world is in a highly antagonistic position in relation to that of the village. It is a world which is incomprehensible to the *cafoni* and likewise the language in which it expresses itself. What the *cafoni* can understand is that the official language of the bureaucracy and law stands for and imposes a rigid, social hierarchy.

"See" - says one of the *cafoni* of Fontamara to a government official - in the city, lots of things happen. In the city, at least one thing happens every day. They say that a newspaper comes out every day and speaks of at least one happening. At the end of the year how many things have happened? Hundreds and hundreds. And after several years? Thousands and thousands. Imagine, how can a *cafone*, a poor *cafone*, a poor worm from the earth know about all these things? He can't. But what happens is one thing, who is in charge is another. Authority is always the same.[11]

The space outside the village is therefore impossible to decode and is full of traps.

The *cafoni* realise this world is hostile and oppressive, but otherwise incomprehensible to them and even more incomprehensible when it tries to communicate through *language*. In other words maximum incomprehension occurs where one would expect full clarity, that is when language is used for communication. This happens because, as we will see, official language always appears as a tool of power.

The problem of language is first mentioned in the introduction to the book, where the author asks himself in which language he ought to tell the story of Fontamara.

Don't think that the people of Fontamara speak Italian. The Italian language for us is a language learned at school, similar to Latin, French or Esperanto. For us Italian is a foreign language, a dead language, a language whose dictionary and grammar have been developed without considering us, or our way of being and of expressing ourselves. Obviously, before me, other *cafoni* from the South have spoken and written in Italian, in the same way that we dress in shoes, shirt and tie when we go into town. You only need to look at us, to see our awkwardness.[12]

The relationship between the official language and the dialects is, in reality, a problem which should have been resolved long before. The Fascists tried to influence the evolution of the national language: in 1926, for example, the use of foreign words was prohibited by law in all sectors and dialects were excluded from schools.

At that time, the official language was heavily rhetoric and standardised. It used a lot of hyperbole which created the image of a strong and self-confident regime.

If we consider, however, that dialects were the mother tongue and commonly used language of about four fifths of the population of Italy, we realise that the regime did not use language to communicate meanings and ideas, but to stimulate uncritical emotive consensus.

The awareness that there is a gap between words and their true meaning is present in other authors of Italian literature, contemporary to Silone, whether the writer is opposed to Fascism or not, but perhaps, in no other work of this time is it declared so dramatically, that the official language was in direct opposition to the language of the people.

This idea is certainly the consequence of the experience of living in exile, when the linguistic barriers which are normally high, appear in full force, accentuating the feeling of isolation.

One of the most significant examples of the perverse use of language by authority is that of the farcical contracts which the inhabitants of Fontamara make, concerning the use of a water course which is vital for their agriculture.

To calm the people who are exasperated by the latest injustice, the village lawyer intervenes, seemingly to support the villagers, but in reality to confirm the injustice through an unscrupulous use of the language.

The women - says the lawyer - claim that half of the stream is not enough to irrigate their land. They want more than half, at least that is how I interpret their wishes. There is only one solution. We need to give to the authorities three quarters of the water from the stream, and the three quarters of water that remains will be for the villagers. That way both will have three quarters, that is, a little more than half. I understand that my proposal will cause the authorities great problems, but I appeal to your kind hearts.[13]

The deceit, masqueraded by the play on words (three quarters plus three quarters evidently doesn't make one) is accepted, even if everybody knows that they haven't understood the terms of the agreement.

Then, when the fraud is discovered and the rebellion threatens to reach explosion point again, it is quelled by a new agreement, which once again is based on the repressive use of incomprehensible language: it is established that the loss of the water source will last—literally, '*ten lustri*' (one *lustro* is a period of five years, so ten *lustri* are equal to fifty years).[14]

No one understands the meaning of the expression and furthermore, in this, as in other cases, no one thinks of asking for an explanation because it is clear to everyone that when the authorities use official, bureaucratic language, it is not to start a dialogue, but to confirm an act of force, to sanction an injustice that has already taken place. Thus the people of Fontamara show themselves incapable of organising a protest.

True redemption for them will come, but through an absolutely personal choice. At the end of the novel, one of them, the best of them, the one who has always been their point of reference, goes to the city to look for work, and meets a clandestine political activist. He is arrested with him by the Fascist police, who find anti-fascist propaganda in the restaurant where they were eating. In prison, the hero matures his own revolutionary conscience and decides to take onto himself the responsibility of possession of the material of propaganda, even if he has no idea what it is about. He is tortured for many days by the police but accepts his destiny, saying:

> If I talk, everything is lost. If I talk, Fontamara's damnation will be eternal. If I talk, a hundred more years will pass before another such occasion will present itself. And if I die? I will be the first *cafone* who doesn't die for himself but for others.[15]

In the concluding chapter, the parallels with Christianity are very strong. We see it from the language of the previous quotation which projects the individual's story into the eternal time of religious dimension. Like Christ, the protagonist dies through the fault of others and to save humanity from eternal damnation. This imitation of Christ is a theme which Silone uses for the rest of his life and from which the strongest characters of his books are created.[16]

Silone tries to return to active politics several times after his exile, but every time he has to give up because the fracture between himself and every form of social, political and religious organisation, which matured during his years in exile, cannot be repaired.

Translated from Italian by Anne Marino Thomson

NOTES

* This article is a token of my homage to Anna e Nino Battaglia, victims of Fascism.

1. See Elisa Signori, "Ignazio Silone e l'editoria dell'esilio", in *Nuova Antologia*, fasc. 2195 (1995), pp. 120-146.
2. "La diffusione dei miei libri in Italia, posso affermarlo senza tema di essere smentito, avvenne senza il mio concorso: di solito sono stati letti e diffusi nelle edizioni inglesi, tedesche e francesi, che fino al 1939 potevano circolare liberamente, ma so che anche degli originali italiani circolano copie scritte a macchina e riprodotte col torchio per iniziativa di persone a me del tutto sconosciute." I. Silone, *Memoriale dal carcere svizzero*, ed. by Lamberto Mercuri, Cosenza, 1979, pp. 16-17.
3. "Se ha fatto il giro del mondo, non si può negare che l'abbia fatto con le sue gambe". I. Silone, *Parliamo di me*, in *Nuova Antologia*, fasc. 2127 (1978), p. 50.
4. In Archivio centrale dello Stato (ACS), Direzione Generale di Pubblica sicurezza, Divisione Affari Generali e Riservati, serie Atti speciali, f. 58.
5. G. Amendola, *Un'isola*, Milan, 1980, pp. 233-236.
6. See Giacinto Spagnoletti, *Storia della letteratura italiana del Novecento*, Milan, 1994, p. 472.
7. "... un antico e oscuro luogo di contadini poveri..." I. Silone, *Fontamara*, IV ed. Gli Oscar, Milan, 1949, p. 19.
8. "... racchiusa in un cerchio immobile saldato dalla chiusa morsa delle montagne e dalle vicende del tempo." I. Silone, op. cit., p. 21.
9. "In pianura, questo si sa, molte cose cambiavano, almeno in apparenza; ma a Fontamara nulla mutava." I. Silone, op. cit., p. 24.
10. "... all'improvviso, davanti a noi, ci trovammo la pianura del Fucino, vastissima e dorata di messi mature, spartite da filari di pioppi giganteschi, l'emozione ci tagliò il respiro. Fucino aveva un aspetto nuovo: l'aspetto della terra promessa." I. Silone, op. cit., p. 134.
11. "Vedi ...in città succedono molti fatti. In città ogni giorno succede almeno un fatto. Ogni giorno, dicono, esce un giornale e racconta almeno un fatto. In capo all'anno, quanti fatti sono? Centinaia e centinaia. E in capo a vari anni? Migliaia e migliaia. Immagina. Come può un cafone, un povero cafone, un povero verme della terra conoscere tutti questi fatti? Non può. Ma una cosa sono i fatti, un'altra è chi comanda. I fatti cambiano ogni giorno, chi comanda è sempre quello. L'autorità è sempre quella." I. Silone, op. cit., p. 47.
12. " A nessuno venga in mente che i Fontamaresi parlino italiano. La lingua italiana è per noi una lingua imparata a scuola, come possono essere il latino, il francese, l'esperanto. La lingua italiana è per noi una lingua straniera, una lingua morta, una lingua il cui dizionario, la cui grammatica si sono formati senza alcun rapporto con noi, col nostro modo di agire, col nostro modo di pensare, col nostro modo di esprimerci. Naturalmente, prima di me, altri cafoni meridionali han parlato e scritto in italiano, allo stesso modo che andando in città noi usiamo portare scarpe, colletto,

cravatta. Ma basta osservarci per scoprire la nostra goffaggine." I. Silone, op. cit., pp. 29-30.

13. I. Silone, op. cit., p. 88.
14. I. Silone, op. cit., p. 197.
15. "E se io tradisco, tutto è perduto. Se io tradisco...la dannazione di Fontamara sarà eterna. Se io tradisco passeranno ancora centinaia di anni prima che una simile occasione si ripresenti. E se io muoio? Sarò il primo cafone che non muore per sé, ma per gli altri." I. Silone, op. cit., p. 247.
16. See Rosario Cantarino, *Il Mezzogiorno contadino e il silenzio della storia*. In *Letteratura italiana. Storia e geografia*. Vol. III: *L'età contemporanea*, Turin, 1989, pp. 768-770.

MIRCEA ITU

God was Born in Exile : Mircea Eliade and the Recuperation of the Sacred

The concept of exile gives a new perspective not only to literature, but also to culture and moreover to humanity itself. It bring into view the transnational dimension, a new vision of the world, not confronting the traditional aspect with the modern one, but unifying them in a special synthesis.

There is an exterior exile and an inner exile. There are plenty of causes as concerns exile: political, social, economical and so forth. It is a question of time and, of course, of place. These two fields define the exile, together with its characteristics. We do not consider it necessary to insist on these well-known points. We would like to give a new value to exile, beyond the deprivation and nostalgia, the hardships and the hopes, the profound pessimism and the futuristic optimism. We see exile not in the sense of a retreat, a refuge or an emigration from cruel reality, but as the reality itself. Exile, like life, starts with a bad cause, the traumatic experiences and restrictions to be compared with *du:kha* (pain), but goes towards a good aim, the feeling of freedom and the liberty of creation to be related to *mokṣa* or *nirvāṇa* (liberation).

In the modern age, universal culture and spirituality can be seen as a land of exile in front of the materialistic and egoistic existence, the profane experience of daily life. If we admit that the life of pleasures and pains is but *māyā*, mere illusion, not a reality in the end, it means that exile is, in fact, the true reality. Everyone who builds up his personality through love and altruism, in the quest of truth, following the path of knowledge, is an exiled human being. In this lost world, when people are interested in money, power or other profane goals, the individual discovers herself or himself alone, exiled. It is this kind of exile that we try to emphasize as the main idea of our paper, giving the example of a universal spirit, Mircea Eliade. The exile of the Sacred from the profane.

We shall deal with the Romanian exile and then we shall give the example of Eliade, which stands for both the exterior and the inner exile and proves the complexity of the concept.

First of all, we shall discuss the concept of exile in Romanian literature which has a very strong literature of exile in the twentieth century. Most of the national literatures in the world contain the examples of some personalities who belong, by birth, to another state. At the beginning of the thirties, Romanian Peter Neagoe wrote an anthology of the american literature abroad, with the title *Americans Abroad*. Two hundred and fifty German writers decided for exile rather than to sign the document of loyalty to Hitler and Thomas Mann said "*German culture is here, where I am*".

One of the foremost works in literary criticism in Romanian culture is *Leptuariul romanesc* (The Romanian Reading), by Aron Pumnul. The book comprises six volumes dealing with the belief in the unity of Romanian language and culture, despite the historical borders of the state. It takes into consideration the Romanian writers from the land of old Dacia as well as from Pind, Epir and Olympus, Thesalia and Macedonia, Moravia, Istria, even Poland and Swizerland, to other states and teritories. On the other hand, in 1925, Nicolae Iorga, historical scientist and savant, says the following words : "*All the nations gather inside their spiritual life what has been written in other languages by personalities belonging to them*".

From the historical point of view, there are five big periods in Romanian literature: 1) the preRomanian old culture; 2) the medieval Romanian culture; 3) the national Renaissance of Romanian culture; 4) the Romanian culture between the two world wars and 5) the Romanian culture during communism until today. Of course, there is a post communist Romanian culture which tries to define itself nowadays and, from the axiological point of view, we should mention Romanticism in Romanian literature, a period characterised by the five classical models: Mihai Eminescu in poetry, Ion Luca Caragiale in theatre, Ion Creange in novels, Ioan Slavici in short-stories and Titu Maiorescu in critics.

As concerns the exile, in the first historical period of Romanian culture, we would like to mention Publius Ovidius Naso, Latin poet exiled by Emperor Augustus at Tomis, in Dacia, old Romania. At the same time, there were some writers in the Greek culture who were Thracians, ancestors of the Dacians, ancestors of the Romanians, such as: Anacharsis, Istros, Satyros, prince Cotys, Niceta of Remesiana, considered the prophet of the Dacians.

In the second historical period of Romanian culture we take the examples of Dimitrie Cantemir who wrote in Latin language *Descriptio Moldaviae* (The Description of Moldavia) at the request of the Berlin Academy and Antioh Cantemir, who lived in Russia; and Miron Costin, who studied in Poland and wrote in Polish. They were not usual cases of exile, but of writers expressing their identity, both national and individual, abroad or in a foreign language.

In the period of national Renaissance, Shcoala Ardeleana (The Transylvanian School) showed an interesting case of exile inside the country, expressing through historical and linguistic works the attitude against the Austro-Hungarian Empire and the treatment of Romanians in Transylvania by the imperialistic rulers from the Austro-Hungarian Empire, who were refusing to consider the Romanians, despite their majority in the province, as a nation, not even as a nationality. The representatives of the Transylvanian School, intellectuals who studied at the Universities of Berlin and Viena, tried to prove the Latin origin of the Romanian language, together with the Roman origin of the Romanian people. It was a case of political, as well as social exile. In the nineteenth century, Moses Gaster, a personality in the folklore culture, went to England, his works becoming a chapter in English culture while Countess Anne de Noailles (Ana Brancoveanu) went to France and wrote poems in French.

In the period between the two world wars, the Romanian exile became more and more clear. Among the examples of Romanian culture in exile during this period, there were Elena Vacarescu, Benjamin Fondane, Marcel Iancu and Tristan Tzara, who invented the dadaist movement in modern poetry, the musician George Enescu, who composed *The Romanian Rhapsody,* the well-known cubist artist, sculptor Constantin Brancushi, who created *The Unending Coloumn, The Table of Silence* and *The Gate of Kiss* etc., masterpieces of sculpture. Most of these personalities of Romanian culture lived in France, like Panait Istrati, the author of *Codin, Kira Kiralina and Ciulinii Baraganului,* called *"a Balkan Gorki, a genious story-teller"* by Romain Rolland. The exile in these cases, as in many others to follow, was the same, with the idea of the deprovincialization of Romanian culture in order to express the universal feature of their personality and work. This type of exile is present in the situation of Mircea Eliade, too.

The most evident instances of exile was happening in Romanian culture in the later part of the twentieth century, during and after the communist period. Thus, there was an exile inside the country and culture became the way of expressing protest, more often allusive than direct, against soviet opression, against communist opression, against the dictatorship of Ceaushescu and the policy of the Communist Party, the only one legally existent during the communist years. Romanian literature became like the other literatures of the Eastern countries in Europe, a literature of the opressed, a literature of exile. The same process took place in Poland, Cehia, Slovakia, Hungary, Croatia, Bosnia and Herzegovina, Macedonia, Serbia, Bulgaria, The Soviet Republics etc. At the same time an exile outside the country sprang up.

An interesting Romanian literature of exile flourished in Basarabia, at present The Republic of Moldavia, as well as in Bucovina, at present a territory in Ukraine, in the South of the Danube river and in other neighbouring countries of Romania. On the other hand, important Romanian cultural schools or individual personalities lived abroad and they represented, in fact, not only the *Diaspora*, but also the most brilliant exile in Romanian culture.

In France, a lot of personalities of Romanian exile gathered around the Radio Post called *The Free Europe and the Post Radio France International*. They had a remarkable anticommunist and antidictatorship activity and contributed to the liberation of the country, achieved by the revolution of December 1989. In the universe of culture, there are a lot of names to be mentioned as concerns the Romanian exile in France. There are journalists and literary critics, such as: Monica Lovinescu, Virgil Ierunca, who, together with Ioan Cusha, publishes the magazines *Ethos* and *Limits,* Victor Frunza, Alexandru Papilian, Mircea Iorgulescu, Virgil Tanase, Max Banush, Paul Barbaneagra. There are writers in the field of the theory of literature and in the history of literature, for example: Ion Negoitzescu, Emil Hurezeanu, Peter Neagoe and in the field of aesthetics: Pius Servien (Sherban Coculescu, by his Romanian name), representative in the field of mathematical poetics and informational aesthetics, with his studies upon the rhythm as the basis of the creation in works like: *Principes d' esthetique* (Principles of Aesthetics), *Science et poesie* (Science and Poetry), *Sagesse et poesie* (Wisdom and Poetry) etc. and Matila C. Ghyka, who considers the relation between science and art as seen by Pytagora the basis for the modern aesthetics and wrote: *Les rythmes* (The rythms), *Le nombre d'or* (The Golden Number), *The Geometry of Art and Life* etc. There are poets like: Dumitru Tzepeneag and Ilie Constantin, writers in prose like: Petru Dumitriu, Virgil Gheorghiu, who wrote *The Hour 25*, subject of a movie with Anthony Quinn in the leading role, Paul Goma, who expressed by the means of the prose in the novel *Ostinato* the tragic experience of the prison, the political and inner tensions as parts of exile, then Bujor Nedelcovici, who dealt with the tragic condition of the man who was confronting a foreign space, making efforts to communicate in a foreign world, becoming the tamer of the dogs in a western city and becoming more and more isolated till he lost his speech, in the novel called *The Tamer of the Wolfs*. As concerns the theatre, Matei Vishniec and the famous Eugène Ionesco are to be mentioned. Eugène Ionesco became a classic, writing in French language *The Chairs, The Bald Singer* and *The Rhinoceros,* the last play being a metaphor of the fascist movement, emphasizing the fall from the human personality to the rhinocerous condition. In the field of essay, Emil Cioran is an important writer. He became one of the stylists of French language. His poor life in Paris, but moreover his existentialist philosophy as brought into view by his works are interesting to learn about. *La tentation d'exister* (The temptation to live), *Le mauvais Demiurg* (The bad Demiurg), *L'inconvenient d-être né* (The Inconvenience of being Born) etc. are some of the titles. He always felt himself exiled in this world. Last, but not least, is Mircea Eliade in the field of the history of religions.

In Germany, Horia Stamatu is a poet and an essay writer, Nicolae Balota and Marian Popa create in the field of the theory of literature and literary criticism, Virgil Mocanu and Viorel Roman - in the field of philosophy, aesthetics and the theory of politics, Cicerone Poghirc, who lives in Paris, but taught in Bochum University, is an outstanding linguist, and Eugen Cosheriu received recognition from universities all over the world for his works and activity in the field of linguistics and romance studies.

In Spain, the most important personalities of Romanian exile are Vintila Horia and George Uscatescu, the head of the Department of Aesthetics and Philosophy of Culture for many years at the University of Madrid and the director of the magazine *Fate*.

In Italy, we would like to mention Mihai Vulcanescu, Angelo Moretta (Dan Petrashincu, by his Romanian name), Iosif Constantin Dragan, who publishes in Rome the magazine called *We, the Thracians* and, of course, Ioan Petru Culianu, famous philosopher and disciple of Mircea Eliade, writing a book with the name of *Eliade* as title. He published a lot of books, among which one of the most important is *The Dualistic Gnosis of the Occident*.

In England, lived Michael Titus and Petre Tzutzea, one of the greatest philosophers of Romania, who preferred, like Socrates, the oral form of expressing his knowledge.

In Sweden, there is the poet John Moish, in Rusia the novelist Ion Drutza, in Canada the drama and essay writer George Astalosh and in Hawaii lived the poet Shtefan Baciu, who wrote studies about the Brazillian literature as well and became a citizen of honour at the city of

Rio de Janeiro. The Romanian writers in Israel published an anthology of their works in 1971.

In the USA, Virgil Nemoianu is a remarkable writer in the field of theory of literature, for example, his book *The Taming of Romanticism,* in which he distinguishes between High Romanticism and the Biedermayer Romanticism as the two major forms of the cultural movement. Romanian exile is also represented by Dorin Tudoran, Petre Popescu, Mihai Botez, Dan Deshliu, Maria Manoliu Manea, Matei Calinescu and Norman Manea who received the prize of the Foundation MacArthur for his short-stories and novels. In the USA is the school of Mircea Eliade, teacher of history of religion in Chicago University, where the department headed by Wendy Doniger O'Flaherty bears forever the name of the Romanian savant after his death in 1986.

We chose for the first part of the title of our paper the name of a famous novel written by Vintila Horia in French language *Dieu est né en exile* (God was born in Exile). The author received the Goncourt prize for literature as an appreciation of his novel. It was composed on the occasion of the celebration of two thousand years from the birth of the Latin poet Ovidius. The book treats the story of an exile in the manner of a diary. Being in love with the daughter of the Emperor Augustus of Rome, Ovidius was exiled at Tomis in ancient Romania. Exiled because of love. He lived eight years here, each year being the title of a chapter of the book. The novel began with the Getic winter and ended in the same, in a cyclic structure. The winter season, with its cold, was the symbol of exile. But one day Ovidius discovers, through an initiation trip, the religion of the supreme God Zalmoxis, of the people from the Carpathian mountains. At old age his love turned to love for God, to spiritual love. His loneliness, his exile had then a deep meaning and the pain was washed away.

We intended to prove that for Romanian culture "God was born in Exile" and even today if political exile seems to be over, there still is a strong economic cause among others which may produce cases of exile. In order to outline the importance of exile we chose one special example of one of the greatest Romanian personalities and a universal spirit as well, Mircea Eliade.

Mircea Eliade (1907-1986) was a savant in comparative religion. He wrote many scientific studies and books in French, English, Romanian and other languages, short-stories and novels, diary and travel memorials and articles. He was the editor in chief of *Encyclopedia of Religion*, in 16 volumes, published by MacMillan Publishing-House, New York, 1987. He taught History of Religion at École des Hautes Études in Paris and at Chicago University. He studied Sanskrit, Bengali and Indian

Philosophy, especially the theory of yoga, with Surendranath Dasgupta in the University of Calcutta and practical yoga with Swami Shivananda in an *ashram* in Rishikesh and lived in India during the period 1928-1931. In his talks with Claude-Henri Rocquet, Eliade confessed that India taught him three major lessons: 1) the discovery of the philosophy of religion, 2) the interest in the primitive and archaic cultures; 3) the cosmic religion. We could add the main concept used by him, *coincidentia oppositorum* (the coincidence of the oppositions), existent in the concept *ekatā* (unity), the essence of Indian spirituality. Mircea Eliade is well-known for the travel memorial called *Indian* and especially for his novel *Maitreyi* (La nuit bengali), although he wished that he would not be read only as the author of this love story. Fascinated by *Rinascimento* (Italian Renaissance) and the personality of Pico della Mirandola, he went to study in Rome. While in Rome, he fell in love with Indian culture and published many books about India, out of which the four on Yoga, including his doctoral thesis *Yoga. Essai sur les origines de la mysthique indienne* (Yoga. Essay on the Origins of Indian Mystics), were outstanding and earned him recognition as a specialist in the theory of Yoga. He worked in Romanian Embassies in London and Lisbon, where he wrote the study *Os Romenos, Latinos do Oriente* (Romanians, Latins of Orient), translated from French by Eugenio Navarro.

When Communism took its roots in Romania, he protested and decided to emigrate. He lived all his life ever since in exile, with the wish unfulfilled that one day maybe he will return home. But in the socialist Romania his name was on the black list, like other Romanians from abroad, all of them being considered by the leaders of the Communist Party as traitors and sentenced to life imprisonment in their absence. At first Eliade lived in Paris, then in Chicago. His life was a clear expression of the pain in exile.

In his works, exile was not so obvious, yet we may find the inner exile. The exterior and the interior exile existed both in the life and creations of the Romanian historian of religions.

Mircea Eliade taught liberation of man from the terror of History and the abolition of Time. The ideal for the man was the transcendence of the human condition in order to be free and immortal. This vision could be related to Indian spirituality, the concepts of *mokṣa* and *nirvāṇa*. In his book *Images et symboles. Essai sur le symbolisme magico-religieux* (Images and Symbols. Essay on the magico-religious Symbology), Eliade made the distinction between the profane time, which was transient, dynamic, historical and linear; and the sacred time, which meant the moment equal to eternity, it was static, mythical and cyclic. Anicius

Boetius uses the concepts *nunc fluens* (the moment which flows) and *nunc stans* (the moment which stays). Eliade spoke about the terror of History and Time. There was an exile of the human being in front of the profane time, of the fear of death. The solution proposed is "*la sortie due Temps*" (the exit from Time), the profane one and to rediscover, through true knowledge, the sacred character of Time, the cosmic and reversible Time. "*Le Temps peutêtre maîtrise*" (Time can be ruled), said Eliade in the book *Aspects du mythe* (Aspects of Myth). He suggested the trip towards the origin for the recuperation of the sacred Time. This kind of practices can be found in Yoga and Buddhism. The aim was "*guèrir l'homme de la douleur de l'existence dans le Temps*" (to cure human beings from the pain of existence inside the Time) and to get free from *saṁsāra*, to liberate. The cure from Time signified the cure from death, from bad in general. It was a step beyond the time, a taste of immortality. The method was called *retour en arrière* (return backwards) and comprised a spiritual trip to the origins, the recuperation of the sacred, the reconstruction of the supreme unity separated into a multiplicity of forms. On the other hand, *Ie mythe de I'éternel retour* (The Myth of eternal Return), part of a title of another book, had a negative value, meaning the return to the wordly existence, the passing from a life to another, from a condition to another, tied up in *saṁsāra* (the eternal cycle of life and death). In the book *Le Sacré et le Profane* (The Sacred and the Profane), Mircea Eliade praised the idea of the fly, present also in the legend of Master Manole from the ballad *Argesh Monastery*, a masterpiece of Romanian folk literature and in Eminescu's poem *Luceafarul* (Bright-Star). The fly represented a way to exile as well as to freedom. Extatic or enstatic, the fly was to climb to the infinity of space. It was the abolition of relativity, as the writer emphasized in the book *Mythes, rêves et mystères* (Myths, Dreams and Mysteries). The transcendence of human condition does not mean the entrance into a superhuman condition, into a divine condition, but freedom itself. Later on, Eliade suggested the breaking of the top of the roof, the mark of an inner exile, as a symbol of liberty. His last book has this symbolic title: *Briser le toit de la maison. La creativité et ses symboles* (To break the Roof of the House. Creativity and its Symbols). It was about the transcendence of the limits towards liberation and the Absolute. The historian of religions referred to the yogic-tantric practices and believed that, at the moment of death, the human soul leaves the body through *brahmarāndhra* (the top of the head).

Mircea Eliade, exiled from communism, exiled from contemporary profane world, dedicated all his life for the quest and the recuperation of the Sacred. He revealed it to us. Not by the pride of the philosopher, but by the gentleness of Wisdom. The motto of his work and life could be the following phrase, from an interview: *"Si Dieu n'existe pas, tout est cendre..."* (If God does not exist, everything is ashes..) *Asato mā sad gamaya. Tāmāso mā jyotir gamaya. Mṛtyor mā amṛtam gamaya (Bṛhadāranyāka Upaniṣad* I, 3, 28) - Lead me from the Nonbeing to the Being. From Darkness to Light. From Death to Immortality.

BIBLIOGRAPHY

Douglas Allen - *Structure and Creativity in Religion. Hermeneutics in Mircea Eliade's Phenomenology and New Directions,* Monton Publishers, The Hague-Paris-New York, 1978

N.N. Bhattacharya - *History of the Tantric Religion,* Manohar Publications, New Delhi, 1982

Madeleine Biardeau - *L'hindouisme. Anthropologie d'une civilisation,* Flammarion, Paris, 1981

G. Calinescu - *Istoria literaturii romane de la origini pana in prezent,* Editura Minerva, Bucureshti, 1982

Ananda K. Coomaraswamy - *Hindousime et bouddhisme,* translated from English by René Allar and Pierre Ponsoye, Gallimard, Paris, 1949

Surendranath Dasgupta - *A History of Indian Philosophy,* Motilal Banarsidass, New Delhi, 1988, vol. I-IV

Mircea Eliade - *Le Sacré et le Profane,* Editions Gallimard, Paris, 1956

Mircea Eliade - *Aspects du mythe,* Editions Gallimard, Paris, 1963

Mircea Eliade - *Mythes, rêves et mystéres,* Editions Gallimard, Paris, 1957

Mircea Eliade - *Le mythe de l'éternel retour. Archetypes et répetition,* Editions Gallimard, Paris, 1949, II-nd edition

Mircea Eliade - *Images et symboles. Essais sur le symbolisme magico-religieux,* Editions Gallimard, Paris, 1952

Mircea Eliade - *Briser le toit de la maison. La creativité et ses symboles,* Editions Gallimard, Paris, 1986

Mircea Eliade - *Encyclopedia of Religion,* MacMillan, New York, 1987, vol. I-XVI

Jean Haudry - *La religion cosmique des Indo-Européens,* Arché-Les Belles Letters, Milan-Paris, 1987

Ion ITU - *Primii noshtri poetzi,* Editura Orientul Latin, Brasov, 1994

Ion ITU - *Literatura romana pentru clasa a XII-a,* Editura Orientul Latin, Brasov, 1995

Mircea ITU - *Indianismul lui Eliade,* Editura Orientul Latin, Brasov, 1997

Carl Olson - *The Theology and Philosophy of Eliade,* MacMillan, London, 1992

Cicerone Poghirc - *Philologica et linguistica,* Studienverlag Dr. N. Brockmeyer, Bochum, 1989

S. Radhakrishnan - *Indian Philosophy,* Motilal Banarsidass, New Delhi,

1930, vol. I-II

Louis Renou - *L'Hindouisme,* Presses Universitaires de France, Paris, 1979

MacLinscott Ricketts - *Mircea Eliade. The Romanian Roots, 1907-1945,* Columbia University Press, New York, 1988, vol. 1

Roberto Scagno - *Libertà e terrore della storia: genesi e significato dell' antiistoricismo di Mircea Eliade,* Torino, 1982

Rabindranath Tagore - *The Religion of Man,* Harper Collins Publishers, New Delhi, 1993

Jean Varenne - *Aux sources du Yoga,* Editions Jacquelinc Renad, Paris, 1989

Swami Vivekananda - *The Complete Works of Swami Vivekananda,* Motilal Banarsidass, New Delhi, 1937, vol. I-III

Heinrich Zimmer - *Maya, der indische Mythos,* Stuttgart, 1936

PRATIBHA BHATTACHARYA

Exile Blossomed—The Case of Yiddish Literature

The word 'exile' in the dictionary means banishment, expulsion from one's own country, long absence abroad, permanently living away from one's home or country. My paper, explores the case of a community which has been in exile for several centuries and as second class citizens have served the countries of their domicile faithfully, but almost always have been turned away empty. Yet by their sheer determination and perseverance they have nurtured this exile into an intellectual and linguistic paradise. Today while touching upon their pain briefly, let us turn to their achievement. I use the singular form 'achievement' because all their efforts were united in keeping themselves with all their gifts alive. They, among other things, created a new language which move within its fabric all the West European language strains, made for, by and of them. They are the Jews and the language is Yiddish.

In order to arrive at Yiddish we have to necessarily go back a little historically and briefly touch upon the Jewish history of Europe because the history of Yiddish is also the history of the Jewish people. The earliest Jewish settlement in Europe was in Italy, going back to the second century B.C. Pompey's conquest of Jerusalem in 63 B.C. brought some more Jewish groups to Italy. From the humble beginnings of slavery they soon became free Roman citizens. They were mostly traders and there was no active Jew-baiting although the intellectual Romans regarded them with contempt. The strict interactional code and the monotheistic faith of the Jews segregated them as outlandish and clannish people. However the Jews and the non-Jews shared an amicable relationship. With the advent of Christianity to Europe paradoxically began the saga of Jewish persecution, paradoxically because Christ had died for the promotion of love between people. The destruction of the second temple in Jerusalem in 70 A.D. made the community draw further inwards. All along this period the Jews had spoken Greek and

Latin but their mother tongues Hebrew and Aramaic were not and had not been allowed to be forgotten. The Jewish life which had been built around the sacred word of God through the Torah, spanning the Old Testament which covered all areas and aspects of human existence in the form of Laws, was guarded, followed and taught assiduously, and the languages were maintained and protected zealously. From fifth century onwards a more intense Jewish spirit and sentiment developed in the Italian Jewish community. The European Jewish people seemed to be mentally suspended between Palestine on the one hand and their settlements in Africa and Europe on the other. The development of Talmud studies initiated by Al Fasi in Spain and the homilectical material compiled by Nathan the Sicilian in Rome and the Talmud commentary known as 'Rashi' in northern France are some examples which witness the inner turmoil of the exile, guarding their scriptures and themselves against their assimilation in the larger society, a threat which they have always taken seriously. Marx (1945) mentions a Jewish community in Cologne at least a century before the onslaught of the Germanic people on Central Europe. He calls it an organized community with its roots going back to the very foundation of the city administration. After Clovis, the first Christian king of the Franks (481-511) the security provided by him to the Jews was shattered and from 535 A.D. Jewish persecution began in earnest in France and Gaul.

After the treaty of Verdun (845) the German nation separated from the Frankish empire. By this time there were Jewish settlements along both banks of the Rhine and along the Upper Danube, the Upper Elbe in Bohemia, in Bavaria, Austria. The post-Byzantium Jews had also largely settled in cities like Cologne, Augsburg, Metz, Worms, Merseburg, Magdeburg, Speyer etc. By this time they had been forbidden possession or land (ninth and tenth century) and had to fall back totally on commerce. Their intellectual life during this period is highlighted by the commentary on the Babylonian Talmud in which not only did Aramaic find Hebrew expression but also vernacular French—the process of assimilating a European vernacular in Hebrew and Aramaic had already begun. With the beginning of the Crusades came the decree of Pope Urban II (1095) giving the Jews the 'either-or' choice. The French Jews fled to the Rhine area. Pillaging of Jewish psyche went on well into the twelfth century. In the years 1348-49 the Jews were enclosed in separate quarters, the gates of which were locked each night. Here is where the negative meaning of the world 'Ghetto' begins, the inner exile comes to join the outer.

The majority of Jewish groups almost from all the countries of their West European domicile gathered together in an area which they called 'Loter'. This area was situated in Northern Germany and Mainz, Worms,

Cologne, Regensburg, Speyer were some of its cities where, we have already seen, the Jewish roots were really old. There are even special Jewish streets mentioned in the city records. Loter is the birth place of Yiddish. I have a theory, that more the persecution, more rigid the monolingual and mono-religious structure of the majority society, the more the minority withdraws and turns 'inwards'. The Jewish community at this temporal and historical juncture turned 'inwards' and created Yiddish as a passive but a very powerful protest against the persecution of the majority. The Jews had their unique philosophy, their scriptural solidarity—I do not use the word 'religious' because religion for them was a way of life and not an 'ism' at all. They also had their inherited languages which had crystallized and strengthened their ethnic identity. Reaction to persecution was geared towards underlining their Jewishness. Landmann (1922) feels that their forced isolation helped the Jews to emerge stronger as a community and Hebrew and Aramaic dominated the other 'functional' languages imbibed by them. Their inherited languages influenced their social and intellectual life in its entirety including their linguistic expression. But then Landmann speaks about how the inherited languages affected their German linguistic expression and there is much more to Yiddish than merely that. Yiddish encompasses not only the lexical or the phonetic world of the people but also their value world. Because of this intricacy that it poses, we need to borrow a definition for it. Herder calls a language the expressive vehicle of the national soul. Wisse (1985) says about the Yiddish language'... in its distinctiveness it is comparable to the vernaculars of the European nations'. (31)

The most detailed and indeed the most forceful work done of the Yiddish language is by Max Weinreich (1969) *The History of Yiddish Language*. He goes into the details of the formation of the language and yet does not fail to argue that it was not just a language but also the cry of aspiration of a tortured people, a mark of their Jewishness. In fact he emphatically maintains, that had the Jews not come to the Rhine valley as a part of the segregation policy and the second exile born out of extra-linguistic reasons, there would have been no Ashkenazi Jewry and no Yiddish language. Born in alienation, it signified 'Yiddishe verter un Yiddishe Vertn' (Jewish words as well as Jewish values). It was already conceived of by the time the Jewish groups had begun to migrate to Loter, evidenced from certain glosses going back to ca. 1100 found in the Rashi commentary. Because of our inability to ascertain when exactly it 'left' the other languages, one has to accept it as being a very gradual process. For Weinreich, Yiddish is not just recasting German in the Jewish manner but while speaking German, drawing from the indigenous sources of the community. He emphasizes the fusion character of Yiddish throughout his work highlighting the expression 'fusion' as against 'mixture' to describe the way in which various sources consolidated into this new language. He while refining and describing the vocabulary is arguing on behalf of Yiddish to be accepted as a cultural document underlining the 'national Existence' of the Jewish people. The organic term 'fusion' presupposes the absorptive as well as the creative capacities of the Jews. He rejects outright any aspersion of it being a 'piebald mix' or a 'sackful of borrowings' as he calls it. He explains his stand thus: Ashkenazi Jewishness (expressed in Yiddish) is NOT general German life plus a number of specific Jewish supplementary traits but a distinct sphere of life, a culture system (28). He characterizes the language as 'Derekh haShas' (derekh=way, Shas= a popular synonym for the Talmud which is the logic and philosophy of the Torah=way of Life). Though at first glance this term may appear to be linked with religion, Weinreich makes it very clear, that the concept of religion per se, i.e. 'Judaism' , is a comparatively recent concept, a product of the era of Enlightenment, when the sacred and the secular were drawn apart. His coinage of the world 'Derekh haShas' then assumes the existence of a sphere beyond the boundaries of religion. Wisse (1985) describes Yiddish very succinctly and beautifully as '...the rich distillation of centuries of growth.'

Weinreich traces four main components of this fusion characterizing Yiddish- i) the Hebraic-Aramaic element which he calls the Loshna - Koydesh ii) the Loez originating from Latin and manifest in Romance languages (Ladino[1] now rarely spoken, was a Jewish fusion language, a strain of Yiddish) iii) the Germanic iv) the Slavonic. The Slavonic was the last element to fuse with Yiddish. The original creation of Yiddish situated in Northern Germany is referred to as Ashkenaz I. When Yiddish migrated eastwards around the late fourteenth/fifteenth centuries, it absorbed the Slavonic element establishing the strong foundation of Ashkenaz II. Weinreich calls these four components as 'stock languages' because they provided the 'raw material' for the fusion character he feels. Thus Yiddish was definitely a product of linguistic pluralism, they had not shifted their linguistic loyalties to the majority community and for them language, ethnicity and culture were inseparable. As such when we consider Yiddish, we must look at it as the silent protest of a people in exile in its total sense, we have to take cognizance of the social, the cultural, the philosophical, the psychological and the ethnic aspects of the Jewish existence, their community through the ages.

Even today, with a nation of their own and no more needing to be exiles and second class citizens[2] they have apparently not forgotten the place of Yiddish in their lives. Dr. Hagar Salamon of the Hebrew University Jerusalem says, that even today the extra-religious people of Israel speak in Yiddish and the Jewish community of New York speaks three languages:

(a) English as a functional language.
(b) Hebrew as a religious/ritualistic language.
(c) Yiddish as the language of the heart, spoken at home and with friends and relatives.

II

Modern Yiddish developed steadily from mid nineteenth century or in fact from the time of European Enlightenment the Jews had made conscious efforts to free themselves and Yiddish from its multiple nuances and had tried to make Yiddish an insignia of their cultural autonomy alone. They were proud of their achievement of producing a good secular literature which could compete with any of the European vernaculars. Modern Yiddish had been a part of the process of Jewish modernization. The secular European culture had attracted the Yiddish writes to such an extent, that they had wanted to reject their own indigenous literature and intellectual tradition for being too drab and insular.

It had generally been a period of great confusion. From the turn of the century the ugly and frightening tread of the marching boots of Fascism could already be heard. The largest Jewry in the world the Ashkenaz II enamoured by secularism and modernism had turned to their new 'friends' — the Communist International who in turn had asked them to assimilate the Jewish International with them to avoid Pogroms. This was a cruel blow. Glatstein, one of the founding editors of *Inzikh* and the writer of *Yidishitaytshn* opposed this suggestion, opining that a people should be able to demand the right to live without pogroms and remain themselves, self dissolution of a people should not be the price they would have to pay for survival. That those very people who had vowed to fight for the rights of the downtrodden and the oppressed should demand the price of their identity was blood— money indeed. The very idea was overwhelming. The Jews had once more become political exiles. The result was *Yidishtaytshn*. (1921)

The dream and tryst of the Jews with Enlightenment and modernism, promising equality to all came very abruptly to an end, when men of knowledge, culture and intellect like Knut Hamsun and Gerhart Hauptmann, who had been greatly admired, displayed indulgence towards Fascistic principles. The rejection and betrayal of Yiddish intelligentsia hit them both socially and intellectually, sending them to another exile. Writers like Leivick and Sholem Asch are some of the stalwarts of this period of disillusionment with their works like *Abelard un Heloise* (1936) and *Der man fun nasaret* (1936). These works turn 'inwards', away from all worldly considerations, finding spirituality as a refuge from the bald and ugly face of reality. Abelard and Heloise seek a spiritual union! *Der man fun nasaret* brings in Jesus to express the extent of human pain and makes Him identify with the East European Jews. Jesus stands for the Jews as a nation being purified through adversity. The traditional European Jew seems in his work to embody the experience of Jesus in His poverty, turning the other cheek, giving good for evil. Wisse (1993) says:

> Asch was... inspired by the historical sweep of the subject and by the challenge to his imagination of the most famous and universalised instance of Jewish Martyrdom. (91)

Many Jewish families because of understanding secularism as anti-religious and godlessness had suffered turbulant times. The pendulam had entirely veered away from God's word. God, who had been alive for the older generation, was lost from the world of the younger people, their road backwards into the Eternal Time which had been the mainstay of the older people, an escape, a promise, a solace from the bitterness and ugliness of day to day life, was closed to the Enlightened, the Messaiah whom they sought in their desperation was a fraud. Left bereft and hopeless because of godlessness had pushed them into a spiritual exile and whatever they sought solace in turned to ashes. This feeling is beautifully projected by the brothers Singer,- Israel Joshua and Isaac Bashevis, through their works '*Di brider ashkenazi*' and '*der sotn in Goray*'. The first book talks about the rapid growth of the city of Lodz, the unhealthy competition between bothers. Every person is jinxed, killed or betrayed, like the two brother or the honest socialist thrown out of his job by the Bolshevik militia....It is the story of betrayal at the hands of progress, mass-exodus of threatened people from Europe, the dimmed and depressing lives of the once enthusiastic and positive youngsters, a story of spiritual exile. The second book talks about the 'Massaiahzation' of Shabtai Zvi, the fraud, the Satan who arrives in the little Jewish Polish town of Goray. The whole narration when read against the back drop of the socio-political milieu of that time is heavily pregnant with fearful and threatening reality, rocked between surges of hope and anger, fear and despair. The prospect of salvation for the lost and godless people enmeshed in the false dream of secular fredom at all levels, is lost forever. Looking at the literary content of this period the words 'our sweetest songs are those that tell of saddest thoughts' seem to be very true.

I would like to quote two small references, one from *Yidishtaytshn* and the other from *Abelard un Heloise*.

The translations are from Wisse (1993):

(a) Who can bear
The wail of a young orphan?
Or the tears of a needy widow?
Who can endure
the loneliness-like a stone's—
of a woman who is barren?
Or the shame of an ugly wife
Whom a husband has deserted?
Worst of all is the dumb misery
of a beaten horse.
The whip crackles
on the pelt.
The heavy head bends lower
without reproach; without opposition
or resistance.
Such anguish should come before God's majesty
and there make its plaint.'
"Master!
Master of the Universe-
Why?"
Yosl Loksh cannot bear it.
He would gladly get in the shafts.
Giddy-up, Giddy-Up
he would run, year after year,
taking those blows-
like bracing lashes, stinging basoms-
like
an atonement.

ii) I am not Heloise of once upon a time.
Neither the maiden nor the woman
of tender velvet body.
I am the equal partner of your pain....
Let the light we cast on the monastery walls and on
the walls beyond
be not the glow of our bodies,
but the angry glare of chains; steel rings
and bony fists that pound
against the cruel forehead of the world.

NOTES

1. Ladino is the form of Yiddish created by the Spanish Jews of the Sephardic stock, which later merged with the Yiddish created in Loter.

2. There is an argument offered by people that the Jews were always the money bags as banks, business houses were owned by them. Money could control anti-semetism upto an extent but being a second class citizen/ remaining a second class-citizen has nothing to do with it.

BIBLIOGRAPHY

Asch Sholem (1939)
Der man fun nasaret.
(Ref. Ruth Wisse, 1993)
The Nazarene (Eng. Transl. M. Samuel) NY. 1939
Printed again in Yiddish, NY. 1943)
Glatstein Jakob (Jankev glatshteyn) (1937)
Yidishtaytshn
New York:
The poem quoted was scored by H. Kon as
Yosl Loksh fun Khelem, 1944, NY.
The work was transl. "*Rabbi Yussel Luksh of Chelm* by N. Halper in '*A Treasury of Yiddish Poetry*" (Ed) I. Howe & E. Greenberg.
New York/Chicago/San Francisco, 1969.
pp. 246-256.
Leivick H. (1936)
Abelard un heloise.
pp. I-93.
Warsaw
Marx Margolis and Alexander Marx (1945)
A history of the Jewish people.
Philadelphia: The Jewish Publication Society of America.
Singer Israel Joshua (1936)
Di brider ashkenazi.
(Transl. Eng. M. Samuel, 1936, NY.)
Warsaw:
Singer Isaac Bashevis (1935)
Der sotn in Gray—A mayse fun fartsaytns.
(Foreword by Aaron Zeitlin)
Singer Isaac Bashevis---
Warsaw
Transl. Eng. M. Samuel, 1936, NY.)
Weinreich Max (1969)
History of the Yiddish Language.
(Tranl. Schlomo Noble)
Chicago/London: The University of Chicago Press.
Wisse Ruth R. (1985)

The Politics of Yiddish.
In Commentary, The American Jewish Committee, Vol. 80, No. I, pp. 29-35.
-------------- (1993)
Studies in Jewish Culture in honour of Chone Shmeruk.
(Ed) Israel Bartel, Ezra Mendelsohn, Chava Turnianski, Jerusalem: The Zalman Shazar Center for Jewish Study, pp. 83-103.

VIJAYA VENKATARAMAN

Exile as Recuperation of the Past in Augusto Roa Bastos' *El Fiscal*

What is utopia? The perfect place? It's not that. More than anything else, for me, exile is utopia. There is no such place. Exile, exodus, a space suspended in time, between two times. We have the memories of the country that have remained with us and then we imagine how it will be when we return. This dead time, between the past and the future, is utopia for me. Then: exile is utopia.

Ricardo Piglia in *Respiración Artificial*

Defining exile as utopia, or a space suspended in time, between two times, is the only manner in which the protagonist of Ricardo Piglia's novel, Marcelo Maggi, feels capable of coping with the problem of exile. He longs to reconstruct the history, not of the past but of the future as he dreams of writing a *relato* to be read a hundred years later. Though, paradoxically, even if he were to succeed in doing so, the reader of such a *relato* may not understand it for lack of sufficient co-ordinates. For Maggi, the present in exile is suspended time and only useful for projecting the past onto the future. This has been the project of many a contemporary Latin American writer—to understand and interpret the past in order to decipher the present and to use the present to understand the past and project the future. The exiled writer finds himself in an (un)enviable position, distant from his past and his present and only the future to look forward to.

Exile can be perceived as a double-edged phenomenon—a balance between the positive and negative aspects. On the one hand, it is an experience leading to self-marginalisation and self-pity, as feelings of nostalgia, anguish, pain of separation from friends, family and homeland, the exclusion or marginalisation in the adopted space predominate in the mind of the writer. It is perceived as a loss. On the contrary, feelings of nostalgia may be backgrounded and adaptation becomes possible and the new geography and history of the writer become a vehicle for understanding the self. Very often, it may help to review the past and the present from a distance in order to reconstruct the future. The feelings of an exile are clearly difficult to identify. While on the one hand, there is an attraction to the new situation and surroundings of the adopted country, at the same time there is also a feeling of suspicion and rejection, mainly propelled by feelings of loyalty to one's homeland and the fear of betraying it. This double movement of attraction and rejection and the accompanying tension can be said to configure all exile.

In the case of Latin America, one can say that the phenomenon of exile is an extremely important one in the 20th century, given that a large number of writers and artists have spent a greater part of their lives outside their countries, fleeing from situations of terror, violence or torture under repressive regimes. The increasing brutality and violence in the society they live in, where 'disappearances' are as commonplace as death, has been one of the main reasons for exile. Culture had become the target of the military dictatorships as was witnessed in Argentina during the "Guerra sucia" (dirty war)[1]. Many writers were forced to go to other countries for overtly or covertly opposing these repressive and undemocratic regimes. Exile in Latin America is not mainly a 20th century phenomenon, as it was fairly common even in the 19th century. But what differentiates 20th century exile from that of the earlier century is what Julio Cortázar describes as "voyage en Europe". He says:

> What we perceive today as a constraint was then a voluntary and happy decision - the mirage of Europe as the catalyst of forces and of talents not yet born. That voyage of a Chilean or Argentine to Paris, Rome or London was a voyage of initiation, an impetus without substitute, access to the Holy Grail of Western Knowledge.[2]

The voyage to Europe in the 19th century was to gain access to knowledge, or to gain consciousness, as Terry Cochran puts it, deriving from a colonised mentality whereas the present day voyage is not a choice but an imperative. Cortázar describes this imperative to exile as a constraint and a violence inflicted upon oneself: "The notion of exile, for me at least, carries with it a constraint and very often a violence." One has no choice but to react and the way in which one reacts is determined by the very conception of exile, thus confirming the loss that it implies. Therefore, exile is seen as:

> . . . a denial, a derogation, a mutilation against which one reacts. . . . One almost always departs from the negative (...), making use of the poor trampoline of denial, one tries to leap forward and recuperate what has been lost.[3]

This recuperation of what has been lost is important in that it does not signify an idealisation of the past in the present, but helps in changing the negative aspects of exile into positive ones by refusing to conceive exile as a loss and by facing this situation in a way that the adversary could not possibly imagine. As Cortázar puts it: "Those who exile intellectuals believe this act to be a positive one because it leads to the elimination of an adversary. But what if those who are exiled also consider their exile as positive?"[4] Exile is not simply the distance separating one from a cultural, linguistic and geographic origin. It signifies the struggle of the writer to transform the negative into the positive. The act of writing, then, becomes an act of rebellion and is considered a metaphor of exile by many writers and critics.[5] Very often, the writer (as in the case of Roa Bastos) delves into history, reaffirming and reasserting the loss of history, but at the same time recuperating this loss.

In this essay, we wish to examine the case of the Paraguayan writer, Augusto Roa Bastos and the treatment of exile and specifically, the use of his exiled condition to recuperate the loss of history and, thus the use of history in his novel *El Fiscal*. Many of the dictatorial regimes of the 19th century, which were the cause of many an exile, were hard to describe in clear terms, as the project of national liberation was closely linked to their agenda. In Paraguay, for instance, many historians believed Dr. Francia to be a benevolent dictator and at the same time he was also a hero of the indigenous people for several reasons. First of all, his policies of political and economic isolation for Paraguay helped to avoid military tensions with Argentina and Brazil. Paraguay had never had easy relations with either of these countries because of their expansionist policies. Secondly, Francia hated the Creole elite and in order to dispossess them, he carried out land reforms, and in some ways became the saviour of the underprivileged and landless indigenous people. He systematically attacked the Creole class in many ways. Roett and Sacks describe it so:

> He (Francia), smashed the network of social bonds that defined the peninsular Spaniards as a class by criminalizing marriages between Europeans, forcing them, in effect, to marry mestizos, Indians or mulattos. In the years after he became *El Supremo*, Francia arrested, exiled, jailed, or shot hundreds of Paraguay's Spanish and Creole elite.[6]

Very soon Francia usurped power and elected himself the "Perpetual Dictator" of Paraguay, thus becoming a cruel and tyrannical dictator, who controlled people by propagating fear. There was no freedom of expression or movement. He ruled from 1811 till his death in 1840 and during this period, paradoxically, there was relative progress and peace in Paraguay. To quote Roett and Sacks again:

In 1818, he closed Paraguay's borders to the contaminating influences of the outside worlds, allowing no one to enter or to leave without his permission. (...) Francia derived his power by crushing his elite opponents and by intimidating the Paraguayan masses. ... His rule was a period of personalist autocracy and intense social conservatism, not social transformation.[7]

Carlos Antonio López who ruled till 1862 succeeded Francia. He carried forward Francia's isolationist policies. He was succeeded by his son, Francisco Solano López, one of the most colourful characters in the history of Paraguay. He continued the same personalist legacy and almost pushed Paraguay to the brink of extinction with the War of the Triple Alliance. Solano López wanted to ally with Uruguay against their formidable neighbours, Argentina and Brazil. In 1864, Brazil decided to intervene in Uruguay to protect its interests. Using this opportunity, Solano López tried to create a third power by allying with Uruguay. But he failed tactically because he sent his troops through Argentina to attack Brazil. George Pendle describes the situation arising out of this tactical error thus:

The immediate result of this campaign was the formation in 1865 of a formidable anti-Paraguayan alliance: Argentina joined Brazil and its satellite Uruguay, in a solemn pact to destroy Solano López. Once more, Paraguay was trapped behind an iron curtain.[8]

The results of the Great War or the War of the Triple Alliance were disastrous for Paraguay in terms of its population and territory. It nearly lost the area of the Chaco to Argentina and a large part of its population in the war, which left it demographically, politically and economically decimated. The total male population of Paraguay after the war was 28,000, including children. This period saw a large-scale emigration of workers, especially to neighbouring countries on account of lack of resources in Paraguay. A period of political instability ensued after Solano López was killed in the war. The first part of the 20th century till the War of Chaco in 1932 was a seesaw between the liberals and the conservatives. Though this was not a period of prosperity, there was relative peace but both the liberals and the conservatives failed miserably in governing the country. The War of Chaco with Bolivia over a piece of land, thought to be rich in petroleum, was mismanaged by the liberals. The end of the Chaco War was to signify in some ways the beginning of a series of military dictatorships in Paraguay for more than half a century. This was also marked by the next wave of emigrations, which continued till the late 40s due to various reasons, primary among them the oppressive and dictatorial regimes.

Augusto Roa Bastos (1917), one of the foremost Paraguayan writers of the twentieth century, has lived in exile since 1947. This year could be described as the year of the great exodus[9] from Paraguay after the end of the civil war when Natalicio González - described by Roa Bastos as one of the biggest public thieves in the history of Paraguay - took over. Roa Bastos was ordered to be captured dead or alive. His 'crime' was that he was the editor of the only independent daily in Asunción, *El País*. He took refuge in the house of the Cultural Attaché of Brazil and later went to Buenos Aires. The successive dictatorial regimes in Paraguay ensured that he would never return. He lived in Argentina for almost thirty years, where he wrote the most part of his earlier works. In 1976 he moved to France fleeing from Argentina in the wake of the 'disappearances'. He joined as Professor of Guaraní and Latin American Literature in the University of Toulouse II, which became his home during the second phase of his exile.

The first phase of exile in Buenos Aires for Roa Bastos turned out to be an enriching and positive experience — as he himself concedes in an interview[10] — he tried his hand at several activities, from writing scripts for cinema and television to teaching and delivering lectures on literature in academic circles. He did not consider exile as a loss of identity or feel nostalgic because of his faith in the universal man and the solidarity he received from the people he came in contact with. As he says:

> I am interested in the universal man, which is the great lesson I owe to exile. I will never be able to complain about exile because it was a great school for me. [...] I systematically tried exterior and interior exile, and I always thought that the latter was true exile. In any case, amongst exiles there is a principle which I think is one of the most encouraging things I see, there is inextinguishable element in the people: solidarity. This has comforted me in moments of extreme depression. It is hard to be far away, but I have always had the people's solidarity, openly or subtly. People have what can be called human understanding and this, for me, is what has saved me in exile. Nostalgic exile does not exist [...][11]

The position of an exile, though vulnerable, is also a vantage point from which the writer can make his writing an act of opposition to oppressive regimes. According to Roa Bastos, interior exile is a manifestation under extreme conditions of political or social oppression, where one loses the ability to communicate. The inability to communicate could become so overpowering that one may lose oneself in such a situation. This is possibly what happened to Roa Bastos when he was not allowed to return to his country for several decades during the dictatorship of Alfred Stroessner. In 1982, he tried to visit Paraguay with his wife and daughter but he was violently expelled by the authorities and deported for 'harbouring Bolshevik ideas and trying to indoctrinate the youth'. He was further accused of being a communist and of visiting Cuba, which he never did. Augusto Roa Bastos was most affected by the Stroessner era (1954-89), which, despite coming after nearly a hundred years after Dr. Francia's rule, had many striking similarities with that period in Paraguay.

Many historians have described Paraguay as a geographically or physically and culturally exiled country because of its peculiar geographical location. Being one of the only two countries without a coast and therefore playing no significant role in international trade, it had to depend largely on friendly relations with its neighbours out of economic compulsions. The isolationist policies of dictators like Dr. Francia and Carlos López ensured that Paraguay remained 'exiled' economically, politically and culturally from the rest of Latin America. This so-called exile of Paraguay has parallels with the political, physical, cultural and linguistic exile suffered by Roa Bastos as argued by Brent Carbajal.[12]. Roa Bastos' native language was Guaraní and since the language did not have a script, he had to use Spanish to write. He consciously addressed the issue of writing in Guaraní not only as a rejection of the language of the coloniser but also as an expression of the indigenous people of his country. He found an answer to this question by attempting a fusion of Guaraní with Spanish, which found expression in the creation of "absent texts".[13] D W Foster refers to this linguistic dilemma faced by many a writer in post colonial times:

> Roa Bastos finds himself isolated, at least from the practical and editorial point of view, from the popular language of his people, guaraní, and resigned to the need to express himself in what is still considered in many parts of Latin America as the language of feudal oppression: Spanish.[14]

Political exile, in the case of Roa Bastos, is directly related to the physical and cultural alienation of his country. Although he does not present this from the point of view of a nostalgic romantic, it is certainly true that his forced exile from rural Paraguay to urban Buenos Aires gave him the opportunity to reflect upon aspects of Paraguayan history and culture and the role of the writer in society.

Roa Bastos is best known as a novelist — his major novels being *Hijo de Hombre* (1960), *Yo el Supremo* (1974), *Vigilia del Almirante* (1992) and *El Fiscal* (1993) which forms a trilogy on power and repression along with the first two novels. He also has several collections of short stories and poems written mainly during the earlier part of his exile in Buenos Aires. The dictatorship of Alfred Stroessner and his subsequent exile to France had such a deep impact on Roa Bastos that he did not publish anything for almost twenty years. The author himself destroyed an earlier version of *El Fiscal* as an immature fruit. He says:

> After almost twenty years of silence, the first version of this book was written during the last years of one of the longest and most ferocious dictatorships of Latin America. In 1989 the dictator was overthrown by an insurrection. The novel was out of place and had to be destroyed. The fruit was immature. ... The world had changed just as the author's world vision. ... In four months, from April to July, a totally different version emerged from these changes. [15]

He also felt that he had been too harsh in *El Fiscal* not so much on the dictatorial regime but on the people of Paraguay for having tolerated him. When he was suddenly faced with the possibility of the restoration of democracy in Paraguay he felt he owed it to his people to not publish 'such a demoralising work for the sake of the entire collectivity'[16], which was precisely negating what he was depicting in the novel.

In his first novel, *Hijo de Hombre* he depicts Paraguayan society and the struggle for freedom and justice in a society which constantly negates these values. In the novel, Roa Bastos tries to examine the reasons and the effect of the War of Chaco on Paraguay. It is divided into nine parts, which can be read as independent episodes or stories but for the fact that Miguel Vera is the common narrator through most parts. The first episode begins with a reference to the appearance of Hailey's comet in 1910 and the last episode ends with the end of the War of Chaco in 1935. Spanning almost a quarter of a century of Paraguayan history, the novel describes man's solidarity with his people in his struggles. Nowhere is present any autobiographical reference, either to Roa's participation in the War of Chaco or his subsequent exile in Buenos Aires, although as he says:

> Distance from my country imposed the theme of this novel, a theme that has hurt my sensibility in the long years of reflection on my land and its problems. Whenever I wanted to remember or recover the essential image of our country, I met with the desire of resistance, to persist at all costs, despite the misfortunes and vicissitudes which has been a prodigal part of our history.[17]

Roa Bastos uses the motif of crucification in the novel as another character, Gaspar de Mora, is shown to be the Christ figure, whose sacrifice redeems the people. This motif reappears in *El Fiscal*, which we shall see later.

In 1974, he completed *Yo el Supremo*, a novel dealing with the dictatorship of Dr. Gaspar Rodríguez de Francia. This novel reconstructs the history of Paraguay under Dr. Francia. The novel is not written but 'compiled' by a compiler, who uses a variety of archival documents—declarations, orders, promulgation and letters. As the writer puts it in the compiler's note: "This novel was first read and then written". The act of writing in *Yo el Supremo* becomes an act of rebellion and that of questioning official versions of history.

Roa Bastos' exile in Buenos Aires proved to be rather fruitful as he came into contact with Argentine intellectuals and writers, many of whom encouraged him to write. In the acknowledgements to his novel *Vigilia del Almirante*, he thanks some of his friends in Argentina who carefully preserved his initial notes and sketches of the novel for more than forty years and also those who saved his life and his writings. However, he does accept the fact that exile dried up his pen and imagination for seventeen years between *Yo el Supremo* and *Vigilia del Almirante*. As he says:

> The long exile or forced *trastierro* - despite the examples to the contrary - is not fertile or healthy for lesser ingenuities; losing one's language abroad tends to distort the life of a common human being, his world vision, his notion of history of a country, which - in the words of Luis Cernuda - 'he visualises according to his image'.[18]

Vigilia del Almirante was Roa Bastos' response to the polemics around the Fifth Centenary of the so-called Discovery and he participated in the discussion in the only way he considered fit in his capacity as a writer and a Latin American, belonging to 'two worlds' as he likes to call himself—by writing a novel on Columbus' voyage. He evokes the two visions of history which contradict and negate each other constantly and the novel has been defined as not only ahistorical but also anti-historical.

I now wish to examine some aspects of the novel *El Fiscal*, which relate to the condition of exile of Roa Bastos. As mentioned earlier, Roa Bastos' second exile was in France, where he taught Guaraní and Latin American Literature in the University of Toulouse-Le Mirail. Although the novel is a reflection on the Stroessner regime, the themes of exile and the impossibility of return are constantly present and highlighted throughout the novel. It may be mentioned that Roa Bastos tried to visit his country on several occasions but he was refused permission and on the one occasion that he was allowed to visit Paraguay to deliver some lectures, he was unceremoniously picked up and deported because of his allegedly inflammatory speeches against the government amongst university students. He could never return to Paraguay while Stroessner was in power. Maybe, this is what he refers to as 'internal exile' - a condition described as one in which one finds oneself incapable of communicating with his other countrymen.

The protagonist of the novel *El Fiscal* is Félix Moral, who lives in exile in Nevers in France with a Spanish exile Jimena. The protagonist's obsession with the pain and suffering of exile and the impossibility of return is symptomatic of Roa Bastos' exile. He constantly makes reference to his exile. He says:

> The obsession of every exiled person is to return. I cannot return with a face of a proscript. I have had to adopt a pseudonym and a pseudo body that would make my own one unrecognisable, I wouldn't say the real one, because that also does not exist. One can invent another way of life, but one cannot disguise oneself and remain the same. Now my name is Félix Moral, Associate Professor in the University of X.[19]
>
> Exile is the greatest destroyer of souls - wrote my grandfather Ezequiel Gaspar during the first days to comfort me. Any kind of exile, even that where one goes to buy cigarettes in the corner and never returns, as if he himself had disappeared into smoke. And political exile, even of those who do not do politics, like you, is the worst of them all...[20]

The narrator is Félix Moral — the inter-alia of the writer himself—and he reflects on the condition of exile, which is no longer isolated to any one part of the world. The whole world is a victim of exile. Félix Moral concedes that the only way to live 'well' is by not maintaining any contact with other exiled people from the country of origin. Exile, for Félix Moral, is both interior and exterior. He is in exile for political reasons and the only person with whom he is able to communicate is Jimena, for the simple reason that he finds her in a similar predicament as his. The novel is written in the form of a personal diary maintained by the protagonist, to be revealed only after his death. It takes the form of an epistolary addressed to Jimena who is responsible for saving his life. He repeatedly expresses his gratitude to Jimena and France for saving him from the depravities of an exiled life. As he writes:

> Exile, effectively, is the worst of the diseases that could inflict a human being. The contact with other afflicted only worsens it. It is not only the consumption of the body and spirit, it is the moral degradation that an individual can suffer to extreme limits and which lead him to madness, crime, mystical or political delirium and finally to physical or moral suicide. There comes a moment when the ill person stops suffering. He is reduced to a tranquil and satiated shadow...[21]

Jimena and France have helped in bringing him out of the deep depression and moral degradation he was going through and are responsible for bringing about a radical transformation in his physique and character.

Félix Moral gets an opportunity to visit Paraguay as a participant at the Congress of History, Culture and Society in Latin America in the XX Century, organised by the Dictator - or Tyrannosaurus as Moral calls him - of Paraguay. He takes upon himself the mission of doing away with the dictator and prepares an ingenuous plan to kill the dictator. Jimena tries to persuade him not to go, but he insists as his identity is recognisable only as Félix Moral - the exiled other. He would enter Paraguay as any foreigner with his "schizophrenic character". The plan is to kill the tyrannosaurus using a ring containing a poison, which would be injected when he would shake hands with the participants of the Congress. Jimena fears that he may be recognised, in which case, his life could be in danger but Moral brushes aside her fears as he sees in himself the inter-alia of the 'real' threat to the dictator. The plan does not succeed as Moral is recognised, imprisoned and tortured. He dies in prison and this time, Jimena is unable to save him despite her visit to Paraguay to rescue him. In the meantime, the dictator is overthrown by a military coup and he flees to Brazil. Jimena returns to Paris to publish the manuscript and Félix Moral dies in the Paraguayan jails.

The novel is in the form of a long oral narrative, an uninterrupted letter with only one addressee - Jimena - and the protagonist calls it his *Papeles póstumos* (Posthumous Papers). The people who would ultimately get around to reading it, he says, would always be voyeurs, furtive eavesdroppers into a private correspondence. He tries to write it with all the openness and frankness that Jimena deserves. The epistolary as a genre seems to be quite appropriate to the expression of exile as a utopia, thus described by Marcelo Maggi, the protagonist of *Respiración Artificial*:

> Why have I been able to discover that my utopian romance has to be an epistolary novel? Firstly, correspondence in itself is already a form of utopia. To write a letter is to send a message into the future; to talk from the present to an addressee who is not there, of whom we do not know how he is (in what mood, with whom) while we are writing to him and above all, later, when he reads us. Correspondence is the utopian form of conversation because the present is annulled and the future is the only possible space for dialogue.
>
> But, moreover there is a second reason. What is exile but a situation which forces us to substitute with written words the relation with our dear friends, who are far away, absent, spread out in different places and cities? And moreover, what relation can we maintain with a country we have lost, the country we have been forced to leave, what other presence is there of this absent place except the testimony of its existence which is brought to us by the letters (sporadic, elusive, trivial) which come with family news?[22]

So, as Maggi, Moral also sees in the epistolary the genre par excellence to deal with the theme of exile. The novel ends with a letter too, not Félix Moral's but Jimena's letter to Félix's mother in which she tells her of Félix's last visit to his country and sacrifice. His visit has a mission, which unfortunately fails and he is forced to concede defeat. In the process, he becomes the martyr.

Roa Bastos insists on the fictional character of the novel but the parallels between the author and his narrator in *El Fiscal* are so close that comparison is unavoidable. Most of the first part of the novel contains autobiographical elements, like his relationship to France and Jimena to whom he dedicates the book, his feelings in the second part of his exile, where he suffered from what he terms internal exile or "the inability to write". He seems to be thoroughly disgusted with his work as a Professor of Guaraní and Latin American Literature, as an extremely superficial activity for he does not have any contact with his country or his continent or what is being written there. What reaches him from there seems distant.

> I did not know anything of what was being written in Latin American countries, most of them submitted to dictatorships, persecutions and repression of all kinds. Its culture of resistance, fighting for survival, could do little for an art and literature that was only useful for spreading amongst children of well-to-do families. It did not have any immediate practical utility. It did not exist. I used to invent these books of contemporary writers which I was forced to read, but which I would probably never read or which would never be written. Some names, some books used to reach me. I did not know who they were. I never used to touch those books, which used to stink of interior exile, repressive asphyxia. [23]

I would like to consider now the treatment of history in *El Fiscal* and link it to the relationship between history and fiction in contemporary Latin American novel. The role of counter memory as a way of reconstructing the past is considered very important by many contemporary Latin American writers as the rewriting of history can be defined as 'counter-memory'. María Cristina Pons[24] describes the recent upsurge in historical novels in Latin America, denominated the New Historical Novel, as a critical and demystifying re-reading of the past through the rewriting of History. This rewriting, going beyond historical events, incorporates an explicit mistrust of historiographic discourse in the official versions of History. This is manifested in diverse manners: understanding, interpreting or reconstructing the past, filling in the blanks or silences of official history, defamiliarising the past as a rejection of official historiography and centring on marginal figures or episodes from History. In Latin America, writers and thinkers have always been conscious of the role of the narrative in recuperating lost traditions and history. As Andrés Bello puts it:

> But when the history of a country does not exist except in incomplete, sparse documents, in vague traditions, which have to be put together and judged, the narrative method becomes obligatory. Let the person who denies this cite one specific or general history which has not begun thus.[25]

Dorris Sommer[26] highlights the importance of filling in the gaps in historical knowledge, which the contemporary novelist does using the possibilities of intertextual play, absorption of a heterogeneous variety of languages and breaking purely historical or purely literary frameworks and opening the discursive field to all kinds of texts. History is shorn, thus, of its scientific aureole and subjected to invention. In this sense, new versions can be proposed when the concept of a single correct version is demolished. The classical historical novel consciously used historical data, but the post-modern novel involves history in an act of subversion and violation. *El Fiscal* does precisely this: by bringing to us the mediated past and its non-contemporary problems, it focuses on contemporary obsessions and conflicts in an oblique manner.

Although most of the novel is a reflection on the condition of exile and the life of two exiles, there is a brief incursion into the history of Paraguay and Félix Moral narrates the conditions and the reasons leading to the War of the Triple Alliance. Roa Bastos presents the historical events leading to the defeat of Paraguay in the War of the Triple Alliance. The War of the Triple Alliance and Solano López's role in it is reconstructed in the novel through *Cartas desde los Campos de Batalla del Paraguay*, the memoirs of Sir Francis Richard Burton, published towards the end of 1870. The translator of *Thousand and One Nights*, Sir Richard Burton describes in detail the holocaust of a "people who are going to disappear without leaving a trace". Roa Bastos wonders if Burton was recreating what he actually saw or simply putting in words the paintings of Cándido López. Burton was representing his country in Brazil and he had the opportunity of travelling extensively through Paraguay and knowing Solano and his Irish mistress Madame Elisa Lynch closely. Burton portrays Solano as a cruel tyrant, but whose motto in the war was to win or die. He aspired to be known as the "Napoleon of America". His close aide, the priest Maíz, helped him to get rid of his adversaries or anyone who dared to oppose him. Maiz was the one who played an important role in converting Solano into the "Paraguayan Christ". Burton justifies such a measure as he says:

In the wake of the tragedy facing the people— reasons the Counsellor— the people needed the man as a charismatic messiah, enveloped in the aureole of the immortality of religious faith.
(Ante la tragedia que estaba padeciendo el pueblo - razona el cónsul - este tenía necesidad de que su jefe militar se convirtiera en un Mesías carismático, envuelto en la aureola de inmortalidad de la fe religiosa.) (275).

The painter Cándido López who is supposed to have painted the most expressive paintings about the war is a metaphor of the Paraguayan people decimated by the effects of the war. Successively losing a part of his body as the war progresses, he continues to paint with whatever part that remains. The last painting by Cándido represents Solano López as the figure of Christ - the redeemer of the Paraguayan people. He is represented in the novel as the Christ figure who represents salvation for his people although Moral is the martyr. The dictator in his death becomes the redeemer of his people and his death also signifies the hope of the people in a new tomorrow free of bondage and tyranny. The actual dictator does not die, Moral loses his life, and Solano López becomes the redeemer of the people only in death.[27]

As is known, the war ended with the assassination of Solano López by the Brazilian troops in Cerró-Cora. The historians Roett and Sacks describe Solano López in the following manner:

Since the nationalist revival of the 1930s, López is officially Paraguay's greatest hero, a patriot who mobilised the nation to fight its enemies to the death. But others say that López was a tyrant who used nationalism to disguise his megalomania, a man who was willing to lead his country to death and destruction in his quest to become the "Napoleon of South America".[28]

The purpose of including this incursion into a particular moment in the history of Paraguay is explained within the novel as a means of understanding the present, although it is too late for Félix Moral. He confesses to Jimena or Morena that the profundity and complexity of these events unfold at a moment when he views them as a foreigner through the eyes of another foreigner (Richard Burton). Maybe, they are clearer from the outside as the exile's position allows him insights and an objectivity, which proximity blurs or confuses. The history of the past from the point of view of an outsider becomes a pretext to study the history of the present, also from an outsider's perspective.

In conclusion, we can say that Roa Bastos' exile, though long and arduous was extremely productive in many ways. Not only did he continue to write—which he felt was the only weapon he had to fight the repressive and dictatorial regimes—but he also stood beside his people. The interior exile which expressed itself as an inability to write was probably more painful than the earlier part of exile. Seventeen years of silence and the end of Alfred Stroessner's rule in Paraguay gave him added strength to come back with a renewed vigour, expressed in novels like *Vigilia del Almirante* and *El Fiscal*. Writing, for him therefore, becomes an act of subversion, defiance in the face of repression and of reliving the utopia that is the dead time between the past and the future.

NOTES

1. The war was dirty because the weapons were dirty just as the goals were dirty.
2. As quoted by Terry Cochran in the Foreword to Djelal Kadir: *Questing Fictions. Latin America's Family Romance*. University of Minnesota Press, Minneapolis, 1986, p. xiii.
3. Ibid. p. xiv.
4. Ibid. p. xiv-xv.
5. Cf. Augusto Roa Bastos: "Writing: A Metaphor of Exile" in John King: *Modern Latin American Fiction*.
   Also see Roberto González Echevarría: *The Voice of the Masters*.
   And James Whitlark: *Literature of Emigration and Exile*
6. Riordan Roett y Richard Scott Sacks: *Paraguay: The Personalist Legacy*, Boulder, Westview, 1991, p. 26.
7. Ibid. p. 20
8. George Pendle: *Paraguay*, New York, Oxford UP, 1967, p. 21.
9. The country witnessed mass-scale exodus as the people tried to escape the witch hunt.
10. Cuadernos hispanoamericanos
11. Paco Tovar: *Acordar la palabra*..., Premio, p. 69 - 70.
12. Brent J Carbajal: *Historia ficticia y ficción histórica:Paraguay en la obra de Augusto Roa Bastos*, Editorial Pliegos, Madrid, 1996.
13. The transcription of Guarani words in predominantly Spanish texts were the absent texts in his writing.
14. D. W. Foster: *Augusto Roa Bastos*, Boston, Twayne, 1978. p. 113.
15. Roa Bastos, Augusto: *El Fiscal*, Editorial Alfaguara, Madrid, 1993, p. 9. (All translations are mine unless stated otherwise).
16. Semana de autor. *Augusto Roa Bastos*, ICI, Madrid, 1986, p. 40.
17. As quoted in Vera Kuteischikova and Lev Ospovat: "Paraguay: el destino del pueblo y el hombre" en *Ensayos sobre novelistas latinoamericanos*, Editorial Arte y Literatura, La Habana, 1987, p. 259.
18. Roa Bastos, Augusto, *Vigilia del Almirante*, Cal y arena, México, 1993, p. 319.
19. Roa Bastos, *El Fiscal*, op. cit. p. 14.
20. Ibid. p. 15.
21. Ibid. p. 18.

22. Ricardo Piglia, op.cit. p. 85.
23. Ibid. p. 69.
24. María Cristina Pons: *Memoria del Olvido*, Siglo XXI Editores, 1996.
25. Andrés Bello: *Obras Completas*, Vol. XXIII, Caracas, Venezuela, 1957.
26. Doris Sommer: As cited in Daniel Balderston: *The Historical Novel in Latin America*, Ediciones Hispamérica Gaithersburg, 1986.
27. The theme of salvation and martyrdom is a constant in Roa Bastos' writings, especially in *Hijo de Hombre* and in *El Fiscal*. The Christ figure is used to reinforce the idea of sacrifice not so much from a theological perspective but from a secularised social perspective of man who must always struggle for salvation in a pattern which continually repeats itself in history in an unending cycle of renewal. Cf. Beth Dublinsky: *The Function of the Christ Myth in three Latin American Novels*, University of Colorado, Boulder, 1987.
28. Roett and Sacks: op.cit. p. 30.

SONYA S. GUPTA

Exile as Ex-centricity: Juan Goytisolo's Rehabilitation of Moorish Spain in *Reivindicaiòn del Conde don Juliàn*

In a secular and contingent world, homes are always provisional. Borders and barriers that enclose us within the safety of familiar territory, can also become prisons, and are often defended beyond reason on necessity. Exiles cross borders, break barriers of thought and experience.

Edward Said[1]

In an article entitled *Celebration of Vacuity* ('Celebraciòn del vacío'), written on the eve of the 1992 quincentennial commemoration of Columbus' voyage to the Americas, Spanish novelist Juan Goytisolo had pointed to the vacuity of the official celebrations which were explicitly intended to celebrate Spain's new, 'modern', democratic national identity. Goytisolo's objection was to the present-centeredness of the 1992 celebrations that stood for him as a symbol of the most sterile aspect of the Spanish (post) modern condition in that they effectively precluded any real engagement with history. Goytisolo wrote:

The assumption of modernity by today's Spain has been done at the cost of a lobotomy which consisted in extirpating from its consciousness, the awareness and the experience of its past... In a society which silences its best fruits, recuperative festivities like these do not help in unblocking the future nor in providing a clearer idea of who we were, are and want to be... This lobotomy on our brains makes a *tabula rasa* and homogenizes our historical, literary and human landscapes.[2]

As far as Spain is concerned, the Quincentenary of 1492 was a commemoration not only of Columbus's voyage to the Americas but also of the conquest of Granada from Arab rule and the subsequent expulsion of Jews and Moors from Spain. As Helen Graham and Antonio

Sànchez have noted, the politics of commemorating 1492-1992, that is,

> the 'relationship between a nation's encounter with its imperial past and its current political, social and cultural practices' —points to 'the way Spain's continuing historical 'amnesia' prevents the assimilation of meaning of empire in terms of the devastating experience of otherness visited not only on the colonized, but also on those cultures expelled from peninsular Spain.'[3]

Nancy Vogely has pointed out in the context of Spanish Orientalism, that Spanish historical experience suggests the formation of several Others. Apart from the Other that was demonized when official policy expelled the Jews and the Moors from the country in 1492, and the distant colonial Other which as a scapegoat had transferred to it the hatred and guilt the dominant Self left for an aspect of itself, there was the internal Other which generally was ignored, silenced or expelled.[4] The presence of these centrifugal tendencies prevented the emergence of an integrating national identity and the theme of duality, whether external, that is, "Europe-Spain "or internal, that is "the two Spains" has been a constant in the philosophical thought and literature of Spain since its very emergence as a nation-state. This "dissenting conscience" voiced itself with greater intensity in moments of socio-political crisis such as the exodus of liberals and romantics in the 1820's, the disaster of 1898 when Spain lost its last colonies, and above all during the Spanish Civil War and the Republican exile of 1936-39 in which several writers and intellectuals fled from Spain to all over the world after General Franco's military victory in April, 1939. While within Spain, Francoist rhetoric orchestrated the dictums of 'Eternal Spain' and one nation, race, one religion,' revealing an interesting apposition of nationalism and fascism in the way in which the nation was imagined, writers of the 'Peregrine Spain', the 'Other' of the oficial Postwar Spain replaced the topos of 'nationalism' by that of 'exile' and undertook a renewed inquiry into the Spanish Self and its various Others.

In the present paper, we shall attempt to read Juan Goytisolo's discourse concerning the Spanish nation and its historical past through a reading of the novel *Revindicaciòn de Conde don Juliàn*[5] — as well as his ideas as reflected in some of his non-fictional works. We will underline his constant engagement with historian Américo Castro's discourse on the rehabilitation of Moorish Spain as a product of his condition as exile.

Américo Castro's works written in his post-1939 exile represent a severely critical posture towards the way in which the Spanish people define themselves. He questions the concept of millenarian continuity of the Spanish essence sustained by historians such as Menéndez Pidal and

Menéndez y Pelayo and his thesis affirms the importance of the Jewish and Arab culture in the formation of the Spanish character. Juan Goytisolo belongs to the second wave of exile and immigration that took place in the 1950s. Born in 1931, he had witnessed the Civil War as a child and lived his adolescence in Francoist Spain. Generationally, he belongs to the group of social realists whose works started appearing in the middle of the decade of 50s. In his voluntary exile to Paris in 1956 and later to Algeria and Morocco he wrote several works, mainly his trilogy of autobiographical novels: *Señas de Identidad* (Marks of Identity, 1966) *Revindicaciòn de Conde don Juliàn* (Vindication of Count Don Julian, 1971) and *Juan sin Tierra* (Juan without Land 1975). These novels take head on the myths of Spanish history. From the distance of exile Goytisolo sees Spain as a nation whose historically characterstic obsession with political and religious righteousness (the Reconquest, the Inquisition, the 'discovery' and usurpation of the New World, the insistence upon monarchy as the most virtuous form of government, the Civil War) is built upon a series of beliefs, stories, and legends that seek to deny an integral part of peninsular culture-the Islamic Orient.

Despite later protestations of 'Impieza de sangre' (purity of blood), Spanish historical experience was one of racial mixture and thus the Muslims were not a distant people but, as result of extensive intermarriage and cultural borrowing during the long centuries of the Middle Ages, part of the Spanish Self. Spanish Medieval, Renaissance, Golden Age and Enlightenment literature contains numerous examples of Arabic influences, as well as Oriental representations.[6]

After the Civil War in Spain, the main tenets of historiography under the new Francoist culture and correlatively much of the literature promoted by the State, was embedded in a discourse that was largely mythic and monologic. This cultural discourse attempted to construct and impose a claustrophobic model of national identity grounded in the fifteenth, sixteenth and seventeenth centuries, that is, the age of medieval Reconquest, Counter reformation and Empire reinforced by an anachronistic Catholic ideology. The concept of race, identifying Spaniards as of 'one blood, one race and one religion' was central to Phalangist rhetoric which celebrated the myth of 'La Espana eterna'. The Civil War was projected as a machination of the Red-Jewish-masonic international axis. To give an example, José Maria Peman, the bard of Nationalist Spain, warns in the beginning of his *Poema de la Bestia y el Angel* (Poem of the Beast and the Angel, 1938) of the arrival of "the easterly wind, that is, the threat of Red and Semitic Orient". This Orient, which threatens the essence of Western Christianity and which was defeated in the Battle of Lepanto - "*La media luna tuvo la forma de una hoz*" ("The half-moon had the form of a sickle") - is "*el mismo/oriente pecador*" that is, "the same/sinful Orient" now embodied in the perverse will of Lenin. The Nationalist victory, in Manuel Machado's words, was seen as having elevated Spain "to the height of a new sacrifice for the sake of Western civilization, of heroism for the sake of the Catholic, that is, the universal ideal as in the times of Granada and Lepanto..."[7]. The accent on the heroic which we find evident in Machado was well in conformity with the ideological exigencies of fascism and was promoted by Phalangist writers: The short lived Phalangist magazine *Jerarquía* that appeared in the very midst of the Civil War, as José-Carlos Mainer has noted, "represented perfectly the ideological dimensions of the particular moment of the Phalange: fervent heroism and defence of religious values..."[8] Another example of the same is anthology *Poesía heroica del imperio* of Luis Rosales and Luis Felipe Vivanco published by the Phalangist publishing house 'Jerarquia'. In fact, as Shirley Mangini has noted, one of the most popular forms of narrative in the early post-war period were biographies that not only exalted the epic and the heroic but also sustained a view of history according to which "*la historia la hacen los hombres excepcionales, los 'caudillos' como Napoleon*", that is, history is made by exceptional men, by 'caudillos' like Napolean.[9] Franco himself presented the Nationalist victory as "the triumph of Spain against the anti-Spain, the heroic reconquest of the father land that was moving headlong down the path of destruction".[10] 'Anti-Spain' was all that had to be disaffirmed and excluded from memory. As Manuel Tuñon de Lara writes,

> ... the victors of 1939 wanted to make a *tabula rasa* of the entire tradition which they did not consider as their own, which was not dogmatically institutionalised and identified as the national; the rest was marginalised and expelled from intellectual co-existence.[11]

That the concept of race permeated the entire cultural programme of Franco regime can be seen, for example; in popular culture: *Raza* (Race) was in fact the title of a notorious film scripted by Franco himself in 1941. The Nationalist comic, *El Guerrero de Antifaz* (The Masked Warrior, 1944) set in the Middle Ages in Moorish Spain, licensed racist violence against alien (Arab) antagonists. David Herzberger points out that in historiography too the idea was to affirm the regime's morally correct role by arresting dissonance in the discourse of history as well as to assert continuity between the glories of an imperial Catholic Spain and the illustrious present of the Franco era.[12] Franco himself frequently linked his regime to the birth of Spain:

> In order that the History of Spain not become distorted — History of Spain that is also yours (the peoples') — it is necessary for us to remain loyal to that spirit which illuminated the awakening of Spain.—[13]

Nationalist historiographers insisted that a diversity of discourses on the past would compel the dehiscence of all that was held noble and authentic. Though there were attempts by historians such as Vicens Vivens and Tierno Galvàn towards a more objective approach to history, historiography in the 40s and 50s continued to prop up the myth of a monolithic, Castilianized construction of Spanish identity upon which the Franco regime had been constructed. This construction borrowed heavily from the philosophers and writers of the early twentieth century - the Generation of 98, Menéndez Pidal, Menéndez Pealyo and José Ortega y Gasset — who, following the "Disaster of 98" and the subsequent challenges thrown up by the process of Spain's modernization, had presented exegeses strengthening a monolithic conception of national identity constructed on a supposedly archetypal Castilian character. Ortega, for example, maintained that the Arabs are not "an essential ingredient in the genesis of our nationality".[14] Critics have pointed out the affinity between Goytisolo's historical and cultural vision and that of historian Americo Castro. Though Goytisolo never mentions Castor specifically in the main text of *Don Juliàn,* he has acknowledged, on several occasions, his affinity to Castro's ideas. Americo Castor's main contribution to Spanish historiography, in his several books written in the exile has his rehabilitation of the Jewish and Moorish Spain. His dissenting vision of Spain revolves around the concept of *morada vital* (dwelling place of life), i.e. the collective consciousness of a society or cultural group. According to Castro, the Spanish *morada vital* created the tripartite caste system: Jews, Christians and Muslims and the interrelationship and conflicts between these three groups is the key to the structure of Spanish history. Further, Castro considers the intransigence on the part of the ruling Christian community and the phobia of any contradictory or non conforming element as giving rise to Spain's tendency to "vivir deshaciendose" — i.e. to a regenerating process of self-destructiveness.[15]

Like Castro, in his non-fictional works Goytisolo has insisted that Arab rule in Spain cannot be dismissed as a "deviation" from an "authentic destiny". He considers that the fanaticism, the obsession with an internal enemy and the fear that they may be equated with Jews or Arabs, which the Spaniards carried since after 1492, precipitated the country's intellectual and moral ruin.[16]

Don Juliàn is an explicit attack on the official version of Spanish history given by Nationalist ideology: so much so that novel was banned in Spain till Franco's death. In the novel, the author goes back to the very moment at which the Arabs enter Spain from the coast of what is now Morocco and extend the northern border of the African continent into Europe. From the very first line of the novel, the anonymous narrator establishes his condition of exile vis-a-vis Spain:

ungrateful land, petty and spurious, amongst all, never will I come back to you... *(Don Juliàn,* p.83).

From Tangiers, he looks on at the Spanish coast, and identifies himself with Count down Julian — Visigothic Governer of Tangiers - the Great Traitor of Spanish history alleged to have opened the doors of the Peninsula to the Muslims in vengeance of Visigothic king don Rodrigo who had violated his daughter La Cava. Why did Goytisolo write this novel? In one of his essays Goytisolo says:

> The justificatory and mythical interpretation of Spanish history had obsessed me since years. It is difficult to live in a city like Tangiers confronted with the close presence of the Spanish coast without evoking the legendary figure of don Julian and dreaming of a grand "treason" like his. My disenchantment with the official values of my country had reached such an extreme that the idea of its profanation, of its symbolic destruction accompanied me day and night.[17]

Apart from the context of exile, another vital context for the writing of *Don Juliàn* is the Algerian War. As Goytisolo has explained in an interview with José Miguel Ullan, this War forced him to "rabidly demythify that old and moving image of (...) Western Civilization, embodied in the French society" and participate" with the groups maintained by the Algerian FLN".[18] Thus the first seeds of *Don Julian* and its fictional reappropriation of several precepts of official Spanish historiography are a product not only of Goytisolo's disenchantment with official Spanish culture but also of awakening to European ethnocentrism.[19] Goytisolo's obsession with the betrayal of the legendary Cunt Julian and his complete identification with this figure was also occasioned by his own experience of living with the epithet of 'traitor' which the Spanish Press continuously used against him in the 1960's. Linda Gould Levine has noted that if eight centuries ago Alphonse the Tenth, in his *Cronica General,* had condemned Don Julian as a traitor, in 1961 the Spanish Press classified the permanent opposition of Goytisolo as 'betrayal's and situated the 'resentment' of the writer in a long tradition of equally 'unjust', 'irritating' and 'intolerable' 'attacks' launched against Spain by other parias and dissident since the Counter-reform and thereafter till now.[20] But who exactly was Count don Julian? Historical data are not clear though legends abound. The numerous ballads collected by Menendez Pidal attributes the loss of Visigothic kingdom to the Muslims to the lust of Rodrigo and the betrayal of Julian in 711 AD. The legend soon became 'history' as it was incorporated into the 'First General Chronicle of Spain' by Alphonse the Tenth and later versions included at the end of the ballad, the penitence of the king who shut himself up in a tomb where he was castrated by a serpent. Subsequently, what Goytisolo refers to as "the infantile favouritism towards Romans and Visigoths and morbose phobia against Jews and Muslims"[21] which characterises much of Spanish historiography and works of contemporary thinkers, legitimized the truth of the legend. According to Goytisolo's interpretation in the legend of don Julian we can see a variant of the fable of original sin and paradise lost in which , instead of the apple the device was the beauty of the daughter of don Julian. Similarly, the role of Adam would correspond to the last Visigothic king because

> due to his fault, the Spaniards would lose forever their innocence, and in their eyes, the invading Moor would symbolize the evil and the sinful[22]

And thus the original carnal sin of King don Rodrigo has had to be expiated by the Spaniards with all the myths and symbols of chastity on which Spanish identity has been constructed since the times of Catholic King: i.e. the theme of sexuality in a punitive context, the dialectics of honour, the perfect Christian gentlemen/knight, the exaltation of austere and funerary, the tragic sense of life and stoicism.

In *Don Julian* Goytisolo attacks this Freudian mythology through the interior monologue of the unidentified narrator who will undertake a new invasion of Spain:

> A ship sails away rapidly into distance while, with your elbows on the window, romantically, lermontovially you recite the black psalm: Goodbye, stepmother, country of serfs and lords: goodbye, three cornered hats and you, people who tolerate them: perhaps the sea of the Strait will liberate me from your guardians: from their eyes that see everthing....patience, the hour will come... the cruel Arab is brandishing his lance; warriors with crisp hair, Bedouins of pure blood shall cover one day the spacious and sad Spain with a dense concert of ayes, of screams, of laments: sleep, sleep tranquil: nobody suspects you and your harmoniously mature plan: reliving the memory of your humiliations and insults, accumulating drop by drop you hatred: without Rodrigo, or Frandina, or Cava: new Count Don Julian, confabulating new treasons." (*Don Julián,* p. 89)

The process of confabulation is coupled with another avowed mission of Goytisolo: that of attempting "a national psychoanalysis through a reading of the traditional collective discourse on Islam in our literature and in our history"[23]. Showing simultaneously a decidedly post-modernist interest in mass-culture, Goytisolo invades the territory of cinema, songs, newspaper advertisements, television programmes, IBM computers and so on and creates a delirious world where the characters metamorphosize continually into others by the novelist's continuous shifts between pastiche of mass cultural forms and abstruse intellectual discourse. Goytisolo had one said that the primordial task for the Spanish writer of his times was to be a 'mythoclast' since "despite the profound transformation of our socio-economic structures the old myths continue to operate and prevail."[24] Thus in *Don Julian* all the myths of Sacred Spain — from Seneca to the editorials of *ABC* - are ferociously violated by a vindicated traitor as we reach the last chapter of the novel in which the chaste Spanish child, symbol of Christian Spain, identified by the narrator as "you yourself a quarter of a century before." (*Don Julian,* p. 282) is violated and sodomised by the furious Muslim who occupies his grandmother's bed.

The anonymous narrator/traitor who has taken to exile and lost and all his marks of identity cannot, however, shed one aspect of it that continues to link him to his country— and that is his language. As Goytisolo himself says for the exiled, language is the only possession that remains, and seizing upon Castilian as it exists in its written texts as the only authentic fatherland, he can embark on the mythical destruction of the one which figures on the map.[25] He is convinced that the 'sacred' essences of Spanish identity cannot be destroyed if he does not destroy is mythical language. In the novel, Julian can reject Castilian in his Tangierian surroundings in favour of Arabic,

> happy to forget for some moments the last chord which despite you unbeatably binds you to the tribe:---language of the Poet, necessary vehicle of the betrayal, your beautiful language... (*Don Julian,* p. 143).

Language thus becomes the agent as well as instrument of the destruction of Sacred Spain. Carlos Fuentes has underlined the revolutionary critical power of Goytisolo's linguistic enterprise in *Don Juliàn* in the following words:

> Goytisolo's implacable critical intention is to demonstrate the falsehood and corruption of traditional literary Spanish language and to show up to what extent the moral, economic and political institutions of Spain are grounded in the consecration of rhetoric in which the values of 'purity' and 'tradition' justify a hermetic culture and a system of dependencies and values of submission...

Moreover, the imposed moral order of Sacred Spain can be destroyed only by violating its sacralized literary canon. The novel has been described as an intertextual dialogue between Goytisolo and a plethora of Spanish writers whose texts appear all through the novel. The novel ends with an 'Advertencia' where it is stated that the novei been written with the "posthumous and involuntary participation" of a host of writers listed thereafter (p. 305-6). Goytisolo has mentioned :

with *Don Juliàn,* I meant to produce a work which would simultaneously be creation and criticism, literature and discourse on literature[27].

From this point of view of one of the key passages in the novel is the scene in the library in Tangiers (*Don Julian,* p. 104-114) which presents "in miniature the entire intertextual construction of the novel" (Levine, 'Introducciòn', *Don Julian,* p. 30) and which can be described as tirade against authors and the historico-literary premises as well as genres which are the founding tradition of the millenarian Spanish essence. The destruction of the literary and linguistic structure would mean removing the obstacles for the imposition of a truly revolutionary semantics. Thus, the new 'treason' of Don Julian has to be carried out through a morally and sexually totalizing polisemic language. And this leads us to another important aspect' that of sexuality and its role in the novel. All through its text *Don Juliàn* reveals most audacious forms of sexuality: sodomy, rape, masturbation and homosexuality. Goytisolo agree with Americo Castro and Xavier Domingo that after the expulsion of the Moors the Hispano arab erotic tradition of rich of rich sensuality was eliminated from the future literary creation of Spain. He shares with Castro his insistence on the crucial influence of the sensuality of Arab culture on erotic medieval texts such as *El libro de buen amor.*[28] He considers 'pathological' the hatred for the erotic that characterizes some of the most consecrated writers of the Spanish literary canon from Quevedo to Unamuno and Menendez Pidal.[29] In an interview to Claude Couffon shortly after the publication of the novel *Goytisolo* had pointed out:

Spain is a living example of the fact that repressing sexuality is equivalent to repressing intelligence and vice-versa. That is why in *Don Juliàn* sex plays such an important role. The narrator tries furiously to eroticise Spain.

And hence, Goytisolo's attempts in the text to us the 'robust serpents' of the Arabs to 'sodomize' all the myths of Sacred Spain. The old Christian Spain thus stands destroyed by the new Arab invasion.

Having reached this point is has probably become clear that in *Don Juliàn* the topic of Goytisolo's commentary is not Spain itself, it is rather the written versions of the myths of Spanish history, including Spain's literary production that concern him. The considerable body of critical studies on the novel have identified the authors, texts and aspects of Nationalist ideology parodied in it. Jo Labanyi has, however, argued that Goytisolo's use of parody, while debunking Nationalist mythification, creates a new mythology rather then contrasting it with an alternative view of history.[31] Michael Ugarte, too, points out that in such an undertaking there is no pretense of offering the 'real' picture of Spanish history, for the repulsive myths are just as real (or unreal) as the new ones.[32]

Don Julian , the Count of Ceuta in 711, is recast; he is placed in a contemporary setting and his story is told in a way that subverts the fiber of the original myth. Yet the old myth remains intact as the new one emerges; the result is a struggle between the two, the outcome of which is ambivalent. For example, Goytisolo rightly holds that the Nationalists claimed to be descendents of an 'Eternal Spain' represented by the Celts, Iberians, Romans and Visigoths in order to dismiss the ensuing Arab presences as a 'usurpation.' But, as Labanyi suggests, Goytisolo's dismissal of Castilian dominated Spain as a 'mask' imposed on an 'authentic' Arab Spain conforms to the same mythical pattern: the Arab 'usurpers' are simply recast as a 'founding tradition', turning Castilian rule into a 'usurpation'. In the novel, the figure of Seneca — exalted in Nationalist ideology as the symbol of an innate Spanish stoicism — is subjected to continual metamorphosis implying that identity itself is a shifting concept. It may be argued that such an endeavour could create the effect of experiencing history not as linear time but as synchronicity and that the shifting nature of identity encompasses plurality and contradiction challenging a fixed stable identity. But, in *Don Julian,* the multiple incarnations of Seneca are versions of the same stoicism which is supposed to be an essential facet of Spanish national character suggesting thereby that Spain is condemned to an eternal repetition of Senecas. The narrator himself is, however, "dueño proteico de tu destino" (Protean master of your destiny), having a flexible identity which is neither inherent nor imposed nor condemned to eternal repetition. Such a construction of identities suggests that the narrator, having taken to the exile in Tangiers, has escaped this circle of eternal repetition and achieved the freedom to negotiate his own identity. But the ahistorical nature of the narrator's enterprise is soon clarified: "*dueño proteico de tu destino, sí, y, lo que es mejor, fuera del devenir històrico*" (Protean master of your destiny, yes and, what is better, outside the flow of history, p. 99). Thus the Protean narrator who lacks psychological consistency, is lifted out of historical time to be put to the service of the narrative. Reality is lost in language and in the interplay between the an old mythology and a new one. The collage of intertextual references becomes a metafictional game in the which texts refer only to other texts. In fact, at the starts of the novel the curtain is drawing: the (re) presentation beings" (p.86) and at the end it close (p. 294) turning the entire text into a theatrical representation. The novel, with its stress on representation, coinciding with the postmodernist "death of the real", could be read either as rejection of history or a critical deconstruction of the ways in which reality is packaged for our consumption. Perhaps the ambivalence of

Goytisolo's stance is nowhere more apparent than in his use of Arab male sexuality to violate the traditional symbols of Christian Spain. *Don Juliàn* has been referred to as the fictionalisation of the dichotomous battle between the Occident and Orient in what refers to the 'disjunction' between "*cuerpo y no cuerpo*" that is, between body and soul in the Christian West as against the conjunction of the two in Arab male culture. (Levine, Introducciòn, *don Julian,* P.50). Should the constant glorification of the 'robust' Arab phallus as against the '*lechuguino concepto*' of the Spaniards in the novel be read as the demythification of the Western 'myth of the Arab' or as its inversion? Claudia Schaefer — Rodriguez has criticized Goytisolo for perpetuating the stereotyped Western view of the Oriental as treacherous, violent and sensual.[33] Levine has, moreover, pointed out that the exaltation and the deification of the Arab phallus reminds one of a D.H. Lawrence or a Henry Miller in its crass phallocentrism (*Don Julian,* p.49). Orient thus becomes a site of sexual release. But this sexual release is at the same time just a theatrical enactment, another mask. Labanyi has pointed out yet another problematic aspect is that the narrator of *Don Julian* views the Orient through the lens of European literature: Kipling's *The Jungle Book,* Chateaubriand's, *The Adventures of Abencerage* etc. and reminds that in his essays in *Crònicas Sarracinas* Goytisolo declares that in his novels he has deliberately chosen to depict the Arab world through Western eyes in order to send up "the traditional collective discourse on Islam". She concludes that:

> Goytisolo is not only parodying the European view of the Oriental (specifically the Spanish view of the Moor) as the repressed, monstruous Other of Western civilization, his attempt to 'define himself negatively' by assimilating Arab culture repeats the view of Oriental as Jungian shadow.

The narrator's exile to Tangiers as return to nature can also never be more than a 'second nature', a theatrical enactment, an assumed identity, a utopia. In the next novel of the autobiographical trilogy, however, Goytisolo's displacement is not towards a utopia but towards 'atopia'— to nowhere, to migrancy—which is the attribute of the landless. *Juan sin Tierra* starts in Cuba, and from Cuba the text, the narrator, is displaced— Tangiers, Paris, Istanbul, Nile... It is for this reason that Severo Sarduy has described Goytisolo's work as 'ex-centric discourse',[34] ex-centricity being a centrifugal force that takes one towards the periphery, towards nomadism and migrancy, away from the sedentary centre. It is this ex-condition which Goytisolo' exile took him to and which Carlos Fuentes, in his essay on Goytisolo, recognizes as the attribute of universality.

We are all contemporaries because we are ex-centrics. The old universalist pretension of the European bourgeosie being lost, we are all today exiled in a world without a centre. God is dead and with him his pretentious white, christian, bourgeois and rationalist creature too. Universality today consists in recognising oneself in ex-centricity.[35]

NOTES

1. "Mind of Winter: Reflections on Life in Exile", *Harper's Magazine,* September 1984, p. 54.
2. "Celebraciòn del vací", *El país,* December 21, 1991.
3. "The Politics of 1992", *Spanish Cultural Studies,* O.U.P. Oxford, 1995, p. 416.
4. "Turks and Indians: Orientalist Discourse in Postcolonial Mexico", *Diacritics,* Spring 1995, p. 9.
5. Vindication of Count Don Julian, 1970. Henceforth referred to as *Don Juliàn.* All references to this novel correspond to the edition prepared by Linda Gould Levine for Catedra, 1985. Translations are mine.
6. In this context the following studies are interesting: Lily Litvak, *El jardín de Alàh. Temas del exotismo musulmàn en España,* Granada, Don Quijote, 1985; Victor Morales Lezcano, *Africanismo y orientalismo español en el siglo XIX,* Madrid, 1988.
7. Cfr. *Historia social de la literatura española,* volume 36, Julio Rodriguez Puertolas et al., pp. 55-57.
8. *Falange y Literatura,* Labor, Barcelona, 1971, p. 41.
9. *Rojos y Rebeldes,* Barcelona, Anthropos, 19987, p. 15.
10. *Franco ha dicho,* Madrid, Voz, 1949, p. 21.
11. Manuel Tuñon de Lara, and José Antonio Biescas, *España bajo la dictadura franquista,* Barcelona, Labor, 1982, p. 516.
12. "Narrating the past: History and the Novel of Memory in Post-war Spain," *PMLA* (Jan.1991) Vol. 106, N.1, p. 35.
13. Franco ha dicho, 1949, p. 96-97.
14. *José Ortega y Gasset, España Invertebrada,* Madrid, Espasa-Calpe, 1964, p. 129.
15. Cfr. Americo Castro, *La realidad històrica de España,* Mexico, 1962 and also Stephen Gilman (ed.), *an Idea of History: Selected essays of Americo Castro,* Ohio State University Press, Columbia, 1977, p. 313-334.
16. "Declaraciòn de Juan Goytisolo" in *Juan Goytisolo,* Fundamentos, p. 139.
17. *Disidencias,* Barcelona, Seix Barral, 1977, p. 292.
18. Goytisolo's interview with José Miguel Ullan, "Arabesco para la transparencia", in *Voces,* No.1, 1981, p. 16.
19. See the introduction by Linda Gould Levine to the edition of *Don Juliàn* being cited in this paper, p. 16.
20. Levine, *Juan Goytisolo: la destruccion creadora,* Mexico, Joaquin Mortiz, 1976, p. 125.
21. Juan Goytisolo, "Supervivencias tribales en el medio intelectual español" in *Estudios sobre la obra de Americo Castro,* coord. by Pedro lain Entralgo,

Madrid, Taurus, 1971, p. 146.

22. *Crònicas Sarracinas,* p. 35.
23. *Crònicas Sarracinas,* pp. 32-33.
24. Interview with Claude Couffon in *Juan Goytisolo,* Madrid, Fundamentos, p. 117.
25. "Declaraciòn de Juan Goytisolo", *Juan Goytisolo,* p. 141.
26. Carlos Fuentes, "Juan Goytisolo: La lengua comun" in ***La nueva novela hispanoamericana,*** Joapuín Mortiz, Mexico, 1969, p. 88
27. Interview with Couffon, op.cit, p. 119.
28. In *La realidad historica de España* Castro discusses the link between this Spanish text and Ibn Hazm's *El collar de la paloma,* pp. 413-29.
29. *Juan Goytisolo,* p. 139.
30. Claude Couffon, *Juan Goytisolo,* p. 246.
31 Jo Labanyi, *Myth and History in the Contemporary Spanish Novel,* OUP, Cambridge, pp. 196-213.
32. Ugarte, "Juan Goytisolo: Unruly disciple of Americo Castro", *Journal of Spanish Studies* 7, 3 (1979), pp. 353-364
33. Cfr. *Juan Goytisolo: Del 'realismo critico' a la utopia,* Madrid, Porrua Turanzas, 1984.
34. "La desterritorializaciòn", *Juan Goytisolo,* pp. 175-183.
35. *La nueva novela hispanoamericana,* p. 89.

ANTONIA CABANILLES

I Shall Inhabit My Name or Memory of Oblivion

First part of the title of my essay was a reply that S.J. Perse wrote in the form which was given to him as the plot when he began his exile. The century, which is going to end now, is being named as the century of the homeless man, the century of those without the motherland. It wouldn't be risky to state categorically that this distressing label could equally be applicable to many earlier periods as well. I shall begin by remembering two other great banishments which we have in our own historical memory: the explusion of the Hebraic community in 1972 and the Muslim community in 1609. Literature also offers to us its own memory, that of Cicero, Ovid, Plutarch, Seneca...These would be some of the first manifestations. The Biblical narrative gives some earlier examples. The exodus is located in the period of the fall of the Eighteenth Egyptian dynasty (1350 BC). And if thus continued, perhaps, we would be able to say that the human condition itself is based on an exile. Or to say it in the words of Phythagoric Empedocles, "We all are exiled from the celestial world, banished demons, lost on the route of ferocious living". What is that, which makes this century so different from all the earlier ones? We can note the first and the most evident reason: the discernible increase in the number of exiled persons. Other reasons go along with the new communication possibilities, which this century offers to us. We are in the age of globalisation, free movement, abolition of borders, a common market. However, all these terms have just one valid referent: the capital. We are told about it. The prophets of the new technology sell these theories to us as the 'free flow of information'. The roads that join the North with the South are not of freedom. More often than not, they are filled with tragedy. Those are slippery roads, the ones that come from the North of Africa and go to Spain. Those are the routes of the boats full of Albanians who are unable to anchor on an Italian port. Those are also the routes of the people with wet back who try to reach the North. Those are also the roads of columns and columns of those people who are fleeing away from hunger, misery, war, in many parts of the world. Then there are those who die in an attempt to reach the destination or those who are repatriated in a humiliating manner. And for those fortunate ones who manage somehow to reach a new land there is only the labyrinth of fear, the so-called 'illegal ones'. It is, as Maria Zambrano used to say, *the black night of the history.* At the end of this century the trilogy by Josefina R. Aldecoa: *Story of a Teacher* (1990), *Women in Black* (1994) and *Power of Destiny* (1997) offers us a magnificent set of stories to analyse and reflect upon some of the basic themes of exile: the relationship between an individual and a collective history, memory as the only inhabitable space, the uprootendness, how the time waits, the enrooting or the return. In Josefina R. Aldecoa's works these themes have one reference point - the Spanish exile 1939. Her characters Gabriela and Juana live through the 1931 Republic, the 1936 War and the 1939 exile, the Mexican life and the return to Spain in 1975 after the death of the dictator.

STORY FOR ALL

The first aspect with I am going to deal with is the way in which personal history gets interwoven with the collective history to the extent that it becomes one and the only history for the exiled. Dr. Jose Solanes Vilaprenyo, a psychiatrist and a victim of 1939 exile, having researched this theme from different angles, has pointed out that "the exile converts the motherland into an intimate matter. Its history is confused with one's history, with one's autobiography and one is compelled to distance oneself from it." (1993-191) The very title of the novel which opens Josefina R. Aldecoa's trilogy *Story of a Teacher* shows the willingness to interweave both the dimensions. "To narrate my life", thus begins the novel and this first persons narration is a well thought out technique impelled by intimate notes. Gabriela begins to narrate her life so that her daughter Juana, who left for exile as a child, could construct her story — a history linked with the history of Spain. The addressee is introduced with a view to show the extent to which the narration belongs not only to Gabriela, but also to Juana: "If you take the responsibility of looking for explanations of so many things which are so dark for me, we may try" (HM:13).[1] Implanting the addressee into the story makes the narrative a shared work, where the addressee could also have the word and above all, where the narrator does not claim to possess all the knowledge. In fact, in the second novel, *Women in Black*, it will be Juana who will carry on the narration, returning to many of the events already narrated in the first book. However, she offers here another point of view and another interpretation of the events already narrated.

The double plot, personal and collective, of the novel gives way to a double beginning. By way of this narrative strategy it is shown as to what extent two totally different stories and projects are interlinked. Gabriela's story begins just after she finishes her teachers' training course, precisely, in October of 1923, the day when she would join her school friends at Oviedo:

At 10 O' clock I shall once again see my name written amongst many others: Gebriela López Pardo, Teacher...End of the first stage of life and the beginning of a dream. (HM: 14).

One of the most significant episodes of the autobiography and of memory - the childhood and adolescence - is found missing from the story. But there is a manifested desire not to impinge upon the private history, not to resort to individualism. Quite on the contrary, there is an attempt to depict a social project, a dream: the commitment to teaching in the Spain of 1923.

The beginning of the other story, which initially looks like an anecdotal incident, corresponds to the description of an event, celebrated in Oviedo this very day i.e., a wedding. The narrator describes a spectacle organised in the centre of the city before the arrival of the cars full of bridegrooms. This description includes some comments of the friends of the bride, who refer to the disapproval of the marriage from the side of her family. However, the narrative technique used to represent the character is quite extraordinary. As in the best portraits the focus on two points serve to show the main features of the character, here as well, by showing bride's hands and bridegroom's look, the real expression is obtained. After having found out the identities of each character, the reader will be able to verify for himself/herself the reality of the portrayal and, above all, the relevance of this double beginning:

I have recollected that wedding later several times. A few days later I read a news item about it in the paper, but those names did not say much to me ... Miss Cermen Polo and Martine. Valdes and Lt. Col. Don Fanisco Franco Bahamonde...

Those names did not say anything to me then. Years later, I shall hear them all over, and without my noticing it, they will mark my destiny for all times to come. (HM:16)

The temporal duality of the story is also reflected in the narrator's return to the time of the statement. From the present it turns to the past through a 'before'. An anaphoric 'then' corresponds to that 'before' which carries with it a 'later'. Through this strategy the narrator can allude to future, because the parallel development of the stories belongs to the future. The use of prolepsis will also serve the double beginning of the story.

As the title shows, the novel will concentrate around the story of a collective, even though it is a narration in first person. The delivery is very important: the dreams - the debate amongst those who thought that education would change the society - are all quite relevant. The ambition of an army man, his individual story, were in the beginning a simple anecdote. Nevertheless, at the end of the story we can see how an official history has been constructed at the back of those dreams. The name of his character will reappear in the newspapers, but now he is converted into a General. Thirteen years have gone by and the story is located at the end of July 1936. The dream evolves between those two dates, i.e., 1923 and 1936: the dream of having a more free and just country thanks to education - dream shattered in July 1936. The novel ends by showing the convergence of these two stories.

> In front of our seat I saw a man who had opened a newspaper. From above his back I saw a photograph:
>
> General Francisco Franco... I remembered, unexpectedly, that face, that morning in Oviedo, that wedding and his name in the newspaper. I remembered his look, which floated beyond that Avenue from above people' head. I was very young and I believed in my dreams, which were unfolding that day. I could not imagine, where, in which horizons would his dreams be lost. (HM, 232)

The narrator ends her story by giving way to another voice, to that of her daughter Juana, who till this moment had only been an addressee of her mother's narrative. This is the moment of change. Juana will be the narrator of the next plot, because "what follows is as well known to her as it is to me, she remembers it better than I. Because it is her own life." (HM, 232).

All the three novels are permeated by a wish to bring about a fusion between the history of the country and that of its protagonist. The most intimate events will take place on very emblematic dates. Juana is born on April 14, 1931, Ezequiel, Gabriela's husband is assassinated on July 18, 1936. In the second novel, the dates seem to fade away, perhaps because the exile time span is only the time of wait. The exact reference corresponds only to the beginning : Gabriela's mother's death coincides with the day of the fall of Madrid, Gabriela's new marriage and her exile take place in 1939. Juana's independent life, which would make the separation of destiny from her mother's a personal option, will occur at the end of the second World War, in Mexico City, and later in Madrid, in 1950, where she returns to begin her university education. The third novel *The Power of Destiny* begins on November 20, 1975, the day of Franco's death, and the day of the end of Gabriela's exile. Her return to Spain marks the beginning of doubts. Thirty six years out of her own country make her feel as if she had committed a mistake because the present reality -"the feeling of freedom" - had been constructed by others, by those, who had stayed back; or by those, like her daughter, who returned to carry on the struggle: "My country is being reborn, it is entering a new era of opening up to the world, it is moving. And I want to be there... ..," Juana had said (FD:119) Thus, the narrator, once again, foregrounds the question of the confluence of the two currents of thought, two destinies: the personal and the collective.

I ask myself:

> Am I the victim of my individual destiny or the destiny of the collective? Had the Republic not fallen, I would not have become a widow and I would not have gone to Mexico. Juana would not have married Alejandro. Miguel would not have been born. And Octavio would not have existed for me. I don't want to go on with my doubts. The historical destiny depends upon all of us; it is a reflection of the collective's behaviour. But my personal destiny depends only on me. Why did I not stay back and fight together with others in order to reach this freedom, constitution, democracy? I am tired to think again and again about the destiny. I have arrived at this point of my life because I was born in a country and during a time which have compelled me to choose. But I am my destiny. (FD:61).

Though I shall return to this point later in my essay, I would suggest in advance that the experience of return, as it is presented in Josefina R. Aldecoa's work is an obvious reflection of the sense of loss. When one returns after such a long period of exile like that of 1939, the exile that had been lived through as a time of wait or as a non-time, virtually makes the real return impossible. As is pointed out by R. José Solanes:

> This scarcity (of time) makes him (exiled) to be without a "before" to support him in order to live though the "present" which he has to suddenly confront. From the "before" he is only left with the most remote one, like the window which opens on history without a vision of the present day. (Solanes, 1993:258).

Gabriela felt like being twice exiled: first time in Mexico and second in her own county. In the best of the Beckettian tradition the return is converted into an experience of absence:.... return?.....*to the absence perhaps.* The past or the remote past is the only part of collective history to which she belongs. The present and the future do not fit into the collective project. Even now, she does not renounce her eagerness, her dream of a just society, which had dominated her young days. Even at the last stage, in order to meet her goal she has no dearth of reference to recent history of Spain. On February 23, 1981 Gabriela begins to note the first symptoms of her illness and dies in June, 1982, a date when the socialists triumph, when here own daughter triumphs. Again the dream begins.

MEMORY OF THE OBLIVION

A poem by Hölderlin titled *Mnemosyne* (2nd vision) allowed Felix de Azua (1996) to make a remarkable commentary on exile and language. Even though the poem refers to an ontological exile, I would like to recollect some of Azua's reflections. In the first place, memory is taken as a mysterious spiritual faculty, which keeps together our individual as well as collective coherence, and thus provisionally liberates us from disintegration. It is not strange, from this perspective, that Lotman and Uspensky would define culture as a non-hereditary memory of a society. Only by remembering as to what we had been, says Azua, we can continue being what we believe to be. Obviously, the poem does not say that we should become 'memory' or 'speech' and, therefore, 'meaning'. It says that we are a "sign", like all the signs, without any meaning. Felix de Azua points out that we are like arrows which aim at some place but never at oneself (1996: 23). The commentary of the text of Babel and the difference between the philosopher Hegel and the poet Hölderlin help him to locate this space in a certain relationship. According to Felix de Azua, reconciling with the world (i.e., appropriating the world), which is what Hegel had aspired for and made an attempt to attain through his 'magnificent' system, was not a part of the poem's project. For Hölderlin we were sill a sign, on our own, an insignificant signal. Nevertheless, this signal indicates the relationship between the language (which is not of the world) and memory, which, despite everything else, maintains the coherence of the exiled ones. (1996:32)

After having mentioned the above works, I will now place the question of memory in the exile land, concretely with reference to the Spanish exile of 1939 as represented in Josefina R. Aldecoa's texts. The author feels the need of constructing memory in the first place. The uprootedness produced by exile was lived through very differently by Gabriela and by Juana. It is the latter (Juana) who feels the need to construct a memory. The children of the exiled ones, those who had left their country at a young age, as children, or those who were born in a country where they had a provisional status, are the ones who construct their identity in absentia. Their parents saw the Republic, the war. These are points of history for them so far as they keep a vivid memory of those events. We would even note that the very survival, the socialising, would mean to them a good dose of oblivion. However, the same does not happen to their children. The loss of a space goes along with the loss of the past, especially when they need it most, when they believe that it was here, it was immobile and it justified the present. Gabriela advises her daughter to write in order to fill this gap. And the result is the novel *Women in Black.*

"Write in order to remember," says the mother while speaking about these things, "and to conjure up the ghost." I write golden boxes, silver boxes, hateful German boxes — symbol of an alien and distant power. (MN:20)

This is the reason for writing the first book as well the novel *Story of a Teacher.* Juana needs to know the signs of her pilgrimage that had marked her life, which also had marked her identity in a new country which was not her own, but all her memory was linked with it. That was the reason why she had requested Gabriela to write her memoirs, much of which she (Juana) was unable to remember, especially her childhood, her father, the lost land. Later in *Women in Black,* Juana herself would explain the need for the same:

Sometimes I am afraid of losing the past. That's why I used to request my mother to tell me about those things, which I did not remember, and I was afraid to forget, and the things, which I had never known. I used to dream about my grandmother. The dream would always appear in the same place, the same country house. In a veiled way I used to reproach my mother for selling that house. If we return one day where shall we go? I used to ask. And she would tell me, "The world is the motherland....you don't cling to small motherlands." But I needed it. I was brusquely transplanted in the other land, I needed the basic sustenance, this nourishment in order to complete the cycle of my growth. (MN:80-81).

The phenomenon of Alejo Carpentier's story *Journey Back of the Seed* is, perhaps, what we are talking about. The narrative strategies are a response to two characters, who represent two different historical moments. As we have shown, in Gabriela's narrative a significant diegetic hiatus is produced, especially, when the infancy and adolescence stages are depicted, which in turn, respond to the wish of narrating only the collective history. Juana's, story however, helps her in filling up the gaps that occur in her memory and carry her tale back to a time which was much further than her personal past, "to those things which I had never known." In her case her personal history cannot, at any point, delink itself, as was shown earlier, from the historical events that have marked our recent history. José Solanes (1993, 148) speaks of a 'retrotime,' a term used by Miguel de Unamumo in *The Other* for explaining a strange journey undertaken in exile called 'autoretro biography.'

The different treatment of time will also affect another dimension, which goes along with it, i.e. space. In Gabriela's case we find the other basic characteristic of an exiled: the appropriation of a space from which they had felt to be excluded and the fact that they discover themselves to be terrestrial human beings. Any land is Land. A characteristic feature that Maria Zambrano has expressed through a famous oxymoron: "Thanks to the banishment we came to know the world." This positive and clear dimension of exile is not perceived in the children of the exiled ones. The younger ones, perhaps due to an identity problem, as explained by Juana, opt for one of the two spaces. However, in her case there is a sense of loss, and perhaps worse, a sense of forgetting. This causes the mythification of a lost land: the land of birth. In these circumstances the phytomorphic representation of the exiled is another aspect. In the *Power of Destiny* Gabriela will remember the need of knowledge for her daughter, who had converted her into a narrator of a "retro life" story. In order to underline the force of this desire, this need and also in order to justify her own story, the protagonist's voice is introduced through a discourse. The effectiveness of this discourse is based on the convergence of three features which allow a clear distancing between these two voices: the change in verbal time, from past to present, the use of volitive verbs, and above all, the use of *dicendi* verbs at the end of the first sentence in order not to reduce the eruption of a new voice which makes the change in discursive level explicit:

> When we were in Maxico, Juana always wanted me to tell her about the things of the past. She had a real obsession with memory. I don't want to forget what we lived, she used to say. And I want to know what you lived through when I was not yet born. This desire to know and to remember was caused by our state of exile. She was afraid of losing the roots, the family, names of plants and children's games. (FD: 35)

TO REMEMBER FOR OTHERS

To keep alive the historical memory is not born so much from the desire to narrate all what had been lived through but from the need to know what had not been lived through. That's what happens to Juana and was that's what will happen to her son Miguel, who was born in Mexico and later transplanted to Spain due to the return of his mother. In the last novel *Power of Destiny,* Gabriela is once again converted into a narrator of the history of the Republic and the civil War.' However this time, the addressee of her story is her grandson Miguel. Now, along with Miguel's need to know the unlived side is Gabriela's need to justify her exile, to perpetuate a memory which will give coherence to her past and her present. To remember for others, but to remember also for herself.

The continual return to the same events in the works of Josefina R. Aldecoa give way to the fact that the elements, that Genette has called the narrative frequency, get a special importance. The relation of repetition between the story and the diegesis are one of the essential aspects of the narrative temporality. I shall refer only to one event, which I have just mentioned: the fall of the Republic and the death of Ezequiel. The recurrent headlines turn one single event into a ritual story. Undoubtedly, the repetitive character is an abstraction because each time the story is narrated a change occurs because the situations, under which the declarations are made, vary from one another. However, the use of the narrative frequency does not limit itself to the respective story, rather it broadens itself into the so-called iterative story, wherein one narrative emission covers in one go various facets of the same event. In the following example we can appreciate how both types of frequencies are combined. Here in the first place we are dealing with a repetitive story, once again an event is being narrated, which had already been told by Gabriela and her daughter Juana was the addressee. In the second place a temporal frequency of an iterative type occurs ("on a certain day"... "It always begins like this....", "Once more than other times when we spoke about Ezequiel....") which depicts a restoration of certain routine referred to the repetition of the story:

> Every now and then, as if by chance, Miguel asks me about his grandfather. He is very much interested in his political ideas, his activities, which led him to prison in '34 first and then to his death in '36 (...). Your grandfather was a good man....*I always begin like this.* I don't know what was the need to allude to Ezequiel's kindness (...) *once, when more than other times, we spoke about Ezequiel,* I went to look for things that I had inherited from his grandfather: his Socialist party card, a portrait of Pablo Iglesias and a copy of the programme with the republican flag, inside which there was an announcement of a meeting in which Ezequiel was going to participate, I was going to hand them over to him (emphasis added. FD: 71-72).

AN ANCIENT MEMORY AS A BLOWING TRUMPET

I have talked about the need to construct the memory as the first reason for writing. Now I would like to have a short reflection upon this memory, upon how the story itself goes on complying with it. The memory exists in the story only. *Story of a Teacher* begins with a doubt, which affects its body, its structure. "To narrate my life... I don't know where to begin (HM:13) — a canonical formula for beginning the story of a 'retrolife.' On privileging the image of the protagonists, the autodiegetic narrator goes on to reconstruct the experienced time; however the narrator renounces the premature disclosure of events subsequent to the experienced time. In principle, it will be the addressee of the story, as in the analysed discourse, who will interpret all the loose dates, signs, symptoms, which would eventually give coherence to the story:

Later, you arrange them for putting an order to a pack of cards....If you take charge of looking for explanations of so may things, which are for me still very dark....

The double adventure of being the hero of the story and the narrator of the same has its own attractions. The temporal distance, the rupture between the 'I' of the story and the 'I' of the narration creates a situation wherein the latter can be split into two, running into an address of his/her narration. The memory goes on weaving itself from a series of reminiscences, from unconnected particles, which are now submitted to the logic of the story, to its linearity. The lived one is confused with the narrated one, and thus acquires a new meaning for this split narrator who contemplates and narrates his/her own story.

Suddenly a scene comes to your memory and it illuminates your memory. You see them all transparent, very clear, it even seems to you that you understand it all. (HM: 13).

But hoodwinking is not possible. It is known that memory is a tale which one narrates to oneself in order to explain/support the present:

Memory selects. It places in the archives those versions of the events which are considered good and ejects other possible versions which may be disturbing. (HM:18).

Textual strategies, which give certain coherence to the discourse in the manner, convert themselves into a mechanism, which provides to the story called life necessary linkages. Thus comes the definition of memory by Felix de Azua: A mysterious spiritual faculty, which keeps our coherence together.

In the second novel *Women in Black* there is a different narrator but the model of autodiegetic narrator continues. This time, the narrator reflects upon the material that forms the basis of her memory, she reflects upon the impossibility of distinguishing between different versions and upon the very condition of remembrance. Therefore, at the time of reconstructing the experienced time the narrator does not know where the material, which she is using for construction of memory, is proceeding from:

Actually, it is difficult for me to separate the remembered from the imagined. I confuse the dates of my nebulous childhood. And in this way, perhaps, I evoke instances which I lived through as a very small child but I negate having seen some of the events to which I had been a witness at a sufficiently mature age for giving evidence. (MN:19).

However, it is not only to state that memory weaves with more than one thread but it weaves in the middle of oblivion. It is impossible to relate what had been lived. The narrator is sure of only few sentiments related to time and space. Her reflections serve as an evidence of the etymological meaning of the word 'to remember'. To remember means to return with the heart:

Memory does not work as an organised card-index of objective data. Even though we write what we have just seen or perceived. Nevertheless, it will be contaminated by the consequences of oblivion. For example, if I try to remember what the weather was like in my childhood city on the day of the arrival of the Germans, I would say it was cold. It might not have been so. I could consult books and papers in order to confirm the truthfulness of this fact. But I know that in my memory it was cold. It is a hard, hostile memory. That's why I write the Germans came in winter, (MN:19)

The last novel *The Power of Destiny* is very complex in dealing with the theme of memory. The same model continues, it is again an autodiegetic narrator, but here the narrative time will be different. The narrative time runs parallel to the history and the story begins in an imprecise manner, during the Christmas of 1975, after Gabriela's return from exile in Mexico, and goes on up to her death in 1982. At this last stage, her activities consist in recollecting some of the events, which construct the story of her life. However, remembering does not mean feeling nostalgia for the past, which is the ignominious time. Remember but don't go back. "Present is better" (FD: 197). And this present is constructed thanks to the historical memory:

I tell you: Revenge no, but memory yes, Pardon, but don't forget, (FD:75).

In this process of recollection, once again, a split takes place between the 'I' of the narration and the 'I' of history. But now there is a different narration level. The linearity disappears as also the attempt at organising the memory in a successive manner and constructing an explicative history. At this stage it is not necessary. Now to revise the reminiscences is like "getting off the track." (FD:12). It is inconsequential, however, to live backward, in the past. It is important to propose another version, a more disturbing one, of the events. To livê these moments is to remember, to imagine:

> While my head does not fail me, while I keep going on my track, uncovering the thunder boxes according to my wishes: now.....).. (FD:147).

All through the novel, the use of the image of thread (or track) and memory has been changing. In the beginning it was the thread with which the memory was woven for narrating the story. Later, "to go off the track" is aimed as dismantling this story and propose or imagine another version. At the end, "losing the track" stands for losing the memory, it is an announcement of nothing, of definitive exile:

> Very often I see myself lost in the labyrinth of memory. I lose the track, the thread which leads me to recuperate the world which had fled away, an object which had faded away or had been kept away. Where? When? How? The cloud is gathering. (FD: 177)

Memory was this mysterious spiritual faculty which kept our individual as well as collective coherence together, and it had been provisionally liberating us from disintegration.

NOTE

1. The abbreviations used here are the following: HM for *Historia de Una Maestra (Story of a Teacher)*, MN for *Mujeres de Negro (Women in Black)* and FD for *La Fuerza del Destino (The Power of Destiny)*. The page numbers of the edition cited in the bibliography follow these abbreviations.

Translation by Vibha Maurya

BIBLIOGRAPHY

Aldecoa, Josefina R., (1990), *Historia de Una Maestra*, Barcelona, Anagrama, 1997 3rd ed.

Mujeres de Negro, Barcelona, Anagrama, 1997, 3rd ed.

La Fuerza de Destino, Barcelona, Anagrama.

Azua, Felix de, (1996) "Siempre en Badel" *Archipelago,* No. 26-27, pp. 22-32.

Genette, Gérard (1972) Figures III, Barcelona, Lumen, 1989.

Solanes, José (1993) *Los Nombres del Exilio*, Caracas, Monte Avila Latinoamericana, 1996.

Contributors

Lalitha Subbu, Department of English, Hindu College, University of Delhi.

Dominique Sarfaty Varma, Visiting Lecturer from France. Department of Germanic and Romance studies, University of Delhi.

Hema Raghavan, Gargi College, University of Delhi.

V. Rajakrishnan, Department of English, Kerala University.

Rosy Singh, Department of Germanic and Romance Studies, University of Delhi.

Maria Alzira Seixo, University of Lisboa, Portugal.

Alberto Duarte Carvalho, University of Lisboa.

Fernando Cristóvão, Universidad Classica of Lisboa, Portugal.

Ana Paula Laborinho, Oriental Portuguese Institute, Macau.

Margit Köves, Fellow, ICHR, Delhi.

Manfred Stassen, Former Director, German Academic Exchange Service, New Delhi.

Shaswati Mazumdar, Department of Germanic and Romance Studies, University of Delhi.

Stefano Fossati, Visiting Lecturer from Italy, Department of Germanic and Romance Studies, University of Delhi.

Mircea Itu, Visiting Lecturer from Romania, Department of Germanic and Romance Studies, University of Delhi.

Prathibha Bhattacharya, Lecturer in German, Hansraj College, University of Delhi.

Sonya S. Gupta, Department of Spanish, Central Institute for English and Foreign Languages, Hyderabad.

Antonia Cabanilles, University of Valencia, Spain.